ONE, HOLY, CATHOLIC, AND APOSTOLIC

KENNETH D. WHITEHEAD

ONE,
HOLY,
CATHOLIC,
AND APOSTOLIC

The Early Church Was the Catholic Church

IGNATIUS PRESS   SAN FRANCISCO

Material in Chapters 1 and 2 and a portion of Chapter 3 previously appeared in *This Rock*. Material in Appendix I originally appeared in *The Catholic Answer*. Reprinted with permission of the publishers of these periodicals.

Cover art: Titian (ca. 1488–1576) *The Pentecost*
Santa Maria della Salute, Venice, Italy
Cover design by Roxanne Mei Lum

ISBN 0-89870-802-8
Library of Congress control number 00-100238
Printed in the United States of America

To
My nephew,
Father John M. O'Donohue

Ordained to the sacred priesthood in the year 2000,
the Holy Year of the Great Jubilee

CONTENTS

INTRODUCTION

Very often in the history of Christianity, "reformers", by whatever name, have aspired to return to "the early Church". The Church of their own day, for whatever reason, fails to live up to what they think Christianity should be: in their view there has been a falling away from the beautiful ideals of the early Church, perhaps as expressed in such New Testament passages as this:

> And all who believed were together and had all things in common; and they sold their possessions and goods and distributed them to all, as any had need. And day by day attending the temple together and breaking bread in their homes, they partook of food with glad and generous hearts, praising God and having favor with all the people. (Acts 2:44–47)

This blessed vision of peace and loving concord among the early Christians is understandably attractive, especially amid the labor, strife, worries, anxieties, exigencies, and compromises that characterize the daily lives of most of us. To yearn for the alleged perfections of the early Church is only too tempting for anyone who tries to take seriously the gospel of Jesus Christ but sees how regularly the authentic spirit of the gospel of Christ is set aside and forgotten, not only in the world around us, but, unfortunately, even by those who profess faith in Christ.

We do not need to exaggerate. Christianity has brought, and brings, many blessings into the world; it has brought,

and brings, immense consolation and regular encouragement to those of us who have been given the grace of faith;
it is all that enables many of us to live anything like a moral
and hopeful life.

Nevertheless, we must never forget that although Christ
conquered sin and death for us on the cross and has not ceased
to share his divine life with us, especially through the sacraments of the Church—and while the Church through her
appointed leaders does not cease to proclaim and expound
the gospel of Christ to the world—the world, nevertheless,
continually falls far, far short of what a world redeemed by
Christ and in possession of Christ's words and works of truth
and life ought to be.

Nor does the Church always manage to compensate for
the world's failings, in spite of the great good she does do.
Far from it. Sometimes the Church's inability to compensate
here and now for the evil of the world stems from the failures of her members or former members, who ought to have
been able to do better. Even where the seed has been sown,
it sometimes fails to take root and grow and bear fruit, as
Christ foretold in the parable.

This seems to have been true even in New Testament times.
St. John, among others, was obliged to write about those
who "went out from us, but they were not of us; for if they
had been of us, they would have continued with us ..." (1
Jn 2:19).

We must not judge the Church by the failures of her members, certainly not by those of her lukewarm or former members. We must bear with the Church in spite of human failings.
We must remain with her precisely because she is the Church
in which Jesus Christ himself willed that his words and works
should be perpetuated throughout history. Our eternal salvation and hope of heaven, as well as our sanctification in

this world, come from Christ through the Church—and they involve more than merely having "a personal relationship" with Jesus, calling upon his name, or simply accepting him as our "personal savior": *he* it is who wills that we also be members of what St. Paul the apostle consistently called his body, the Church (cf. Col 1:18).

The Church is the community of believers in Christ, to be sure, but she is more than that; she is what in history has been called a *visible* Church, whose members subscribe to her creed and are subject to the authority of her hierarchy— just as the Christians of the first generation accepted the preaching of the apostles and were subject to their authority (as can abundantly be seen in the Acts of the Apostles).

Nor is the Church Christ wills we be members of some ideal body existing nowhere outside the pages of the New Testament. The Church is a living entity, established by Christ in New Testament times, continuing from that time to this, making available to successive generations the salvation and sanctification promised and provided by Christ.

It is the task of each successive generation of Christians in the Church to try to live the spirit of the Gospels. It is most decidedly *not* the task of each successive generation of Christians to try every so often to reestablish the Church anew, perhaps along the supposed lines of "the early Church". It may be tempting to think that whatever we do not like about the Church today or think should not be part of Christ's Church must therefore not have been part of the early Church—we may be in for a surprise when we decide to look more closely and carefully at the early Church.

For the early Church has not disappeared. She is with us still. Reformers, again by whatever name, are not so much needed by this Church as are those who aspire to be saints— those who are determined to follow Christ seriously and to fulfill God's holy will by employing the means of sanctification that Christ's Church continues to provide.

The visible body that today bears the name "the Catholic Church" is the same Church that Christ established to perpetuate in the world his words and his works—and his own divine life—and to bring salvation and sanctification to mankind. Despite superficial differences in certain appearances—and just as an adult differs from a child in some appearances but still remains the same person—the worldwide Catholic Church today remains the Church that was founded by Jesus Christ on Peter and the other apostles in the first century in the Near East. The early Church was—always!—nothing else but the Catholic Church.

Chapter 1

THE CHURCH OF THE APOSTLES

I.

Around the year 58 A.D., Claudius Lysias, a Roman tribune serving in Jerusalem, was forced to intervene with a detachment of troops to save a local man from being savagely beaten by an enraged mob. It was difficult to find out exactly what the man had done to incite the crowd. He had been dragged out of Jerusalem's Temple and was being severely set upon when Lysias arrived on the scene with his cohort of soldiers.

The tribune tried hard to get to the bottom of things, but some excitedly claimed one thing about the cause of the ruckus; others, something else. Jewish religious quarrels were incomprehensible. The rescued man's attempts to justify himself while under the protection of the Roman soldiers only stirred up the crowd further. Lysias thought of having the man examined by the grim Roman custom of scourging—lashing with whips or thongs, sometimes with metal tips—in order to make him confess to why he was being so viciously attacked by his fellow Jews.

Instead, the Roman tribune simply had him imprisoned when he learned that the man, who described himself as being from Tarsus in Cilicia (modern southern Turkey), was a Roman citizen.

This man would remain in a Palestinian prison for the next two years. Who he was and what he was doing would subsequently be brought out in several appearances before the Jewish Council, before two different Roman governors, and, finally, before King Herod Agrippa II, scion of the Herod family, who still, with Roman sufferance, ruled a portion of the Palestinian coast.

A spokesman for the Jewish high priest and the Jewish Council summarized the case against the prisoner to the Roman governor Felix: "We have found this man a pestilent fellow, an agitator among all the Jews throughout the world, and a ringleader of the sect of the Nazarenes. He even tried to profane the temple ..." (Acts 24:5–6).

A subsequent Roman governor, Festus, described the man's case somewhat differently to King Agrippa: "When the accusers stood up, they brought no charge in his case of such evils as I supposed; but they had certain points of dispute with him about their own superstition, and about one Jesus, who was dead, but whom Paul asserted to be alive" (Acts 25:18–19).

King Agrippa expressed the wish to see and hear this prisoner, Paul (his name had originally been Saul), and Festus was happy to arrange the meeting. Before the king, Paul referred to what he claimed was common knowledge. He explained that he had always lived as a Pharisee, one of the stricter Jewish groups, or parties. His crime in the eyes of his fellow Jews, he went on, was nothing else but "hope in the promise made by God to our fathers. ... Why is it thought incredible by any of you", Paul asks rhetorically, "any of you" referring to Jews, "that God raises from the dead?" (Acts 26:6, 8).

The Pharisees, after all, believed in resurrection as an article of faith; so why not in an actual instance of it in the case of this Jesus of Nazareth, about whom the Jews had been disputing?

The prisoner, it turned out, had not always viewed the matter in precisely this light. He freely admitted how zealous he had once been in persecuting the followers of Jesus: "I not only shut up many of the saints in prison, by authority from the chief priests, but when they were put to death I cast my vote against them ... in raging fury against them I persecuted them even to foreign cities" (Acts 26:10, 11).

Then Paul provided Agrippa with a description of how he had been changed and had come to believe in Jesus. It is still the world's greatest conversion story, the prototype of them all. It is also one of the world's greatest love stories— how one man's implacable hatred became transformed into burning, lifelong, self-sacrificing love. The same story is told three different times in the New Testament. Paul also referred to it from time to time in the letters he later wrote to the Churches he founded or visited. But this is how he told the story when he appeared before King Agrippa, more than twenty years after the event had taken place:

> Thus I journeyed to Damascus with the authority and commission of the chief priests. At midday, O king, I saw on the way a light from heaven, brighter than the sun, shining round me and those who journeyed with me. And when we had all fallen to the ground, I heard a voice saying to me in the Hebrew language, "Saul, Saul, why do you persecute me? It hurts you to kick against the goads." And I said, "Who are you, Lord?" And the Lord said, "I am Jesus whom you are persecuting. But rise and stand upon your feet; for I have appeared to you for this purpose, to appoint you to serve and bear witness ... that [people] may turn from darkness to light and from the power of Satan to God, that they may receive forgiveness of sins and a place among those who are sanctified by faith in me." (Acts 26:12–18)

It was going to be a tall order: turning people from darkness to light, from the power of Satan to the power of God. Dispensing forgiveness of sins through faith in Jesus, establishing a place among those sanctified by Jesus. Who could even imagine doing such things?

The reaction of the Roman governor Festus was probably predictable, just as the reaction of many a modern reader might be. "Paul," Festus cried out, "you are mad; your great learning is turning you mad" (Acts 26:24).

But Paul rejoined boldly: "The king knows about these things", he declared, turning to Agrippa. "I am persuaded that none of these things has escaped his notice, for this was not done in a corner. King Agrippa, do you believe the prophets? I know that you believe."

"In a short time you think to make me a Christian!" the king retorted, evidently with some nervousness.

"Whether short or long," Paul replied earnestly, "I would to God that not only you but also all who hear me this day might become such as I am—except for these chains" (Acts 26:26–29).

II.

For the first generation of Christians in Jerusalem, the crucifixion and resurrection of Jesus Christ were not "done in a corner". It was a well-enough-known hard fact that people, including the Herodian king himself, were being directly challenged by the apostles to admit that it had really happened.

And Paul knew very well what he thought about it: he wanted to make all who would listen to him become what he had become. He wanted them to become believers in sanctification and salvation in Jesus Christ, in the very one who had caused such a stir in Jerusalem and, after his resurrection from the dead as witnessed by the other apostles, had eventually singled out Paul, appearing to him in a vision on the road to Damascus.

Paul had already been actively promoting faith in this Jesus for a number of years prior to his arrest in Jerusalem. He had traveled throughout the eastern Mediterranean world with his message—through what today are Palestine, Syria, Turkey, and Greece, including the Greek islands. Many people, persuaded by his message, were converted. He organized these new believers into small communities—Churches—everywhere he went. The letters he would later write to those he had converted and baptized in many of these same Churches were destined to form an important part of what would eventually be called the New Testament. To this day they continue to be read in local churches and are among the best sources of knowledge of Jesus Christ and of the beginnings of Christianity.

Nor was Paul himself any stranger to persecution, to prisons, or to appearing before judges as the accused. He had had to flee Damascus not long after his conversion (cf. Acts 9:23–25). He was stoned (Acts 14:19) and at least three times beaten with rods (2 Cor 11:25). He wrote of "far more imprisonments" (2 Cor 11:23), and we know that he was on trial before Gallio in Corinth (Acts 18:12–17) and imprisoned in Philippi in northeastern Greece (Acts 16:23–39) and at Ephesus on the Aegean Sea in what is today part of Turkey (cf. 2 Cor 1:8–11).

Shortly after Paul's appearance before King Agrippa in Jerusalem, he was sent, still a prisoner, to Rome. As a Roman citizen he had appealed to Caesar and, hence, was sent to Caesar to be judged. He was to be confined within still other prison walls in Rome, and, according to tradition, in about

64 A.D. to lose his head there as a martyr for Jesus Christ in the persecutions launched by the Roman emperor Nero.

What was the message Paul had preached so effectively and so fervently for so long by the time he got to Rome? This is how he himself summarizes it in the first sermon of his that is preserved in the Acts of the Apostles, a sermon he preached in the eastern Mediterranean city of Antioch:

> Men of Israel, and you that fear God, listen.... God has brought to Israel a Savior, Jesus, as he promised.... [T]o us has been sent the message of this salvation. For those who live in Jerusalem, and their rulers, because they did not recognize him nor understand the utterances of the prophets which are read every sabbath, fulfilled these by condemning him. Though they could charge him with nothing deserving death, yet they asked Pilate to have him killed. And when they had fulfilled all that was written of him, they took him down from the tree and laid him in a tomb.
>
> But God raised him from the dead; and for many days he appeared to those who came up with him from Galilee to Jerusalem, who are now his witnesses to the people. And we bring you the good news that what God promised to the fathers, this he has fulfilled to us their children by raising Jesus.... (Acts 13:16, 23, 26b–33)

What Paul preached, then, was "the good news" of salvation in Jesus Christ, whom God had raised up, signifying victory over human sin and death. Salvation was the essence of Paul's message (though he went on to specify considerably more than that). That God had sent Christ into the world to raise us up and save us was the incredible good news that never allowed Paul to rest until he had proclaimed it to everybody he could reach.

Our English word *gospel* derives from the Old English word *godspel*, meaning "good news" (= Latin: *evangelium*; Greek:

euangelion). The four Gospels of the New Testament are distinct but very similar extended accounts of the words and acts of Jesus that constitute this good news.

Even today, Christian faith is nothing else at bottom but belief in that good news. Though reflected upon and elaborated and enriched over the course of two thousand years, it remains the same faith Jesus personally asked of those who heard him in the flesh. His message was not just that we could have a better world by doing good but, specifically, that sin and death can be overcome in us, just as they were in him—and if sin can be overcome in us, then, obviously, we will be able and highly motivated to do good as well.

The difficult question then was the same as it is today: How can anyone really believe that Jesus actually rose from the dead? Jesus had literally had to knock Paul down and then come before him in a vision with explicit instructions before Paul could believe. So how could anyone, then or now, believe simply on Paul's say-so?

Paul thought people could be brought to belief by the preaching of those who witnessed the resurrection of Jesus from the dead. Faith comes from what is heard, Paul confidently declared (see Rom 10:8). Not only was Paul successful in his preaching, he was prepared to go to great lengths to prove his point. Literally millions of people manifestly have been convinced by the preaching of the good news of salvation in Jesus Christ since that day.

But is that all? Is that enough?

III.

There is more—quite a bit more. When Paul left off persecuting the disciples of Jesus at the time of his conversion on the road to Damascus, joining them instead, he became an active member of an existing body of believers in Christ. In view of his evident abilities and his special call from Christ, he was surely not going to play an inconspicuous role within the infant society of Jesus' followers. No: he was a man of high destiny.

Nevertheless, the New Testament makes clear that Paul was never merely an independent operator or self-starting freewheeler. At the time of Paul's vision, Jesus instructed him quite unmistakably: "You will be told what you are to do" (Acts 9:6).

Paul did assume a prominent leadership role in the early Church, but only after being commissioned by Church leaders: "After fasting and praying, they laid their hands on them"—upon Paul and his first missionary companion, St. Barnabas—"and sent them off" (Acts 13:3).

Eventually—perhaps even quite soon—Paul was able to claim the title of "apostle", a name taken from the Greek word meaning one sent out as a messenger. Though selected by Jesus himself, the New Testament is clear that Paul actually was sent out by the early Church.

During his earthly life, Jesus sent out twelve such apostles, a number intended, no doubt, probably, to symbolize the twelve tribes of Israel: "He called the twelve together and gave them power and authority . . . and he sent them out to preach the kingdom of God and to heal" (Lk 9:1–2). After the Resurrection, Jesus sent the apostles out on an even more improbable mission: "Go . . . and make disciples of all nations, baptizing them in the name of the Father and of the Son and of the Holy Spirit, teaching them to observe all that I have commanded you; and lo, I am with you always . . ." (Mt 28:19–20).

The original apostles had been the followers of Jesus during his earthly life. After his death and resurrection, they remained together as witnesses to his resurrection (cf. Acts 1:22). Their number would not be limited to twelve—as is proved by the fact that Paul and others also became apostles. The original group even found it necessary to choose by lot a successor to Judas, the member of the Twelve who had betrayed Jesus and turned him over to his executioners. A group of other followers of Jesus, including Mary, his mother, gathered around the apostles into a small community devoted to prayer (cf. Acts 1:14).

The apostles were clearly the leaders of this community, by virtue of the special relationship they had had with Jesus and specific appointment, or commissioning, by him. One of them, Peter, again by the choice of Jesus, was the leader of the apostles and, hence, of the whole community. While he was still with them, Jesus had instructed them exhaustively, according to the testimony of the four Gospels but with little effect—or so it seemed immediately after his death and even, for a brief period, after his post-resurrection appearances to them.

Then something extraordinary happened. The apostles, along with the whole praying community gathered around them, became changed, transformed, motivated, empowered. Jesus had taught them beforehand that God would send them in his name a counselor, the Holy Spirit, who would teach them all things and bring to their remembrance all that he had said to them (see Jn 14:26).

It is a good thing that Jesus did not depart from this world without making provision for carrying on his words and his works. His chosen followers had not shown themselves to be very zealous or reliable at the time of his arrest and crucifixion. The Gospel of Mark plainly records that "they all forsook him and fled" (Mk 14:50). The outlook for the long-term survival of his teachings and his community was not bright unless something galvanized the members of his group who were familiar with his life and teachings. Something did:

> When the day of Pentecost had come, they were all together in one place. And suddenly a sound came from heaven like the rush of a mighty wind, and it filled all the house where they were sitting. And there appeared to them tongues as of fire, distributed and resting on each one of them. And they were all filled with the Holy spirit.... (Acts 2:1–4)

Extraordinary phenomena accompanied this coming of the Holy Spirit to the assembled followers of Jesus: "[They] began to speak in other tongues, as the Spirit gave them utterance" (Acts 2:4). Such phenomena appropriately signaled a unique occurrence: the conferral of the Holy Spirit upon an organized body of believing worshippers, individually and collectively. Some outside observers, however, thought these first Christians were simply drunk with wine.

But these extraordinary phenomena were far from being the most significant things about this first Christian Pentecost. Most significant was that the Spirit of God had come to dwell in a special way in the community of followers that Jesus had left behind. Among other things, with the coming of the Spirit, the apostles, the leaders of the small assembly, suddenly became *effective* witnesses of the resurrection of Jesus and of the graces that would henceforth flow as a result of it. They began to preach with utter conviction and to bear witness up to the point—in the case of at least most of them, as tradition holds—of giving up their very lives. And what they began then is still going on:

> Peter, standing with the eleven, lifted up his voice and addressed them, "Men of Judea and all who dwell in Jerusa-

lem, let this be known to you, and give ear to my words. For these men are not drunk, as you suppose, since it is only the third hour of the day." (Acts 2:14)

What were the words Peter thought so important for everybody to give ear to and hear? They were almost exactly the same words we have already seen Paul using when he appeared over twenty years later before King Agrippa II in Jerusalem. The preaching of the apostles was nothing if not consistent.

On the day of Pentecost, Peter described Jesus as "a man attested to you by God with mighty works and wonders and signs . . . crucified and killed by the hands of lawless men. . . . This Jesus God raised up, and of that we are all witnesses. Being therefore exalted at the right hand of God, and having received from the Father the promise of the Holy Spirit, he has poured out this which you see and hear" (Acts 2:22–23, 32–33).

As a result of the descent of the Holy Spirit on the first Pentecost, and following the apostolic preaching about the death and resurrection of Jesus, the Acts of the Apostles records that "there were added that day about three thousand souls" (2:41). Moreover, "the Lord added to their number day by day those who were being saved" (2:47). The Lord is still adding to their number.

Pentecost is often, and rightly, considered to be the birthday of the Church, since it was upon the community of believers in Jesus assembled in prayer that the Holy Spirit originally came down. Further careful examination of the New Testament evidence also reveals that the Church upon which the Holy Spirit originally descended at Pentecost in Jerusalem was the same Church we Catholics are part of today—the Church that each Sunday in reciting the Creed, professes to be the One, Holy, Catholic, and Apostolic Church of Jesus Christ the Savior.

IV.

It was Jesus Christ in person who called the apostles to be the leaders of his infant Church, the organized assembly, or community, of his followers. It was Jesus who sent them out to preach his gospel, the good news he brought of the sanctification and salvation that was available in him. Once the Holy Spirit had descended upon the infant Church at Pentecost, the preaching of the apostles very quickly proved to be remarkably effective. Few who heard it remained indifferent; it demanded response, and many responded positively.

More than once, "the Holy Spirit fell upon all who heard the word" (Acts 10:44). The result was belief in the saving message of Jesus and active commitment to his cause, which, from the beginning, always entailed becoming a member of his Church.

Those who heard Peter's very first preaching "were cut to the heart, and said to Peter and the rest of the apostles, 'Brethren, what shall we *do*?'" (Acts 2:37, emphasis added).

Although Jesus had always asked for faith in himself, he was never content with passive acquiescence in his teachings. He always had words of high praise for "those who hear the word of God and *do* it" (Lk 8:21, emphasis added). Jesus did not teach any merely speculative philosophy; the truth he claimed to bring from God was supposed to affect *one's whole life*; what one did after accepting his word tested whether one really believed. This fundamental fact about Christianity has always distinguished it from other philosophies of life and, indeed, from most other religions. From the very beginning of the life of the Church, those who heard the word were immediately anxious about what they should *do.*

What *were* they supposed to do? The head of the apostles, Peter, answered this question as follows: "Repent, and be baptized every one of you in the name of Jesus Christ for the forgiveness of your sins; and you shall receive the gift of the Holy Spirit" (Acts 2:38).

Just as the Holy Spirit had, at Pentecost, come down upon the whole Church, and each member of the Church individually, so the Spirit was to come to each new believer in Jesus who would be added to the members of his Church.

From the very beginning, then, to become a Christian entailed a number of things. It required a conversion, or change of heart, a turning away from wrongdoing and preoccupation with self ("Repent!").

It required participation in a communal sacred act carried out by those who were already members of the community of the followers of Jesus ("Be baptized!"). The "forgiveness of sins" that Peter had also spoken of, by the way, was a *consequence* of the baptism that had to be undergone, according to the head of the apostles; the Holy Spirit further entered the soul of the new Christian as another consequence of the rite of baptism enjoined by Jesus. Through baptism each convert also became a member of the existing community, or assembly, of believing and practicing Christians—the Church.

What were some of the consequences and benefits of incorporation into the already existing Church of Christ? The Acts of the Apostles records that these first Christians "devoted themselves to the apostles' teaching and fellowship, to the breaking of the bread and the prayers" (2:42).

We should take careful note of this brief description of the activities of the early Christians. We can clearly deduce

from it that those Christians who first adopted the faith of
Jesus Christ under the headship of Peter and the other apostles did the following:

1. They subscribed to a specific *doctrine* about what they
   must believe and do in order to be saved ("the apostles' teaching").

2. They belonged to a definite, organized *community*
   ("the Church"), precisely the one led by the apostles ("the apostles' . . . fellowship").

3. They participated in a *sacred rite* that included a meal
   regularly enacted within this same organized community ("the breaking of the bread").

The sacred rite celebrated by the early Church was believed to be a special way in which Jesus continued to remain substantially present in the Church he had founded.
Had he not taught the disciples that "the bread which I shall
give for the life of the world is my flesh"? (Jn 6:51). The
sacred rite celebrated by his Church from the beginning, the
Eucharist (or, as it has more popularly been called for many
centuries in the West, the Mass), was believed to consist in
the sacramental offering, confecting, and consuming of
Christ's own Flesh and Blood. The organized worship carried out in the Church from her earliest days (what Peter in
Acts calls "the prayers") therefore included the substance of
what today we call "the Mass".

One of the most remarkable things recorded in the Acts
of the Apostles concerns what happened to those who responded to Peter's call, underwent baptism, had their sins
forgiven, received the Holy Spirit, were thereby incorporated into the Church, and then partook of the consecrated
Bread that was really the promised Flesh of Christ himself.

They were *changed*—just as the apostles themselves were changed at Pentecost: they no longer acted or reacted merely according to human nature.

For one thing, as the Acts of the Apostles records, they distributed their goods "as any had need"; for another, "the company of those who believed were of one heart and soul" (4:32). In short, their new ideal of conduct, no longer that of mere human nature, was based upon the words and example of their risen Lord, who had taught them that "by this all men will know that you are my disciples, if you have love for one another" (Jn 13:35).

The Lord Jesus himself had been known for "going about doing good" (Acts 10:38); and so the test and proof of authentic Christianity was henceforth to be—in contrast to the mere lip service in favor of the good, which remains a constant temptation in every age—nothing else but "going about doing good" themselves.

It is, of course, true that history has recorded many instances since apostolic times when professed followers of Christ have failed to do the good they should have done; there have been, sadly, all too many instances of their doing the contrary. Christians do not always respond as they should to the graces available to them through the Church. With free will and under the effects of Original Sin that still remain with them, Christians are often untrue to the promises of their baptism.

Nevertheless, what the apostles of Jesus set in motion through an organized institution, the Church—and this Church clearly emerges as what she has been ever since as early as the description of her in the Acts of the Apostles—*has* abundantly resulted, on countless occasions through the centuries, in doing good. And this good would almost certainly not have been done if Jesus Christ had never come into the world and left disciples behind to perpetuate his words and his works and continually lead others to the same discipleship they shared.

This is the legacy, not only of the saints—although, especially of them; it is the legacy also of numberless Christians in every age who, through grace, have tried to be better themselves while doing good to others and in the world.

V.

What kind of thing is it, then, concretely, the entity whose actions are outlined so clearly in Acts—from which we have taken only a few of the more salient and dramatic points? What is it that the apostles set in motion as an organized institution that has lasted until now?

Reading the Acts of the Apostles, we can clearly discern the coming to life of *the Church*. What Jesus left behind to carry on his works and his words was no abstract scheme, outline, plan, or book but rather an organized community of believers. As far as we know, Jesus himself wrote nothing down, except with his finger on the ground when the Pharisees brought the adulterous woman to him for judgment (cf. Jn 8:6).

It is one of the strangest paradoxes in history that many of his sincere followers have imagined that Jesus is chiefly to be encountered *in a book*. Even though the book in question, the New Testament, is an inspired one, and even though Jesus is to be encountered there, the New Testament is far from the only place where Jesus is to be encountered.

We should also bear in mind that not all of the New Testament was written by Jesus' direct disciples; in some cases it was written by *their* disciples. What the New Testament contains, in other words, was handed on. What was then written down has been handed on further in the Church. In other words, Jesus committed his teaching, not merely to the pages of a book, but to living men who handed it on to others.

Even the great apostle Paul, chosen by Jesus to carry the faith to the gentiles, recipient and beneficiary of a special revelation from the risen Jesus—even St. Paul wrote that he had delivered what he also received (cf. 1 Cor 15:3), meaning what he received from the living tradition of the Church already active when he joined Christ's followers.

It is true that Jesus sent his Spirit to St. Paul and to the other New Testament writers in a special way in order to insure that they would deliver his message accurately. That is one of the things meant by "inspiration" in the New Testament. The New Testament books constitute an inspired record of what Jesus said and did on earth among us but this is primarily because they are the record of what the living Church that Jesus left behind continued to teach and preach about him after he ascended into heaven. The Church already was operating before the books of the New Testament were written.

One reason Jesus committed his message to a living Church as he did is that he also committed other essential things to that Church at the same time. Plainly, the Acts of the Apostles shows that the first Christians carried out various rites in addition to hearing the teachings of the apostles. These rites, later called sacraments (another ancient name for them was the mysteries), could only be passed from one living person to another; they could never be gotten out of the pages of the New Testament, no matter how inspired and holy that book is. For in addition to demanding adherence to his words of life, Jesus also said that "unless you eat the flesh of the Son of Man and drink his blood you have no life in you" (Jn 6:53).

Thus necessarily there had to be a living Church in addition to the Scriptures, to dispense Jesus' Flesh and Blood, which he himself said had to be consumed. Otherwise, sharing in his own divine life in this way would have been impossible. For this reason, Jesus, in addition to committing his saving message to his apostles, gave them the power to carry out certain sacred actions instituted by him, which he indissolubly linked to the sanctification and salvation that he had come into the world to bring.

For Jesus not only commanded the apostles to "teach all nations"; he also commanded them to "baptize them" (cf. Mt 28:19-20); he further commanded them to "do this [the Eucharist] in remembrance of me" (Lk 22:19). To put it another way, Jesus not only founded a Church of the word; he founded a Church of the sacraments as well.

What was the essential nature of this Church? It was the "assembly" (in Greek, *ekklesia*), or community, of those "called out" to be his followers. St. Paul habitually employs the word *Church* to designate the entire body of Christians, and he quite explicitly, and often, calls this collectivity "the body of Christ": "You are the body of Christ and individually members of it" (1 Cor 12:27).

One has to be baptized into this Church; the Holy Spirit comes upon one as a result of this baptism. *The Holy Spirit is given to the whole Church, not just to individuals.* Before his crucifixion, Jesus had promised to send the Holy Spirit to guide his followers: "[T]he Holy Spirit, whom the Father will send in my name, he will teach you all things, and bring to your remembrance all that I have said to you" (Jn 14:26). The Holy Spirit was sent to the whole Church: "They were all filled with the Holy Spirit" (Acts 2:4). During Peter's initial preaching proclaiming the resurrection of Christ, he specified that those baptized would "receive the gift of the Holy Spirit" (Acts 2:38).

The intimate relationship between baptism and the gift of the Spirit is regularly seen in the New Testament, for example, in the incidents where Philip baptizes the Ethiopian eunuch (Acts 8) or where Peter baptizes the entire household of Cornelius (Acts 10). Baptism is clearly portrayed in the New Testament as a sacred act of the Church by which the Holy Spirit is conferred.

Thus the early Church was not merely a voluntary association of like-minded people who had come to accept the message of Jesus. She functioned under hierarchical leaders appointed by Jesus himself, who gave them both sacred powers and authority. John's Gospel records that Jesus transmitted the Spirit to the apostles in a special way (apart from Pentecost) and special powers as well: "He breathed on them and said to them: 'Receive the Holy Spirit. If you forgive the sins of any, they are forgiven'" (Jn 20:22–23).

The apostles exercised the powers given to them in dramatic ways. We read that when Paul laid his hands upon some converts at Ephesus in Asia Minor, "the Holy Spirit came on them" (Acts 19:6). Indeed, more than once it is recorded that "they laid their hands on them and they received the Holy Spirit" (Acts 8:17).

Along with the regular powers that they received, the apostles occasionally made use of even more extraordinary gifts. Outside the Temple, Peter cured a man crippled from birth by invoking the name of Jesus Christ of Nazareth (cf. Acts 3:1–9). So great was the prestige of the head apostle that people put their sick out where Peter would pass so that his shadow might fall on them and cure them (cf. Acts 5:15). In Acts 9:36–43 we read of Peter's raising a woman from the dead.

Paul, at Troas, brought back to life a young man who had fallen from a third-story window (cf. Acts 20:7–10). Indeed, "God did extraordinary miracles by the hands of Paul, so that handkerchiefs or aprons were carried away from his body to the sick, and diseases left them . . ." (Acts 19:11–12).

Just as Jesus had done miracles to elicit faith and demonstrate that he made use of God's power, the apostles performed similar miracles to demonstrate the powers Jesus had committed into *their* hands.

When the apostles assembled at the Council of Jerusalem around the year 49 A.D. and made the momentous decision that Christians were to be exempted from the ritual Mosaic law that had bound the Jews, they represented their decision as literally equivalent to the working of the Holy Spirit: "It has seemed good to the Holy Spirit and to us to lay upon you no greater burden" (Acts 15:28). Such was the decision of this protocouncil of Jerusalem.

It is abundantly clear that, already in New Testament times, the Church was consciously carrying out a definite mission as a formed and organized body—a community of believers in Jesus Christ possessing the Holy Spirit and living under appointed leaders dispensing both word and sacrament with an authority they understood they had derived from Christ, and which they also understood they could pass on to others ("They laid their hands on them and sent them off" [Acts 13:3]).

There was nothing in the least vague or ill-defined about what kind of organized, visible, hierarchical community the early Church was from the very beginning. After being commissioned by the Church, Paul and Barnabas in their turn ordained presbyters in every Church they established in Galatia (cf. Acts 14:22).

No doubt this primitive Church did not resemble in every particular of her organization, life, and practice the complex, developed, worldwide organization the Catholic Church is today; but it is quite evident from the New Testament that these differences involve appearances only.

So it is with the Church today by comparison with what she was at the time that Jesus launched her on her pilgrimage through time and space by commissioning the apostles: it is the same Church. The Church is a living entity that has grown and developed steadily from the time of her birth.

VI.

The Church of the apostles resembles in all essentials the Church of today; she already bore the marks, or notes, of the true Church of Christ that are still professed today in the Nicene Creed: the Church is One, Holy, Catholic, and Apostolic.

The Church of the apostles was definitely *one:* "There is one body and one Spirit," St. Paul wrote, "just as you were called to the one hope that belongs to your call, one Lord, one faith, one baptism, one God and Father of us all" (Eph 4:4–5). St. Paul linked this primitive unity to the Church's common Eucharistic Bread: "Because there is one bread, we who are many are one body, for we all partake of the one bread" (1 Cor 10:17). Jesus had promised at the outset that "there shall be one flock, one shepherd" (Jn 10:16).

The Church of the apostles was *holy*: when we say that the Church is holy, we mean among other things that she had the all-holy God as her author. We do not mean that all of her members have ceased to be sinners and become holy. On the contrary, the Church from the beginning has been composed of sinners: "Christ Jesus came into the world to save sinners" (1 Tim 1:15). The Church was founded to continue Christ's redemptive and sanctifying work in the world.

Implicit in the appellation *holy* as applied to the Church is that the Church from the beginning has been endowed with the means to help *make holy* the sinners in her ranks. The Church has been given the sacraments and the truths Christ preached precisely to help make sinners holy.

It was in this sense that St. Paul was able to write:

> Christ loved the church and gave himself up for her, that he might sanctify her, having cleansed her by the washing of water with the word, that he might present the church to himself in splendor, without spot or wrinkle or any such thing, that she might be holy and without blemish. (Eph 5:25–27)

The holiness of the Church of which the Creed properly speaks has always had reference to her divine Founder and to what the Church was founded by him with the power and authority to *do*, not with the condition of her professed members.

The third great historic mark, or note, of the one true Church is that this Church is *Catholic*. *Catholic* means "universal". It refers as much to the fullness of the faith she possesses as to the undeniable extension in both time and space that has characterized her virtually from the beginning. At the very beginning, it was difficult to see how the "little flock" (Lk 12:32) of which the Church then consisted could qualify as "universal". Still, just as the embryo contains in germ the whole human being, the Church already contained within herself the universality that would quickly become manifest.

It is not without significance that the Holy Spirit came down upon the Church at Pentecost at a time when "there were dwelling in Jerusalem Jews, devout men from *every nation under heaven*" (Acts 2:5, emphasis added). The Holy Spirit temporarily enabled the apostles to speak to them in their various languages—a powerful sign that the Church was destined for all men everywhere. At that first Pentecost in Jerusalem, many who had come from afar, the book of the Acts declares, accepted the faith then and there and, presumably, began forthwith carrying "the Catholic Church" back to the four corners of the earth.

The catholicity of the Church resides as much in the fact that the Church is for everybody at all times as it does in the fact that she was indeed destined to spread throughout the whole world, as she has not failed to do. Within a few short years after the foundation of the Church, St. Paul was already writing that "the word of the truth . . . in the whole world . . . is bearing fruit and growing" (Col 1:5–6). This is yet another *process* begun at Pentecost that is still going on.

Finally, the Church that issued from the commission of Christ to the apostles was *apostolic*. Christ founded the Church upon the apostles: "Did I not choose you, the twelve?" he asked them (Jn 6:70). The apostles understood perfectly well that they were not just to set themselves up in their own little community as they pleased, as we sometimes today see "true-gospel" churches set up, whether in storefronts or in the suburbs. No: the testimony of the New Testament is that "one does not take the honor upon himself" (Heb 5:4).

Nothing is clearer than that the Church started out apostolic. The question is whether the apostles had the power and authority to pass on to others what they had received from Christ. We have already seen that they did have this power and authority. New Testament evidence is clear about that. And subsequent historical evidence is equally clear that they did pass power and authority on to successors, the bishops. There are references in the New Testament to the appointment of bishops by the apostles, as well as to the appointment of further bishops by *them* (e.g., Tit 1:5–9).

When, today, we ask *where*, if anywhere, is to be found the Church Christ founded—according to the New Testament, which then describes how that Church perpetuated herself by preaching Christ everywhere and by appointing new leaders as necessary—we have to reformulate the question. We must ask: *What* Church existing today descends in an unbroken line from the apostles of Jesus Christ (and possesses the other essential marks of the true Church of which the Creed speaks)? Further, what Church existing today is headed by a single, recognized, designated leader under the headship of Peter?

To ask these questions is to answer them. Any entity claiming to be the Church of Christ—*his* body!—must demonstrate its apostolicity, its organic link with the original apostles, on whom Christ manifestly established his Church. Nothing less can qualify as the apostolic Church that Jesus founded.

As much for our instruction as for the assurance he intended to give to the apostles to whom he was speaking, Jesus said, "He who hears you, hears me" (Lk 10:16). Do we take these words seriously today? Do we listen to the teachings of the successors of the apostles—the bishops in union with and under the successor of the apostle Peter, the pope—as if these teachings were the words of Christ himself?

If we do, we are properly members of the Church that Jesus Christ founded on the apostles and that has come down to us from them. If we do not, how can we pretend that we take *anything* seriously that Christ said and taught? For he said nothing more solemnly and categorically than those words declaring that the apostles and their successors would speak *for* him in the very serious business of gathering in and converting and sanctifying his people and leading them toward the salvation he offers.

Jesus intended that the fullness of his grace should come to his people in a Church that, from the beginning, was what the Creed still calls that same Church today: One, Holy, Catholic, and Apostolic.

Chapter 2

THE CHURCH OF THE EARLY FATHERS

I.

Sometime around the year 107 A.D., a short, sharp persecution of the Church of Christ resulted in the arrest of the bishop of Antioch in Syria. His name was Ignatius. According to one of the harsh penal practices of the Roman Empire of the day, the good bishop was condemned to be delivered up to wild beasts in the arena in the capital city. The insatiable public appetite for bloody spectacles meant a chronically short supply of victims; prisoners were thus sent off to Rome to help fill the need.

So the second bishop of Antioch was sent to Rome as a condemned prisoner. According to Church historian Eusebius (ca. 260–ca. 340), Ignatius had been bishop in Antioch for nearly forty years at the time of his arrest. This means that he had been bishop there while some of the original apostles were almost certainly still alive and preaching.

St. Ignatius of Antioch was conducted first by land from Syria across Asia Minor (modern Turkey). He was escorted by a detachment of Roman soldiers. In a letter he sent ahead to the Church of Christ in Rome, this bishop described his ardent wish to imitate the passion of Christ through his own coming martyrdom in the Roman Colosseum. He warned the Christians in Rome not to try to save him. He also spoke of his conflicts with his military escort and of their casual cruelties, describing his guards as "ten leopards". The discipline of the march cannot have been unrelieved, however, since Ignatius was permitted to receive delegations of visitors from local Churches in the cities of Asia Minor through which the escorts and Ignatius passed along the way (*To the Romans*, 5:1).

In Smyrna (modern Izmir), St. Ignatius met, not only with the bishop of that city, St. Polycarp, but also with delegations from the neighboring cities of Ephesus, Magnesia, and Tralles. Each delegation was headed by a local bishop. Ignatius wrote thank-you letters to the Christians in each of these cities who had visited the notable but shackled bishop-prisoner. Chiefly through these letters, St. Ignatius of Antioch is known to us today.

Establishing these letters, written in Greek, as authentic and genuinely from the first decade of the second century was one of the triumphs of nineteenth-century British scholarship. Without them, this bishop of Antioch might have remained no more than a name, as obscure as many another early Christian bishop.

Escorted on to the Greek city of Troas on the Aegean Sea, Ignatius wrote yet another letter to the Church at Smyrna, through which he had passed. He also wrote personally to Bishop Polycarp of that city. Finally, from Troas he wrote still another letter to the Philadelphians; the local Church of Philadelphia had despatched two deacons who overtook his party at Troas.

Shortly after writing these seven letters to Churches in Asia Minor, St. Ignatius of Antioch was taken aboard ship. The remainder of his journey to Italy was by sea. Tradition holds that he won his longed-for martyrdom in the Roman amphitheater during the reign of Emperor Trajan (98–117).

But the letters he left behind afford us a precious and remarkable picture of what that Church was like not even two full generations after issuing from the side of Jesus Christ on the Cross.

The adult life of St. Ignatius of Antioch as a second-generation Church leader almost exactly spanned the period of transition between the end of the first Christian generation and the beginning of the third. Thus, his witness about the nature of the Church of his day is of the most profound and fundamental importance.

What was the Church like around the year 107 A.D.? The Church had already spread far and wide since the days of the apostles. St. Ignatius was conducted over a good part of what, today, is Turkey, encountering local Churches in most major towns. At the head of each of these Churches was a principal leader, a bishop. The geographical spread of individual local Churches, each headed by a bishop, is obvious from the fact that Ignatius was met by delegations headed by bishops from each sizeable town along the route.

That St. Ignatius was met by these "official" delegations indicates that local Churches were in close touch with one another. They did not see themselves as independent, self-selected, self-governing congregations of like-minded people; they saw themselves as linked together in the one body of Christ according to an already firmly established, well-understood system, even though they happened to be geographically separated.

The solidarity with which they all turned out to honor a prisoner being led to martyrdom, who also happened to be the bishop of Antioch, tells us something about their respect for the incumbent of that office. Antioch was to become one of the great patriarchal bishoprics of the Church of antiquity, along with Alexandria and Rome—and, later, Constantinople.

The letters of St. Ignatius are even more pointed concerning the role that a bishop ("overseer") held in the early Church. The modern reader may be startled at the degree to which these letters exalt the role of the bishop. "It is essential to act in no way without the bishop", Ignatius wrote to the Trallians. ". . . *Obey* the bishop as if he were Jesus Christ" (2:2,1). "Do nothing apart from the bishop", he wrote to the Philadelphians (7:2). To the Smyrnaeans, he gave the same advice: "You should all follow the bishop as Jesus Christ did the Father. . . . Nobody must do anything that has to do with the Church without the bishop's approval" (8:1).

The New Testament shows the apostles appointing others besides themselves to offices in the Church. Peter and the other apostles at Jerusalem very quickly decided to appoint deacons to assist them (cf. Acts 6:1–6). Paul similarly placed someone in authority in the Churches he founded (cf. Acts 14:23; 2 Tim 1:6). These ecclesiastical appointments were carried out by means of a religious rite: the laying on of hands, either by those who already had authority conferred on them by Christ (the apostles) or those on whom *they* had conferred authority by the laying on of hands. These rites were *sacramental ordinations*.

For a period of time in the early Church there seems to have been no entirely clear terminology designating these ordained Church officers or ministers. St. Paul spoke of bishops and deacons (Phil 1:1), though he also mentions other offices, such as apostles, prophets, and teachers (1 Cor 12:29). St. James spoke of elders (5:14). In the Acts of the Apostles (e.g., 11:30), we hear many times of *elders* or *presbyters*. Sometimes the designations *bishop* and *elder* seem to have been used interchangeably.

In the course of the second half of the first century, however, a consistent terminology for these Church offices was becoming fixed. The letters of St. Ignatius of Antioch make clear that leadership in the Christian community, in all the Churches, is exercised by an order of "bishops, presbyters, and deacons" (*To the Trallians* 3:2; *To Polycarp* 6:1). Of these designations, *bishop* comes from the Greek *episkopos*, meaning "overseer"; *presbyter* from the Greek *presbyteros*, "elder"; and *deacon* from the Greek *diakonos*, "servant" or "minister".

Thus, from that time on, these were the offices in what was already an institutional, hierarchical Church (this is not to imply that the Church was ever anything but institutional and hierarchical, only that the evidence for these characteristics had become unmistakably clear by this time).

By the way, the term *priest* (Greek: *hierus*) does not seem to have been used at first for the Christian presbyter; the nonuse of this particular term in the earliest years of the Church was due to the need to distinguish the Christian priesthood of the new dispensation from the Jewish Temple priests, who were still functioning up to the time of the destruction of Jerusalem and the Temple by the Romans in the year 70 A.D. After that time, the use of the word *priest* for those ordained in Christ began to be more and more common.

St. Ignatius of Antioch did not know of any such thing as a "Church" that was merely an assemblage of like-minded people who believed themselves to have been moved by the Spirit. The early Christians *were* moved by the Spirit to join the Church, the established visible, institutional, sacerdotal, and hierarchical Church—the only kind St. Ignatius of Antioch would ever have recognized as the Church.

And it was for this visible, institutional, sacerdotal, and hierarchical Church—an entity purveying both the word and sacraments of Jesus—that this early bishop was willing to give himself up to be torn apart by wild beasts in the arena. He wrote to St. Polycarp words that were also meant for the latter's flock in Smyrna: "Pay attention to the bishop so that God will pay attention to you. I give my life as a sacrifice (poor as it is) for those who are obedient to the bishop, the presbyters, and the deacons" (6:1). To the Trallians he wrote: "You cannot have a Church without these" (3:2).

St. Ignatius certainly did not fail to recognize that, in one of today's popular but imprecise formulations, "the people are the Church." His letters were intended to teach, admonish, exhort, and encourage none other than "the people". But he also understood that each one of "the people" entered the Church through a sacred rite of baptism, and thereafter belonged to a group in which the bishop, in certain respects and for certain purposes, resembled, on the one hand, the father of a family and, on the other, a monarch—more than some democratically elected leaders.

II.

In what respects and for what purposes does a bishop resemble a monarch? Granted that Jesus came into the world to save us from our sins, sanctify us with his Spirit, and lead us to heaven, how can we imagine that he would also have saddled us with anything like a monarchical bishop who in matters pertaining to Christ's truth and our salvation has to be obeyed?

How can we imagine this when Jesus expressly taught that in the community of his followers, the leaders would have to be the *servants*? "Whoever would be great among you", said Jesus, "must be your servant, and whoever would be first among you must be slave of all" (Mk 10:43–44). This was the Lord's pattern and rule of authority in his Church.

The answers to these questions about why Jesus established an institutional and hierarchical Church are implicit in the reasons for which he founded any Church at all: Jesus wanted (1) to preserve and perpetuate his *teaching*, the truths about God that he came into the world to proclaim; and (2) to provide those he had saved with the sacramental means to share in his divine life. In order to insure the latter, Jesus had to establish within the community of his followers the *power* to reenact the sacrifice of the Cross by which he had saved them.

Prior to the invention of printing in the fifteenth century, books had to be copied by hand and were enormously expensive. Many people were not educated or even literate. There was scant access to the printed word. Thus, committing Jesus' teachings to writing was not necessarily the best means for preserving and perpetuating them. Committing them into the hands of living men charged with faithfully handing them down in the community was a better course, and that is the one that Jesus took. That these living men, or their followers, *also* wrote down the essentials of Jesus' life and teaching in the four Gospels and the other books of the New Testament does not change the fact that Jesus committed the teachings initially into the hands of living men to be passed on to other living men—in a living Church.

To accomplish his second aim, providing the sacramental means for his followers to share in his divine life, Jesus could have acted in no more effective way than by charging others in his living Church with this task: "Do this in remembrance of me" (Lk 22:19)—and providing them with the *power* to do what he asked in his name and on his behalf, through sacred ordination.

The historical fact is indisputable: Jesus chose to perpetuate his teachings and his divine life in this world by committing both to the care of living men, the apostles. He gave the apostles this power and responsibility—along with the power to hand on this power to successors. The apostles and their successors were thus empowered to perpetuate the sacramental presence of Jesus in this world, as well as to teach what Jesus had taught them, with the help of the Spirit (cf. Jn 16:13), and to *correct* any errors that might creep in to what Jesus had originally taught.

If Jesus thus confided this twofold power to a special, set-apart class of his followers, he logically had also to grant them the authority to order the affairs of the community within which they exercised this God-given power to teach and provide sacraments. Thus it was, in an exact sense, that the apostles and their successors, who came to be called bishops, were given the threefold power to teach, sanctify, and rule within the Church (as a later age concisely described the role and functions of bishops).

In these respects and for these purposes, then, Jesus Christ founded a hierarchical Church headed by a "monarchical" bishop in each locality. These bishops appointed others in their turn, presbyters and deacons, sharing with them some of the powers they had from Christ. And Jesus had promised the apostles that they would be assisted in their work in a special way by the Holy Spirit; he said he would pray the Father to send the Spirit to be with them forever (cf. Jn 14:15–17). The historical record shows that the Holy Spirit *has* been with the bishops of the Church when they have acted together with their leader, the successor of Peter, to preserve the truths Christ brought into the world.

What we see in the letters of St. Ignatius of Antioch is that the whole Church "system" for carrying out the mission Jesus gave to the apostles was already firmly established and functioning by the end of the first century. Ignatius, writing no more than seventy or eighty years after the Crucifixion, makes frequent reference to teachings that all Christians are expected to accept as having come from Christ himself. In his letter to the Smyrnaeans, he provides a remarkable yet concise summary of the fundamentals of the faith. What is required, he wrote, is to have

> unshakable faith in the cross of the Lord Jesus Christ.... On the human side, [Christ] was sprung from David's line, Son of God according to God's will and power, actually born of a virgin, baptized by John that all righteousness might be fulfilled by him, and ... crucified for us in the flesh under Pontius Pilate and Herod the Tetrarch. We are part of his fruit which grew out of his most blessed Passion.... By his resurrection, he raised a standard to rally his saints and faithful forever, whether Jews or Gentiles, in one body of his Church. For it was for our sakes that he suffered all this, to save us.... (1:1-2)

Thus was the faith taught around the year 100 A.D. by one of the official teachers in the Church, the bishop of Antioch. His summary accords with the faith derived from the New Testament, on the one hand, and, on the other, with Creeds and other authentic statements of the faith formulated in later ages by the Church of Christ with the special assistance of the Holy Spirit.

As we have seen, one of the things St. Ignatius of Antioch was most insistent upon was the position of the bishop. He held to this because he saw clearly the need for Church unity, which was to be achieved and guaranteed by the bishop. St. Ignatius congratulated the Ephesians on being united to their bishops just as the Church was united to Jesus Christ, "and Jesus Christ to the Father. This is how unity and harmony come to prevail everywhere", he went on. "Make no mistake about it. If anyone is not inside the sanctuary, he lacks God's bread" (5:1-2). And "God's bread", Ignatius wrote to the Romans, was nothing else than "the flesh of Christ" (7:3).

To the Smyrnaeans he wrote that they should only "regard that Eucharist as valid which is celebrated either by the bishop or by someone he authorizes" (8:2). This tells us that by this early date the bishops *were* "authorizing" others, sharing a measure of the authority handed down to them from Christ with priests authorized to celebrate the Eucharist. Similarly, "without the bishops' supervision, no baptisms [were] permitted" (ibid.).

The fruit of all this, for Ignatius, was the personal holiness and uprightness of conduct that was supposed to mark the follower of Christ. "We have not only to be called Christians," he declared to the Magnesians, "but to be Christians" (4:1). To the Ephesians he summarized the way Christians were to act in order to demonstrate that the spirit of the Gospels had indeed been handed down in the Church:

> Keep on praying for others ... for there is a chance of their being converted and getting to God. Let them learn from you at least by your actions. Return their bad temper with gentleness; their boasts with humility; their abuse with prayer. In the face of their error, be steadfast in the faith. Return their violence with mildness and do not be intent on getting your own back. By our patience let us show we are their brothers, intent on imitating the Lord.... (10:1–3)

What we today call "Gospel values" were already fully internalized in the letters of St. Ignatius of Antioch—which means they were fully internalized in the Church of Christ by the first decade of the first century. These letters provide a vivid picture of the Church in action scarcely one generation after the first Christian generation, which included the apostles themselves.

The Church described and reflected in these letters was definitely One, Holy, Catholic, and Apostolic. This Church possessed the four marks, or characteristics, of the true Church that were later to be so concisely summed up in those very words in the Nicene Creed.

For centuries, at every Sunday and holy day Mass, Catholics have proudly professed belief in these four traditional marks of the Church of Christ. Catholics profess this belief by reciting the Nicene Creed, which issued from the Council of Nicaea in 325 A.D. and was further developed by the Council of Constantinople in 381. The Church has consistently applied these words to herself ever since. These two great Church councils were held well over two centuries after the events reflected in the letters of St. Ignatius of Antioch. In chapter 3, we shall look more closely at these two great Church councils as well as at the Church's two subsequent councils.

The words of the Nicene Creed, however, apply perfectly to this earlier period. The Church of St. Ignatius possessed all four of the characteristics specified by the Creed. This Church was manifestly destined to grow and develop in the centuries that followed. Certainly there would be many changes in the Church's *appearance* and how she was perceived by the world around her—even by her own members. Nevertheless, around the turn of the first century, on the evidence of these letters penned by a bishop to local Churches while he was being escorted to his own martyrdom in Rome, the Church already possessed the essential four characteristics that would continue to testify to her authenticity in later ages. This was true because she was the true organic continuation of the Church of the apostles, which possessed the same four characteristics from the beginning.

In strict accord with sacred Scripture, Catholic teaching has always maintained that Jesus founded a specific Church into which all his followers were to be gathered. In the words of the Second Vatican Council of our own day, the Lord Jesus poured forth the Spirit whom he had promised and through whom he called and gathered together the people of the New Covenant, which is the Church.... [A]s the Apostle teaches us: "There is one body and one Spirit, just as you were called to the one hope of your calling; one Lord, one faith, one baptism." (Eph 4:4–5) (Decree on Ecumenism *Unitatis Redintegratio*, no. 2)

The Council Fathers go on to describe this Church established by Jesus Christ as "God's only flock ... this one and only Church of God" (*Unitatis Redintegratio*, no. 3).

St. Ignatius of Antioch had already experienced—and described in his letters—the one and only Church of God.

III.

As we have seen, the One, Holy, Catholic, and Apostolic Church of the Nicene Creed was already present in the first century. St. Ignatius of Antioch, martyred in the Colosseum in Rome before the second century was a decade old, on the evidence of the seven letters he wrote to local Churches in Asia Minor, already considered the Church, in which he was a bishop, to be *one*. His emphasis on the central role of the bishop in each local Church stemmed primarily from his conviction that the bishop was the center of unity in the Church, guaranteeing that it would remain "one".

St. Ignatius wrote to the Philadelphians that there was only "one flesh of our Lord, Jesus Christ, and one cup of his blood that makes us one, and one altar, just as there is one bishop along with the presbyters and the deacons" (4:1). The unity of Christians is a function of the unity of the Church to which they belong; this unity is guaranteed by the bishop of each local Church.

Similarly, St. Ignatius considered the Church to be *holy*, since it is in the Church that "God's bread, which is the flesh of Christ" (*Ep. Rom.* 7:3), is present. Ignatius considered the Eucharist celebrated within the Church to be the means of holiness that also made Christians one. The faithful, he believed, were accustomed to gather together *in order to* obtain a share of God's grace through the Sacrament. He counseled the Ephesians "to gather together more frequently to celebrate God's Eucharist". He believed that by more frequent Communion, "Satan's powers [were] overthrown and his destructiveness . . . undone" (13:1) and the members of the holy Church brought closer to God in holiness.

Looking at the *Catholic*, or universal, character of the Church as described by Ignatius, we find him remarking to the Ephesians that bishops continued to be "appointed the world over" (3:2), as was true in the time of St. Paul (cf. Col 1:6). In his Letter to the Smyrnaeans, St. Ignatius employed a phrase new to Christian writings up to that point, marking this letter as one of the most significant documents of the early Church. If St. Ignatius of Antioch had written nothing else, he would remain a uniquely important witness to the nature of the Church founded by Christ. (This Church, after all, had had so little time to develop between the time of the apostles and that at which he was writing—we are already farther away from the First World War than St. Ignatius of Antioch was from the crucifixion of Christ.) The phrase Ignatius employed in his Letter to the Smyrnaeans was the name by which the Church of Christ was by then known, the unique name by which this Church would be known even to the present day: "the Catholic Church".

"Where the bishop is present," Ignatius wrote, "there let the congregation gather, just as where Jesus Christ is, there is the Catholic Church" (8:2). This letter to the Smyrneans around the year 107 A.D. contains the first extant mention in Christian literature of "the Catholic Church"—the name that the Council of Nicaea would later employ as a matter of course to designate the entity for which that Council professed to be speaking.

According to the Acts of the Apostles, it was in Antioch that the followers of Jesus Christ were first called "Christians" (11:26). When it came to the name of the community into which these Christians were gathered in the name of Christ, however, a name other than Christian came to be used, a name first recorded for posterity in a letter written by the second bishop of that same Antioch, where "Christian" had first been used.

No major historical entity has ever been called "the Christian Church". This term came into use only fairly recently by people unwilling to concede that the entity still known as the Catholic Church—the visible, historic community of professing Christians subject to a local bishop in communion with the bishop of Rome—*is* the Church, the one undivided Christian body to which St. Ignatius of Antioch belonged in the first century, the Church *he* referred to as "the Catholic Church", following an already established usage. Those who speak of "the Christian Church" usually mean a loose amalgamation of the various churches that centuries of schisms and heresies have created by successive splittings off from the one still undivided Church to which St. Ignatius belonged in the first century: the Catholic Church.

In the New Testament, the community of Christ's disciples incorporated into him through baptism and the Eucharist is called simply "the Church"—the body of Christ. In time the adjective that came to be applied to the noun *Church* was derived, not from the name of her divine Founder, but from one of her special characteristics. This characteristic was that this was the one, unique, saving body for everyone, everywhere, as distinguished from the partial or even counterfeit groups or sects that already in New Testament times (cf. 1 Jn 2:19) were springing up in opposition to the true Church and have not ceased to spring up in every age since.

Indeed, these "protesting" splinter groups were usually off-shoots from the true Church; characteristically, they have been self-established communities, whereas the true Church remains Christ-established. "Catholic Church", in a very important sense, has always meant the one, true Church. Other churches, while they may retain elements—both teachings and sacraments—of the true Church, at some point, have elected to be *separated* from her and have *not* insisted on the unity Christ desired when he prayed "that they may all be one" (Jn 17:21).

Not surprisingly, "Catholic Church" caught on and is employed down to our own day—because there has never been a time when the one true Church, the real one, did not need to be distinguished from the many churches, communities, and even sects claiming to be "the Church".

In the generation following St. Ignatius of Antioch, references to "the Catholic Church" become more and more frequent. The ancient account of the martyrdom of St. Polycarp, bishop of Smyrna in the first decade of the second century, referred to "the whole Catholic Church throughout the world". (St. Polycarp was burned at the stake around the year 155 A.D.) No better name has ever been found to designate the Church Jesus Christ himself founded than the Catholic Church, the name that she acquired in her earliest years and that was used both by St. Ignatius of Antioch and St. Polycarp of Smyrna.

St. Ignatius took for granted that the Catholic Church was *apostolic*. In his letter to the Romans, he spoke with the greatest respect of the apostles Peter and Paul, who, he remarked, "gave orders" (4:3). In the salutation of his letter to the Philadelphians, he spoke of the "appointing" of bishops, presbyters, and deacons—by which he clearly meant the handing on of the power of holy orders that the apostles had received directly from Christ.

Actually, we have a witness, even earlier than St. Ignatius, to the fact that the Church was apostolic. About 96 A.D., St. Clement of Rome (30?–100?) wrote in his Letter to the Corinthians that the apostles of Jesus had "preached in country and city, and appointed their first converts, after testing them by the Spirit, to be bishops and deacons of future believers.... They later added a codicil to the effect that, should these die, other approved men should succeed to their ministry" (42:4, 2).

On the basis of such early testimony, there can be no doubt that the early Church understood herself as apostolic, as descending directly and organically, in an unbroken line from the apostles.

IV.

We have looked at evidence provided, for the most part, by one ancient Christian writer about what the Church was like and how she functioned around the turn of the first century. The witness of St. Ignatius of Antioch is of utmost importance. His letters to some of the Churches in Asia Minor testify to the existence, at that very early date, of a kind of Church that many have held to be the invention of later Christian generations, who supposedly modified (and corrupted) the original plan that Jesus Christ had committed to his apostles for the entity that was to carry on his words and his work in the world.

Neither the authenticity nor the early date of the Letters of St. Ignatius of Antioch is in dispute today. All modern scholars accept these letters just as we have them. This scholarly consensus is remarkable, considering the disputes that go on today about authorship and dating, even of the four Gospels.

What Ignatius' letters clearly establish is that by the end of the first century there was already in place in a fairly wide geographical area of the ancient world an organized, visible, institutional, sacerdotal, and hierarchical Church headed in each major city or area by an ordained leader called a bishop. This Church was already firmly in place while some Christians who had personally heard and seen the apostles themselves were still alive.

The Church described in these letters dispensed both word and sacrament to the faithful. From various early writings, we know the members of this Church professed certain doctrines taught by the authority of this Church; they heard substantially the same readings taken from both the Old and New Testaments that are read today and participated in the Eucharist and other rites celebrated by men and ordained within this organized body, the Church of Christ.

The result of this common participation in the body of Christ was to orient those who participated in it toward "doing good" (Acts 10:38). St. Ignatius wrote to the Ephesians that "by your good deeds [God] will recognize you are members of his Son" (4:2).

In short, the Church at the end of the first century and the beginning of the second was not merely One, Holy, Catholic, and Apostolic but substantially the same in nature and function as she is today.

It is important to cite some additional ancient testimony about the Church of the early Fathers confirming what has been cited here from St. Ignatius of Antioch. We have already mentioned St. Polycarp of Smyrna testifying to the Church's catholicity and St. Clement of Rome testifying to her apostolicity. This kind of evidence increases as we move further into the Christian era. By the fourth century it becomes a veritable flood.

In the interests of brevity, we confine further citations in this chapter to the second century. If we can confirm that the Church of the second century was the Church described by St. Ignatius, then all later citations are superfluous for our purposes: the Church of St. Ignatius was continuous with the Church of the apostles. If other early Fathers writing no later than the second century are also found to be in this unbroken line, it is difficult to see where or how the original plan of Jesus for a Church was ever altered, undermined, or "corrupted". The supposedly corrupt institutional, sacerdotal, and hierarchical Catholic Church has existed since apostolic times.

The burden of proof that the Church of the fourth century might somehow not have really been the Church that Jesus founded rests upon those who assert that there was a later, significant deviation. Some may prefer another "model" of the Church—to adopt a fashionable modern term. They may even call it a more spiritual model than the flesh-and-blood Church of history. But they are not doing justice to historical evidence showing what the early Church was really like.

One of the most powerful and eloquent voices among the early Church Fathers was that of St. Irenaeus of Lyons. In his prime he became a bishop in Roman Gaul (modern France), but he too was a native of Smyrna in Asia Minor. Born about 130, St. Irenaeus recorded in his later years his personal memories of the martyred bishop of Smyrna, St. Polycarp. He must have been about twenty-five when the latter was burned at the stake. And St. Polycarp had preserved personal memories, not only of meeting with St. Ignatius of Antioch, but of the preaching of St. John. Thus St. Irenaeus, a second-century bishop, had a direct personal link with the generation of the apostles.

Irenaeus was a respected presbyter at Lyons during the great persecution of Christians there in 177. In that year, he carried out a mission to Rome on behalf of the Church of Lyons. Later he succeeded the martyr-bishop in Lyons. He completed his great work *Adversus Haereses* (*Against the Heresies*) around 189 or 190. This dating is suggested because the last in the list of the bishops of Rome that he includes in this work is Pope St. Eleutherius (ca. 175–189), who was succeeded by Pope St. Victor (189–199?). The tradition is that St. Irenaeus himself died a martyr sometime after that.

It is possible to show that St. Irenaeus understood the Church to be *Holy, Catholic, and Apostolic* from a single passage in *Against the Heresies*. Irenaeus wrote in Book One of this great work that "the Church, although scattered over the whole civilized world to the end of the earth [*Catholic*], received from the apostles and their disciples its faith [*Apostolic*]." It was through this same Church that God, "by his grace gave life incorrupt" to the faithful, whom Irenaeus called "the righteous and holy, and those who have kept his commandments and have remained in his love [*Holy*]." Irenaeus further sees the Church as holy because she offers

> a pure oblation to the Creator. . . . For the bread, which comes from the earth, receives the invocation of God, and then it is no longer common bread but the Eucharist. . . . So our bodies, after partaking of the Eucharist, are no longer corruptible, having the hope of eternal resurrection. (Bk. IV, 15)

Possessing the means of holiness, then, the Church is herself holy. St. Irenaeus is especially insistent, also, that this holy Church is *one*:

> Having received this preaching and this faith ... , the Church, although scattered in the whole world, carefully preserves it, as if living in one house. She believes these things everywhere alike, as if she had but one heart and one soul, and preaches them harmoniously, teaches them, and hands them down, as if she had but one mouth. For the languages of the world are different, but the meaning of the tradition is one and the same. Neither do the churches that have been established in Germany believe otherwise, or hand down any other tradition, nor those among the Iberians, nor those among the Celts, nor in Egypt, nor those established in the middle parts of the world. (Bk. I, 10:1–2)

This passage illustrates how vividly St. Irenaeus saw the Church as necessarily one, since Christ is one. No denominational pluralism here! For Irenaeus, the Church is necessarily one, as she is Catholic, *because* she is apostolic: she is based on "that tradition which has come down from the apostles and is guarded by the successions of elders" (Bk. III, 2:2). "The tradition of the apostles", Irenaeus adds, "made clear in all the world, can be clearly seen in every church by those who wish to behold the truth. We can enumerate those who were established by the apostles as bishops in the churches, and their successors down to our time" (Bk. III, 2:3).

We have noted that St. Irenaeus had a personal link with the generation of the apostles through his mentor St. Polycarp. If toward the end of the second century he thought that an unbroken succession of bishops was the guarantee of the authenticity of the Church, imagine how he would regard the unbroken succession of bishops that has continued through the end of the twentieth century!

V.

As a conclusion to this survey of the Church of the early Fathers, we can now rapidly cite, without going beyond the end of the second century, a few of the other early Fathers in order to demonstrate that saints such as Ignatius of Antioch and Irenaeus of Lyons are not untypical, but in the mainstream of the early Church.

Clement of Alexandria, for example, a second-century Father, was head of the famous catechetical school in Alexandria, Egypt. In bearing witness to the oneness, or unity, of the Church, he alluded equally to her holiness, her catholicity, and her apostolicity. Clement wrote:

> There is one true Church, the really ancient Church into which are enrolled those who are righteous [holy] according to God's ordinance.... In essence, in idea, in origin, in preeminence we say that the ancient Catholic Church is the only Church. The Church brings together [the faithful] by the will of the one God through the one Lord, into the unity of the one faith.... (*Stromateis*, VII, XVI, 107)

To another early Father, one of the first Christian apologists, Justin the Martyr (100?-165?), we owe some of the earliest descriptions of the liturgy and worship of the Church. He is, accordingly, a most appropriate additional witness to the holiness of the Church. Like other early Fathers, St. Justin saw the Church's sacraments as the means to holiness in the Church, and he saw the transformed lives of the members of the Church as results of this holiness. Just as St. Irenaeus stressed that the doctrine, or teaching, of the Church had been handed down from the apostles, Justin emphasized how the power to administer the Church's sacraments had similarly been handed down.

As to the band of twelve men who went forth from Jerusalem, Justin wrote:

> They were common men, not trained in speaking, but by the power of God they testified to every race of mankind that they were sent by Christ ... and now we who once killed each other not only do not make war on each other, but in order not to lie or deceive our inquisitors, we gladly die for the confession. (*First Apology*, 39)

Justin specified that a Christian who bears witness so selflessly has to be "one who believes that the things that we believe are true, and has received the washing for the forgiveness of sins" (66). In other words, the baptized believer necessarily professes a specific doctrine and participates in the Church's sacraments.

Another second-century Christian writer, Tertullian (160?–230?), wrote in a similar vein: "We marvel when a man is plunged and dipped in water to the accompaniment of a few words. ... It seems incredible that eternal life should be won in this manner ... but we marvel because we believe" (*On Baptism*, 2).

The principal sacrament of the Church, according to St. Justin the Martyr, is the Eucharist. The Eucharist is not, he wrote,

> common bread or common drink; but as Jesus Christ our Savior being incarnate by God's word took flesh and blood for our salvation, so we have also been taught that the food consecrated by the word of prayer that comes from him, from which our flesh and blood are nourished by transformation, is the flesh and blood of that incarnate Jesus. For the apostles in the memoirs composed by them ... thus handed down what was commanded them: that Jesus, taking bread and having given thanks, said, "Do this for my memorial, this is my

body"; and likewise taking the cup and giving thanks, he said, "This is my blood." (66; cf. Mk 14:22–24; 1 Cor 11:23–25)

Thus did Justin, who was beheaded in Rome around 165 A.D. for refusing to renounce Christ, testify to the sacramental practice of the Church of the second century—the source of her holiness, then as now.

As for the catholicity, or universal nature, of the Church, we have already noted how Clement of Alexandria called the Church "Catholic" almost as a function of her unity. Earlier we saw that by 155 the phrase "the whole Catholic Church throughout the world" was already current (*Martyrdom of Polycarp*, 8:1), while St. Polycarp himself was called "the bishop of the Catholic Church in Smyrna" (16:2). This kind of testimony, reflecting a period relatively early in the second century, provides sufficient corroboration of the usage of St. Ignatius and St. Irenaeus, for whom the Catholic Church was simply "the Church".

Finally, as to the apostolicity of the Church, we have just seen how St. Justin the Martyr bore witness to this even while writing about her holiness. We can add to this testimony by citing again the second-century Tertullian, who wrote how the apostles "first bore witness to the faith in Judaea and founded churches there.... In the same way, they established churches in every city, from which the other churches borrowed the shoot of faith and the seeds of doctrine and are every day borrowing them so as to become churches" (*De Praescriptione Haereticorum*, 20).

This is not a bad description of how the many local, individual Churches belonging to the "one holy catholic and apostolic Church" of the later Nicene Creed were planted, took root, and grew. What various early Fathers had already written by the end of the second century applies to what is still going on today, thanks to the constant missionary efforts that the spirit of the Gospels inevitably continues to inspire in the Church ("Go therefore and make disciples of all nations, baptizing them in the name of the Father, and of the Son, and of the Holy Spirit" [Mt 28:19]).

The Church of the early Fathers thus described was the flowering and outgrowth of the One, Holy, Catholic, and Apostolic Church founded by Jesus Christ upon the apostles, a Church that has neither ceased to exist nor been transformed but, rather, has lasted intact to our own day.

Chapter 3

THE CHURCH OF THE FIRST
FOUR GREAT COUNCILS

I.

For about the first three hundred years of its existence, Christianity was officially an outlawed and proscribed religion, persecuted by the state. Persecution was sporadic; considerable time could sometimes pass when the state did not actively bestir itself against the Christians. In the earliest years after Christ, active persecution was as likely as not a local affair; later the emperors launched campaigns of persecution on a large, even an empire-wide, scale. Whether active or not, the threat of persecution was always present.

The word *martyr* is derived from the Greek word for "witness". Heroic tales of martyrs losing their lives while bearing witness to the faith were quite naturally handed down. These tales were not pious legends; much of the time they were only too real.

During the approximately three hundred years that followed the crucifixion and resurrection of Christ, the Catholic Church managed to spread throughout the Roman Empire and beyond. Everywhere, though, the Church was only tolerated—when she was tolerated—and for that reason the Church was generally despised by the leaders of society and "right-thinking people".

The great crowds—at the Roman games and spectacles, for example—were only too happy to join in execrating the Christians, especially during active persecutions by the Roman state. Surely the Christians must have been guilty of terrible things to be persecuted so regularly and so savagely! Such has been the judgment of public opinion in many times and places, including our own. However mindless such judgments may be, they are often made in accordance with the ideas and standards of the day, then as now. Only occasionally did or does reality break through and testify to what is really happening behind superficial appearances.

This was the situation faced by the Church while she was spreading nearly everywhere in the Roman world. This was the situation the Church had to contend with until, with the legal recognition of the Church by the state and the respectability that followed, public opinion slowly began to side with the Church.

As Christians grew in numbers and became represented in all walks of life—and as the Churches themselves came to own property and impinge more and more upon the life and society around them—the degree of toleration of the Church in Roman society at large necessarily increased. Nevertheless, official persecutions by a Roman state aimed at curtailing if not wiping out Christianity entirely were periodically mandated. These persecutions became more systematic, severe, and far-reaching as it was perceived that, in spite of efforts by the government to stop her, the Church was spreading everywhere.

The last two great persecutions by the Roman Empire were all-out assaults—total war—against the Catholic Church. They aimed to destroy Christianity, root and branch. There was, first, the one launched by Emperor Decius in 250 A.D., then the even greater one unleashed by Emperor Diocletian in

303. Each of these was intended to be empire-wide, and each was carried forward determinedly for the better part of a decade, either by the emperor who launched it or by his successors. Holy books were confiscated and destroyed, gatherings for worship were forbidden, churches and places of meeting were razed, and Christians in official positions lost them. Some were arrested and forced to offer pagan sacrifices upon pain of torture and death, and the ordinary benefits and protection of the law were withdrawn from them.

When the persecution launched by Diocletian finally proved to be a costly failure, the stage was set for the great reversal of policy made by the Emperor Constantine in 313, when he decided to recognize Christianity officially.

Constantine, a soldier like most of the emperors of that era, at first succeeded his father, Constantius Chlorus, as ruler only of the Western Roman Empire; neither Constantius Chlorus nor Constantine after him had implemented the Diocletian persecutions as seriously in the West as had been the case in the East, where they had been unrelenting and terrible. Then, in 311, Constantine and two of his co-emperors, Licinius and Maximin, revoked the edicts of Diocletian against the Church.

The next year, marching against a usurper in Italy, Constantine had a dream that convinced him he would conquer in the "heavenly sign" of Jesus Christ. ("*In hoc signo vinces*", "In this sign you will conquer"; other versions give "*In hoc signo victor eris*", "In this sign you will be the victor.") Constantine accordingly had his soldiers' shields marked with a cross that also included the Greek letters *chi* and *rho*, signifying Christ; and, with this sign, he did win a resounding victory at the Battle of the Milvian Bridge outside the Flaminian Gate of Rome on October 28, 312.

The dream and victory of Constantine did not lead directly to his own conversion to Christianity. It would be a mistake to compare this Roman emperor's experience with that of St. Paul on the road to Damascus. Constantine was not to be baptized for another twenty-five years, when he was on his deathbed. Even then he was baptized by a heretical Arian bishop. Meanwhile, though instituting policies favoring Christianity, he continued as emperor to be the *Pontifex Maximus*, or supreme head, of pagan worship in the empire. His coins continued to bear pagan images; even near the end of his life, he was known to consult pagan oracles, engage in pagan ceremonies, and issue rulings concerning the pagan priesthood.

Constantine's behavior, both as an emperor and as a man, showed few signs of having been very seriously influenced by Christian ideas or Christian morality. As a ruler, he tended to be unsentimental, even ruthless (although he was sometimes easily influenced by those around him). If he thought the interests of the state or his imperial position were threatened, he was pitiless: he ordered the execution of his own wife, Fausta; one of his sons, Crispus; and his co-emperor and brother-in-law, Licinius.

Nevertheless, the dream of Constantine did mean that the emperor had come to believe, in some sense, not only in "the one God" that even his father, Constantius Chlorus, had respected, but also that this was the God worshipped by Christians. He certainly believed that he was God's instrument for the preservation of the empire. At times, moreover, he evidenced fear of God's anger at the spread of heresy or untruth, and he thought the troubles of the empire might well stem from the "anger of the neglected divine power".

Constantine's new conviction about God and Christ, though far from pure, would nevertheless bring about a complete change in the attitude of the Roman state toward the Catholic Church. Henceforth Christianity could be freely practiced. It was not yet the official religion of the Roman Empire, but in the new climate the Church could carry out her work for souls openly, less trammeled by official constraints.

In March of 313, Constantine and his co-emperor, Licinius, who was married to his half sister Constantia, issued the document known as the Edict of Milan. In this document, the two co-emperors declared that,

> notwithstanding any provisions concerning the Christians in our former instructions, all who choose that religion are to be permitted to continue therein, without any let or hindrance, and are not to be in any way troubled or molested. Note that at the same time all others are to be allowed the free and unrestricted practice of their religions; for it accords with the good order of the realm and the peacefulness of our times that each should have the freedom to worship God after his own choice.

Although the Roman state thus remained neutral, Constantine tended to favor Christianity from that time on. His attitude was to prove decisive, since he was soon, in 324, to become sole master of the Roman world.

If the empire could not destroy the Church, as the failure of the persecutions had shown, then the wisest policy was to attempt to enroll this far-flung, well-organized, and highly motivated body of believers as an ally of a Roman commonwealth increasingly beset by barbarians from beyond the frontiers and steadily declining from within through decay of the old Roman virtues.

This was the policy that Constantine and succeeding Christian emperors followed. This change of policy provided a great opportunity for the Church because she was free to carry out her divinely appointed mission of bringing the word and sacraments of Christ to everyone who was prepared to "repent and be baptized" (Acts 2:38). Although at the time of this great change, Christians constituted no more than ten percent of the population of the empire, the conviction with which the early Church carried out her mission, along with the fervor of the early Christians, soon carried the day in an otherwise decadent Roman Empire.

But the change in Roman government policy also constituted a great danger for the Church. Allied with the state, the Church could only too easily and too often be used by it for purposes other than purveying word and sacrament for the salvation of souls. When allied with the state, some of the Church's leaders were tempted by secular power and prestige. The true religious mission of the Church, thus, was sometimes obscured or deformed.

Unfortunately, these things did occur from time to time, usually with consequences detrimental to the Church and the cause of Christ. The "Christian" emperors constantly tried to control the Church and bend her to the purposes of society and the state as they saw them. In the ensuing decades and, indeed, centuries, the Church was continually obliged to resist state control—basically succeeding in the West though not always in the East.

We should never forget that even amid the fury of some of the controversies, which the state often tried to exploit for its own purposes, the normal, routine sanctifying mission of the Church, purveying word and sacrament to the simple faithful everywhere, did not cease. This has been true in all ages.

We should never mistake manifestations of ecclesiastical politics, however unedifying, for the total life and work of the Church. The Church is not essentially a political entity; she is primarily in the soul-saving business, though her activities necessarily extend beyond preaching, teaching, and sacramental activities. The Church never fails to affect the culture surrounding her, though that is not her primary aim.

We should not conclude that the Church's emergence from an underground and persecuted existence, with the help afforded by Constantine and subsequent Christian emperors, indicated a fundamentally wrong turn for the Church: the Church could not remain in the catacombs if she was to fulfill her mission from Christ to evangelize the world. The indisputable fact is that the Church emerged from the catacombs into a world of Roman state absolutism. Therefore the Church had to come to terms with that absolutism and the power that enforced it, however uneasy those terms might sometimes have been.

For the Church can never renounce the world—not if she is to sanctify and save it through the power of Jesus Christ. No, the Church must always strive to be in, but not of, the world. It is always a temptation to imagine that the Church could, or should, in the name of Jesus, have remained a small, pure, unworldly entity; but it was Jesus himself who commanded the apostles to "make disciples of all nations" (Mt 28:19). In order to carry out that command, the Church had to take advantage of the opportunities afforded by Constantine and his successors, even though this action sometimes cost her something.

In God's providence, legitimate and necessary developments of Church doctrine and life emerged from some of the Church's interactions with the empire, which sometimes were anything but edifying. In the century and a quarter following the liberation of the Church by Constantine, four great gatherings, or general councils, of the Church's bishops were held. Given the times, they had to be convened under the patronage of the Christian emperors. The Church that had operated underground until then scarcely possessed the means on her own to convene all her bishops at a general meeting.

The first four great councils of the Church were called to deal with pressing problems, and all took place under conditions of maximum political turbulence. All four gatherings were almost offensively political. Even at the time, the councils sometimes stirred up more problems than they solved.

Yet in the course of these four ecumenical (worldwide) councils of bishops, the Church of Christ arrived at a definitive formulation of the basic teaching that she had been brought into the world to advance: Who was and is this Jesus Christ upon whom the Catholic Church bases all of her teaching and action? Jesus himself had posed the same basic question when he asked the apostles, "Who do men say that the Son of man is?" (Mt 16:13; cf. Mk 8:27; Lk 9:18). The fundamental meaning of the Christian faith depends upon the answer to this question. Christians clearly have to understand correctly who and what Jesus Christ was and is if they are going to be Christians in the full sense of the word.

Since it was first written down, the New Testament has provided for every generation of Christians all the rich and varied elements that go into finding the answer. By itself, however, the New Testament does not provide the complete answer—or, at any rate, the completely formulated answer—as is proved by the fact that fervent believers in the New Testament have, to the present day, continued to argue about its meaning.

Christians emerged from the age of persecution engaged in many of the same arguments. The Church was obliged to provide answers. Between the Council of Nicaea in 325 and the Council of Chalcedon in 451, and including the Councils of Constantinople in 381 and Ephesus in 431, the bishops of the Catholic Church, possessing the authority passed on by Christ to the apostles, debated, formulated in language impossible to mistake, and then *decided* for the Church the answer to the question Christ had posed to his disciples: "Who do *you* say that I am?" (Mt 16:15, emphasis added).

In the course of the first four great councils the teaching authority of the Church residing in her hierarchy of bishops—the Magisterium—decided the definitive answer to the question of who and what Jesus was and is. The answer hammered out in these councils remains one that Catholics, Protestants, and Eastern Orthodox, despite their differences, generally agree upon.

We must now trace in detail the steps the Church took in formulating her basic doctrine concerning Christ through four great historic convocations extending over more than a century and a quarter.

II.

The Roman emperor Constantine had no sooner won his victory while bearing the sign of Jesus Christ at the Milvian Bridge in 312 and had no sooner decreed the freedom of the Church in the following year, than he became personally embroiled in a raging Church controversy. As emperor he intervened to help restore the rightful bishop to the see of Carthage in North Africa. Ominously for the future, this was the first instance in which the secular arm of the state employed force to back up a Church decision.

In the course of Constantine's intervention in this North African affair, he became personally involved in the established

Church practice of calling together bishops in synods, or councils, to decide important questions. As the Church had grown and spread, these meetings of bishops had more than once proved to be indispensable in regulating the Church's affairs.

After the Council of Jerusalem described in the fifteenth chapter of the Acts of the Apostles, one of the earliest of such councils known was convened in Phrygia in Asia Minor in the year 175. This council condemned the heretical sect of the Montanists, who claimed direct inspiration of the Holy Spirit for their rigorist moral views and exaggerated ascetical practices. These views and practices, however, went beyond the Church's authentic tradition. Convening a council of bishops to decide the matter and reaffirm the Church's authentic tradition proved to be a very practical way to deal with this infection in the body of Christ.

Again, around 190, the bishop of Rome, Pope St. Victor I (189–199), urged the calling of a series of local councils in the East—councils convened by the Churches there—to try to deal with the disputed question of the calculation of the date of Easter. These councils did not meet with complete success. The dispute regarding Easter was not to be resolved for more than a century.

By the beginning of the third century, local Church councils had been convened for one reason or another in nearly every part of the empire. The bishops of Rome had a solidly established custom of convening "Roman synods" to decide Church questions. Similarly, from the 220s on, the convening of periodic councils by the Church in North Africa had become customary. One of Emperor Constantine's first encounters with the Church involved a local African council dealing with what would later come to be called the Donatist schism in that region.

The idea of calling a general council to deal with serious trouble in the Church came easily to the emperor's mind when a problem broke out in the East around the year 323. In this way Constantine became the patron of the first gathering of all the Catholic bishops of the world, a gathering he scheduled for May 325. As the site of the council, he designated one of his summer palaces in Nicaea, some twenty-five miles away from the imperial capital, Nicomedia, and about forty miles from the site of the great new imperial capital he would soon establish on the Bosphorus at Byzantium—the future Constantinople.

The emperor offered the bishops transportation on the imperial Roman road system; over three hundred bishops, responding to the emperor's invitation, attended the Council of Nicaea, the first of the Church's ecumenical councils. They came from the "whole world" (Greek: *oikoumene*).

What was the trouble in the Church that called forth such an extraordinary response on the part of the Roman emperor? Threatening the peace of the Church, as well as her faith, was a novel fundamentally erroneous teaching about Christ that, although superficially plausible, was destructive of belief in Jesus as Savior. This erroneous teaching was spreading with alarming rapidity, especially throughout the Christian East; Christ's cause and the future of his Church, after initially developing in such a remarkable way amid hostile circumstances, were suddenly placed in jeopardy from an entirely different source: from within.

After his resurrection from the dead, Jesus had instructed the apostles to baptize disciples "in the name of the Father and of the Son and of the Holy Spirit" (Mt 28:19). This threefold invocation constituted a summary description of the fundamental revelation about God that Jesus had come into the world to deliver—but that only gradually became fully evident to the disciples as they reflected upon the words, miracles, and other actions of Jesus.

Jesus' fundamental revelation was the basic truth of Christianity itself, namely, that the Supreme Being, the "Lord of Hosts" of the Old Testament, the God of heaven and earth, the Creator of the universe was, in a way not fully comprehensible to the human mind, a *Trinity*, a being composed of Father, Son, and Holy Spirit; three Persons yet still "one God".

Moreover, Jesus himself was the Son in this Trinity of Persons. Although unmistakably a Galilean man with whom the disciples had walked and talked and eaten in ancient Palestine, a man who had suffered and died on the Cross in Jerusalem, Jesus was—again, in a sense not fully comprehensible to the human mind—God.

Jesus' revelation of himself as God had begun to be evident to the disciples even while Jesus was still among them— but in a mysterious fashion that according to the Gospel accounts, the disciples had enormous difficulty understanding: "Have I been with you so long, and yet you do not know me, Philip?" Jesus inquired. "He who has seen me has seen the Father" (Jn 14:9).

Nevertheless the disciples could not help drawing some conclusions about Jesus when they witnessed his walking on water, multiplying loaves of bread, changing water into wine, issuing authoritative commands to evil spirits, taming winds and sea, healing the sick, crippled, and blind; and raising people from the dead.

When Jesus referred to himself as "the light of the world" (Jn 8:12) or "the way, and the truth, and the life" (Jn 14:6), or the "lord of the sabbath" (Mt 12:8), or when he assumed God's exclusive prerogative by asserting that "the Son of man has authority on earth to forgive sins" (Mt 9:6), even the most obtuse disciple could not fail to grasp that Jesus was claiming to be more than just another prophet or "good man".

But it was only after the resurrection that the enormous reality of who and what Jesus was was really brought home to the disciples: Jesus was God. Thomas confessed as much when, confronted with the overwhelming reality of the risen Christ, he said, "My Lord and my God!" (Jn 20:28).

So far from this revelation being something believable only by the ignorant and credulous of ancient times but less so in an era of advanced scientific knowledge, this revelation is probably *more* believable—at least for anyone willing to inquire seriously into it and humble himself to pray for the grace to believe it—for the simple reason that we, after two thousand years of Christianity, have become *used to* the idea of a crucified and resurrected God-man who has saved us from our sins and promised eternal life.

We know that many generations of our ancestors believed in this revelation, including some of the most intelligent and saintly. We know, too, that the allegedly scientific objections to this belief have not disproved it.

When this revelation was first delivered to the world through the words and actions of Jesus, it was a unique and unprecedented revelation. When its truth was finally realized by the disciples of Jesus, the effect must have been overwhelming. We know from New Testament accounts that its effect was staggering. Only the triumphant experience of the risen Christ, accompanied by the superabundant power of the Holy Spirit—whom Jesus had promised the Father would send (cf. Jn 14:16)—could enable the otherwise timid and pusillanimous apostles of Jesus to launch the Church effectively.

Tertullian, a Christian writer who died in 220, well expressed the immense paradox inherent in Christianity, a

paradox only too evident to the ancients who first encountered Christianity:

> The Son of God was crucified; I am not ashamed—
> because it is shameful. The Son of God died; it is immedi-
> ately credible because it is silly. He was buried and rose again;
> it is certain—because it is impossible. (*The Flesh of Christ*, 5)

This, then, was one aspect of the "good news" that the
infant Church was obliged to proclaim in her initial efforts
to convert the world to Jesus Christ the Savior. It was not
the only facet of the gospel of Christ. Many who inhabited
a world increasingly lost in sin and meaninglessness proved
quite responsive to the startling message that God had become man in order to save them from their sins and bring
them to eternal life. Faith in Christ caught on; the Church
began to grow and spread. In spite of myriads of obstacles,
she continues to draw believers today for the same reasons as
in the beginning.

At the heart of the new and hopeful Christian affirmations
that brought light and rejuvenation to a doomed pagan world,
a nagging question nevertheless remained: How could a man
really be God at the same time that he was quite obviously a
man? This question was particularly pertinent to the subtle and
inquiring Greek and Oriental minds of ancient times.

Unfortunately, some of those within the Church who pon-
dered the question reached the conclusion that no mere man
could really have been God, in spite of the clear testimony of
the New Testament writings (e.g., Jn 14).

According to this way of thinking, our Lord Jesus Christ
must have been a creature, however exalted—"the Son of
God" in name only, by adoption only. "The Word [who]
became flesh and dwelt among us" (Jn 1:14) could not, according to this view, have been "in the beginning with God",

though this is what the Gospel according to John, 1:2, plainly asserts. According to this way of thinking, there was a time when he was not.

This was one of the doctrines of Arianism, the heresy that took its name from one of its votaries, Arius, a priest of the see of Alexandria in Egypt. The increasingly widespread preaching of the doctrine of Arius, especially in the Churches of the East, brought about the crisis that impelled Emperor Constantine to summon the Council of Nicaea. The question raised by Arius and his followers had to be authoritatively decided for the whole Church.

The Church's decision at Nicaea was that a first-century Galilean carpenter, Jesus Christ, was "one in being" (*homoousios*) with God the Father. Jesus was, in other words, of the same substance as the Father; that is, Jesus was himself God, as Thomas had testified, as the apostles had preached, as the evangelists had recorded in the Gospels, and as the Church had not failed to affirm and hand down to the faithful of subsequent generations. Just as the apostles at the Council of Jerusalem had decided on the relationship of the old law to the new revelation of Christ, declaring, "It has seemed good to the Holy Spirit and to us to lay upon you no greater burden" (Acts 15:28), so the fourth-century Catholic bishops at Nicaea unhesitatingly decided and declared what the faith of the apostles was, as the Church had preserved and taught it.

A true understanding of the doctrine of Christ admits of no other interpretation than the one arrived at by the Church at Nicaea. Nevertheless the decision made at Nicaea was not, at the outset, universally accepted. Rather, it triggered further questions and controversies about who and what Jesus Christ was. These questions were settled only after three subsequent general councils held over a period of a century and a quarter.

III.

The Council of Nicaea, 325 A.D.

As we have said, Emperor Constantine convoked the first general (ecumenical) council of the Catholic Church, the Council of Nicaea, to answer questions raised by Arius and his followers, who were preaching about Jesus that "there was a time when he was not." The emperor himself delivered an address in Latin, urging the restoration of peace in the Church, which had been upset in many places by this novel Arian doctrine. Otherwise Constantine took no substantive part in the deliberations; it was an affair of the Catholic bishops.

Although most of the more than three hundred bishops at the Council of Nicaea were Eastern bishops, it was probably presided over by a Western bishop, Hosius (sometimes spelled Ossius) of Cordova, Spain. By then Hosius was probably Emperor Constantine's most influential ecclesiastical advisor. Also present at the council and signatories to its official documents were the Roman priests Vitus and Vincentius, sent by Pope St. Silvester I (314–335) to represent him.

Among the other notable bishops present was the "Father of Church History", Eusebius Phamphilus (b. ca. 263), bishop of Caesarea in Palestine from about 314 until his death in 339, who later wrote extensively concerning the gathering. Eusebius recorded that some of the bishops present "bore the stigmata of the Lord Jesus Christ in their bodies" as a result of recent persecutions. Among these was Bishop Paul of Neocaesaria on the Euphrates, whose hands had been paralyzed by the application of red-hot irons. Bishop Paphnutius of Upper Egypt had lost an eye and had had his knees crushed. Another Egyptian bishop, Potamon, had also had an eye torn out.

The contrast between the persecuted Church of only a few years earlier and the bishops now meeting in pomp and splendor under the patronage of the Roman Empire itself could not have been greater. As Eusebius was moved to write, "One might have thought that the whole thing was a dream, not solid reality" (*Vita Constantini,* III, 15). This novel patronage of the Roman emperor would amaze more than one churchman in the years—and centuries—to come.

Eusebius was so dazzled by the imperial patronage that he sometimes raised the emperor to a Christlike level. As Christ had opened the gates of heaven to mankind, so the Christian emperor would purge the world of error with his righteous sword. Eusebius compared Constantine's dining with the bishops to Christ and the apostles at the Last Supper. Eusebius marveled at the Church's new respectability, and he was not alone.

This kind of attitude toward worldly power would continue to be a temptation, an opportunity, and, too often, a source of bitter disillusionment for the Church. Had not Jesus clearly stated that his kingdom was not of this world? (cf. Jn 18:36). He certainly never told the apostles that state patronage and power would clear the obstacles from in front of them! While instructing them to render unto Caesar "the things that are Caesar's", he also pointedly enjoined them to give "to God the things that are God's" (Mt 22:21).

The Christian emperors would many times show themselves determined to domesticate Christ's Church in the interests of Caesar and to enlist her in the cause of this world. Because Bishop Eusebius cherished the illusion that Christ's work could or should be advanced by worldly power, he cannot always be relied upon as an exponent of the authentic faith. Nevertheless, this ancient Christian author is invaluable for providing a history of the first three centuries of Christianity. We are often obliged to rely on the facts reported by Eusebius even when we are unable to share his viewpoint. He often engaged in composing panegyrics, especially where the emperor was concerned, and this ancient literary form cannot be expected to convey precise, "scientific" history.

Among the important prelates present at Nicaea was Alexander, bishop of Alexandria, Egypt, where Arius had begun preaching his heresy. Accompanying Bishop Alexander was his young deacon Athanasius, who would eventually succeed him in the see of Alexandria (serving from 328 until his death in 373). His unyielding defense, over nearly a half century, of the final decision of the Council of Nicaea was to earn him the title of "pillar of the Church". He would come to be regarded as one of the greatest champions of the Catholic faith who ever lived: *"Athanasius contra mundum"*, was the saying: "Athanasius against the world"—with what justice we shall see.

The perpetrator of Arianism, the Alexandrian priest Arius, was allowed to appear before the Council of Nicaea to state his case. Some of the bishops present even championed his cause, most notably the bishop of the then imperial capital, Nicomedia, another Eusebius by name. (That this latter bishop, who was regularly closest to the emperor, was an open champion of Arianism would prove to be a factor in keeping this insidious heresy alive long after it should have been laid to rest.)

The consensus of the bishops at the Council of Nicaea seems never to have been in doubt; that Jesus Christ the Savior could somehow *not* have been fully and truly God was manifestly not the faith that had been handed down in the Church. The faith of the apostles was that Jesus Christ was, indeed, God. The Council Fathers were accordingly obliged to formulate a creed expressing the true faith of the Church.

Formulation of a creed was not a new idea in the Church. Such a profession of faith had been in use in the universal Church from the beginning. A profession of faith had to be explicitly made by each convert to Christianity when accepting baptism. A creed had to be professed *for* the children being baptized into the Church. What the council did in fashioning the original version of what came to be the Nicene Creed was to take one of the baptismal creeds in common use— probably the one being used by the Church in Jerusalem— and add language expressing without error or ambiguity what the true faith of the Church was—as opposed to what Arius and his followers were trying to say it was. The result was the essence of the Nicene Creed that is still professed on Sundays, Holy Days, and other solemnities in the Catholic Church:

> We believe in one God, the Father, the Almighty, maker of heaven and earth, of all that is seen and unseen.
> We believe in one Lord, Jesus Christ, the only Son of God, eternally begotten of the Father, God from God, Light from Light, true God from true God, begotten not made, one in Being with the Father. . . .

This was the principal work of the Council of Nicaea: the adding to the Church's traditional Creed, or profession of faith, of a term that, though not found in sacred Scripture, nevertheless guaranteed correct expression of the faith. This word proved necessary to affirm unmistakably the scriptural truth that the man Jesus of Nazareth is God, and this Jesus of Nazareth, after having been crucified, rose from the dead and sits at the right hand of the Father. We do not know who first suggested the word *homo-ousios* to describe the divinity of Christ. St. Athanasius wrote that it was Bishop Hosius of Cordova. Whoever it was, the word has authentically expressed the true faith of the Church ever since: "one in being".

Writing some thirty-five years after the Council, St. Athanasius pointed out something very important about how the Council of Nicaea reached its decisions. The council, besides decreeing the essence of the Nicene Creed, also decided on a number of other important Church matters. The gathering proved to be a providential means of enabling the bishops to exercise collectively their Christ-given role of teaching, sanctifying, and governing in the Church.

The council issued no fewer than twenty canons, or directives (from the Greek *kanon*, "rule" or "standard"). The issues addressed included the computation of the date of Easter, the manner of receiving back into the Church those who had apostatized during the persecutions, the conditions for ordination to the priesthood and elevation to the episcopate, and many questions concerning the conduct of the Church's liturgy and official prayer. There was even a canon against usury, the taking of unjust interest.

It cannot be emphasized too strongly that, just as the apostles at the primitive Council of Jerusalem (cf. Acts 15) did not doubt their authority to decide for the Church with the assistance of the Holy Spirit, so the bishops at the Council of Nicaea took for granted that they, too, with the assistance of the Holy Spirit, possessed authority to legislate and decide for the universal Church.

However, as Athanasius pointed out, the Council Fathers decided different questions in somewhat different ways:

> The Fathers of Nicaea, speaking of the Easter feast, say, "We have decided as follows." But about the faith they do not say, "We have decided," but: "This is what the Catholic Church believes." And immediately they proclaim how they

believe, in order to declare, not some novelty, but that their belief is apostolic, and that what they write down is not something they have discovered, but those very things which the Apostles taught. . . . (*Epistola de Synodis,* 5)

We here should note the name St. Athanasius employs for the entity for which the Council spoke: the Catholic Church. The Nicene Creed itself, as issued by the Council of Nicaea, originally included a significant additional paragraph that has not been retained. This, with emphases added, is the paragraph:

> As for those who say: "There was a time when He was not" and "before being begotten He was not," and who declare that He was made from nothing, or that the Son of God is of a different substance [*hypostasis*] or being [*ousia*], that is, created, or subject to change and alteration—[such persons] the *Catholic Church* condemns.

For it was, precisely, this first ecumenical council of the Catholic Church that, in addition to its other important acts, also ratified the proper name by which the true Church of Christ had by then already universally come to be known, just as in the later, final version of this Creed the four traditional notes of this same Church—One, Holy, Catholic, and Apostolic—would be professed.

IV.

The Council of Constantinople, 381 A.D.

The second ecumenical council of the Catholic Church was not nearly so dramatic as the first. Only a hundred and fifty bishops attended, all of them from the East. The council was convoked by Catholic Emperor Theodosius I (379–395) in order to reaffirm the Church's fidelity to Nicaea after more than a half century of turmoil, during which the teaching of Nicaea concerning Jesus had many times been called into question, often with the active support of the sons and successors of Emperor Constantine.

The Council of Constantinople was not planned as an ecumenical council; nor was the bishop of Rome, the pope, even represented. It only subsequently came to be recognized as ecumenical, primarily because of the importance of the Creed it promulgated, a Creed essentially the same as that composed in the middle of the fourth century by Epiphanius, bishop of Salamis (b. ca. 315). The *homo-ousios* of Nicaea was by then incorporated into this so-called "Symbol of Epiphanius". This Creed also contained an affirmation of the divinity of the Holy Spirit and listed the already traditional notes, or marks, of the true Church: One, Holy, Catholic, and Apostolic.

In the Creed it promulgated, the Council of Constantinople was to adopt these features in addition to reaffirming the Creed of Nicaea, thus essentially completing the Creed professed to this day in the Catholic Church. The correct name of this Creed is, thus, the Niceno-Constantinopolitan Creed, although it is more often referred to simply as the Nicene Creed. Most Catholics know it by heart, even if they know little or nothing of its history. It represents a classic example of the "development of doctrine" in the Church. Promulgated by a general council, it can never be essentially changed (theoretically, basic truths concerning the revelation of Jesus can be added to it by legitimate Church authority).

The road that led to the formulation and promulgation of this seemingly solid, unchangeable Creed was very rocky.

No sooner had the Council of Nicaea concluded than several bishops in the East revoked their adherence to Nicaea's *homo-ousios* decision. One Arian bishop in particular, Eusebius of Nicomedia (d. 341), not to be confused with the historian Eusebius, was an astute politician who became so influential with the emperor that he was named the first bishop of Constantinople when Constantine established his new capital there five years after the end of Nicaea.

Within ten years after Nicaea, Bishop Eusebius of Nicomedia and his Arianizing allies had persuaded Constantine to banish St. Athanasius, the unyielding defender of Nicaea, to Trier in Germany, nearly as far away as he could be sent and still remain within the Roman Empire. It was the first of several periods of exile from his Alexandrian see for Athanasius in his forty-five years as a bishop.

Remarkably, Eusebius of Nicomedia and his allies persuaded Constantine to allow Arius to return from exile, but the arch-heresiarch Alexandrian priest died very painfully not long after that: his insides ruptured while he was on his way to a church in Constantinople to be reconciled. Nevertheless, the influence of Arius continued long after his death.

In the year 337 A.D., Constantine himself died. Nevertheless the imperial favor being shown to the Arianizers continued, especially after Constantine's son Constantius became sole emperor in 350. He was a convinced Arian and an overweening tyrant who did not hesitate to use his imperial power to try to force his heretical views upon the bishops of the Church. The Roman emperors were generally less interested in truth than in what they called "peace in the Church" (by which they meant often subservience of the Church to state control).

St. Athanasius described how the Arianizing Emperor Constantius, in 355, dealt with a group of recalcitrant bishops at a local meeting in Milan. These bishops were refusing to sign a condemnation of Athanasius and "to communicate with the heretics. And when they in astonishment at this strange order said that there was no ecclesiastical canon for it, he instantly retorted: 'Take my will for a canon! . . . Either obey or go yourselves into exile!'" (St. Athanasius, *History of the Arians*, 33).

In the course of nearly a half century during which he never wavered in defense of the doctrinal teaching of Nicaea, the great Athanasius regularly fought attempts by the imperial power and by bishops allied with it who sought to dictate Church decisions on the basis of considerations other than the traditional faith that had been handed down from the apostles.

St. Athanasius mordantly excoriated in his writings the Arianizing court bishops who spoke of "the eternal emperor" while denying the real eternity of the Son of God! By the end of his life, Athanasius even came to deny the legitimacy of the convocation of Church councils by the emperor and to insist instead on complete independence of the Church from the empire. No one more frequently than he had witnessed the abundant harm that could come from the state's trying to dictate to the Church what her teachings and practices should be.

During the years between the general Councils of Nicaea and Constantinople, more than a half dozen other local councils were held in various cities, usually to try to force the bishops to accept imperial "compromise" solutions on the Arian question. Many bishops gave in under terrible threats and pressures; some were tortured, even murdered. Such were the passions of the time and the misplaced zeal of an absolutist state attempting to impose uniformity on the Church.

Many other bishops, however, especially in the West, where the imperial pressure was generally less felt, resisted the forced distortions of the faith. During this period no fewer than nineteen variations on the Nicene formula were formally proposed for the Church, but none found acceptance.

One of these formulations included the Greek term *homo-i-ousios*, declaring the Son to be *similar* to the Father but not the *same* as the Father, that is, *homo-ousios*, "one in being" with him. The difference was seemingly very small, simply the letter *i* (Greek: *iota*) being added to the variant formula. From this controversy we derive the expression, "There is not an iota of difference." In the history of the Church, that "iota of difference" really has been quite important as the expression of her timeless doctrine of who and what Jesus Christ was and is. The Church could never have abandoned the *homo-ousios* formula once it had been formally adopted, no matter what the pretext or the pressure; abandonment of it would have meant the failure of Christ's promise to the Church.

Competing currents of opinion during the years between the Councils of Nicaea and Constantinople included Arians, who denied the divinity of Christ, and the so-called semi-Arians—perhaps the majority of the bishops at one time or another—who were, in effect, subordinationists. These did not actually deny the divinity of Christ, but they mistrusted the term *homo-ousios* because it was not found in Scripture. Also, they apparently did not understand that, logically, Christ *had to be* one in being, that is, of the same substance as the Father, *if* Christ himself is God.

The same logic applies to the question of the Holy Spirit if, as the Council of Constantinople affirmed, the Holy Spirit is also God. During those same turbulent years, there was an active faction of Macedonians (followers of Macedonius), who specifically denied the divinity of the Holy Spirit, and the council was obliged to address and correct this error.

Then there were the Apollinarians (followers of Apollinaris), who held that in the God-man Jesus Christ, the divine Logos *replaced* the human soul. Jesus, thus, was truly God but not truly man. In a more developed form, this heresy, originally known as Apollinarianism, was destined to play a further role in the way in which the two great Councils of Ephesus and Chalcedon would finally complete the Catholic Church's great work of defining who and what Jesus Christ was and is.

The second ecumenical Council of Constantinople, in 381, explicitly condemned the abounding heresies of that time: Arianism, various forms of Semi-Arianism, Macedonianism, and Apollinarianism. The council then promulgated the definitive Creed of the Catholic Church, which to this day is professed in our churches, proclaiming the Church to be One, Holy, Catholic, and Apostolic.

V.

The Council of Ephesus, 431 A.D.

The Niceno-Constantinopolitan Creed, promulgated by the Council of Constantinople in 381, definitively formulated the Church's doctrine of the Holy Trinity. It also definitively established that the Son of God, the divine Logos, is a divine person within the Trinity, as is the Holy Spirit.

A full half century would pass before further refinement of the Church's understanding of her Creed became necessary. This came about through the work of another great general council.

Arius had doubted that the Son was truly God. Even though that question had been settled by the Church's Magisterium, expressed through her first two great ecumenical councils, questions continued to be raised concerning the relationship of the divine and the human within the God-man, Jesus Christ. For instance, it was asked whether, in Christ, the human remained distinct from the divine or, as the Apollinarians believed, the divine absorbed the human.

Two schools of thought representing the two principal theological traditions of the Church that had developed up to that point contended with each other over these questions. These two theological schools, or traditions, were based in the ancient sees of Alexandria in Egypt and Antioch in Syria, respectively. These sees were considered "Petrine"—as, preeminently, the see of Rome was considered Petrine—since Peter himself had been at Antioch before going on to Rome; and his disciple Mark was revered as the founder of the see of Alexandria. Both would be the sees of future patriarchs when the institution of the patriarchate was developed.

In the meantime, both centers of Christian learning developed distinctive theological traditions. The theological debates carried on in those days were never purely debates but were influenced by human rivalries between these two great sees (and, later, with the newer see of Constantinople as well).

Even more unfortunate for the Church was that these debates generally involved rivalry between some of the powerful ecclesiastical personalities of the day, all of whom had their followers—and some of the latter outdid their masters in partisan zeal!

Where authentic Church doctrine is concerned, we should never forget the inspiration and guidance of the Holy Spirit. The Holy Spirit manifestly assisted the churchmen at these councils to arrive at correct doctrinal formulations even though they were sometimes prone to exhibit an all-too-human side. When God condescends to work through human beings, even those set apart and sanctified by sacred ordination, a human side is inevitably revealed. Nonetheless, these early council Fathers were overwhelmingly sincere in trying to serve God's Church according to their lights.

The Alexandrian theological school, anxious to preserve understanding of the divinity of Christ along with the unity of his actions in saving mankind, stressed the fusion of divinity and humanity in Christ. St. Cyril, the great Alexandrian bishop between 412 and 444, habitually spoke of the one "nature" (Greek: *physis*) in Christ, the incarnate Logos. Although this formulation expressed an important truth, it eventually proved inadequate and had to give way to a more precise formulation. The danger lurking in Alexandrian thought was that Christ's humanity could be totally absorbed by his divinity—as was later to prove unhappily to be the case with the Monophysite heresy (Greek: *monos*, "one" and *physis*, "nature") that eventually prevailed in Alexandria.

By contrast, the theological school of Antioch, anxious to maintain the distinction between the human and the divine Christ—an important truth but inadequate by itself—held that the Logos, "dwells in the man Jesus as in a temple". Thus, the school of Antioch ran the risk of holding that the union between the divine and the human in Christ was simply a moral, not a real, union.

These points might theoretically have been argued thoroughly and amicably by theologians from contending theological schools, but what happened was that Nestorius, a votary of the school of Antioch, became the bishop of Constantinople in the year 428. Nestorius was interested in pushing his views beyond the bounds of mere theological debate. From his commanding pulpit he began to champion a view that distinguished too sharply between the human and the divine in Christ; he also attempted to modify a long-popular devotion invoking the blessed Virgin Mary as *Theotókos*, the God-bearer, or "the Mother of God".

The exertions of Nestorius in this vein soon aroused the ire of St. Cyril of Alexandria, the bishop second in Christendom after the bishop of Rome and one of the greatest theologians of his day. It also stirred up considerable controversy among the faithful, especially among communities of monks. In order to settle this controversy, Emperor Theodosius II (408–450) decided to convoke the Council of Ephesus in 431. Over two hundred bishops eventually took part in this, the third great Church council. It took place in Ephesus in Asia Minor. Some of the sessions were held in the great basilica dedicated to the Virgin Mary, the cathedral of the Theotókos.

One of the most important positions held by Nestorius was that the Greek term *Theotókos* ("God-bearer") could not properly be applied to Mary. Carrying the Antiochian tendency to its extreme conclusion, Nestorius argued that the divine Logos could not have been born of the Virgin, nor could the suffering on the Cross have been suffering by the Word, but only the man in whom the Word dwelt; and it was this man whom Mary bore, not the very Word of God. In accordance with this logic, Mary had to be *Christotókos* only, the mother of Christ, not *Theotókos*, the Mother of God.

The reaction to this viewpoint, which was now being openly preached, encouraged, and patronized by none other than the bishop of Constantinople, Nestorius, was both varied and vigorous. Cyril of Alexandria initially had written about the whole affair to Pope St. Celestine I (422–432), who quickly agreed that Nestorius was in error. The pope therefore authorized St. Cyril to call upon Nestorius in the name of the pope to recant his views and return to the tradition of the Church or be deposed from his position as bishop of Constantinople.

After some delay, St. Cyril produced a list of twelve theological propositions for Nestorius to subscribe to. Refusing to subscribe to them would clearly expose his heresy. In the meantime, the emperor was calling for a general council, mostly in response to an appeal to him by Nestorius (and by the bishop of Antioch among others). Pope Celestine, agreeing to the convocation of such a council under the presidency of St. Cyril, sent three legates.

The Council of Ephesus was a confused and confusing affair. Neither the Roman legates nor the bishops under the bishop of Antioch arrived on time. Meanwhile, both St. Cyril and Nestorius had set up rival parties, or factions, of bishops in Ephesus. At a certain point, St. Cyril formally convened the council, even though not all of the participants had arrived. Under his leadership the council, which had thus been duly inaugurated, condemned Nestorius and deposed him from his see. Unfortunately, the "council" at this point consisted mostly of Egyptian bishops belonging to Cyril's own faction.

Then Bishop John of Antioch arrived with *his* party. These bishops voted to boycott St. Cyril's gathering and to reject its condemnation of Nestorius. They organized their own counter-council (*conciliabulum*), which then proceeded to condemn and depose St. Cyril from the see of Alexandria. People took their theology quite seriously in those days!

At that point the Roman legates finally arrived. They insisted that the council be properly reconstituted under the leadership of St. Cyril, as the pope had originally directed, with the Roman priest Philip, the representative of Pope St. Celestine I, signing the conciliar acts after Cyril (and ahead of all two hundred or more bishops present). The authority of the Roman legates was accepted without question by the Eastern bishops.

Once the council was officially reconstituted, the earlier condemnation of Nestorianism and the deposition of Nestorius from the see of Constantinople were then validated. The pope's own clear condemnation of the views of Nestorius was read aloud and acclaimed by the council Fathers.

The interesting language in which the Council of Ephesus condemned Nestorianism reveals how the Fathers of this early council thought of themselves: as speaking authoritatively for Jesus Christ himself. The council's sentence against Nestorius included these words:

> Since, in addition to other things, the most impious Nestorius has not obeyed our citation, nor received the most holy and God-fearing bishops whom we sent to him, we were compelled to examine his ungodly teachings. And having discovered from his letters and from his writings, as well as from the discourses delivered by him in this metropolis, which have been testified to, that his teachings and opinions are impious, we, compelled thereto both by the canons and by the letter of our most holy father and colleague, Celestine, bishop of the Roman Church, have with many tears arrived at this sorrowful sentence against him: *Our Lord Jesus Christ*, who has been blasphemed by him, *has defined by this holy synod* that the same Nestorius is excluded from the episcopal rank and from all sacerdotal communion. (Emphases added.)

This ecumenical council's own view of itself, then, was that it literally spoke *for* Christ. The same remains true today: an ecumenical council of the Catholic Church speaks for Christ in its authentic, established words and acts.

Emperor Theodosius II was hugely perturbed that the Council of Ephesus had not followed his "orders", which he had communicated to the council through a representative.

Initially, the emperor declared a plague on both houses, upholding both the deposition of Nestorius by the council and the deposition of Cyril by the *conciliabulum*. Further discussions following the council and, no doubt, some conflicting pressures finally tempered the emperor's judgment, and eventually St. Cyril was allowed to return to his see of Alexandria. The exile of Nestorius, however, stood, as did the conciliar condemnation of his doctrine, which condemnation stands to this day.

Thus did the Council of Ephesus reaffirm the Councils of Nicaea and of Constantinople. Fittingly, it did so by reaffirming, in the Basilica of the Mother of God at Ephesus, the popular devotion of the faithful to Mary as the Mother of God.

Unlike the situation that has unfortunately obtained in some later ages of the Church, including, in some ways, our own, the faithful in ancient times seem instinctively to have understood the preeminent position of Mary in the economy of salvation. No doubt they understood this because they also understood that the only way the eternal and omnipotent God could ever have actually become a member of our human race was by having a human mother, Mary. Having no human father, Jesus necessarily derived his human nature *entirely* from his human mother; all of his forty-six chromosomes had to come from Mary; God could not have become a member of our race in any other way.

Thus, in the Hail Mary, when we call upon "holy Mary, Mother of God" to "pray for us sinners, now and at the hour of our death", we are not engaging in some sentimental, sugary devotion; we are expressing profound Catholic truths infallibly defined by an ecumenical council of the Church: that Christ is God and Mary is *Theotókos*, the Mother of God—truths that lie at the heart of our salvation.

VI.

The Council of Chalcedon, 451 A.D.

Within twenty years of the Council of Ephesus in 431, another general council became necessary. In condemning Nestorianism, Ephesus placed a limit upon the degree to which the human in Jesus could be separated from the divine in him without falling into error: Jesus was not just a man in whom God dwelt in a special way; Jesus was himself God. This was the faith the Church had received from the apostles and was obliged to hand on.

Through the definitions hammered out by the first four great councils of the Church—which, after the fourth, the Council of Chalcedon in 451, would ever remain the timeless doctrine of the Church—Catholic doctrine was increasingly able to render a more exact, almost technical, explanation, both of who and what Jesus Christ the Savior was and is, and what the implications of the Church's doctrine about this were for the faith and for the faithful.

Whether or not God really is "in Christ, reconciling the world to himself", as St. Paul so concisely expressed it (2 Cor 5:19), and in what sense this is so, is not merely abstract doctrine unrelated to faith and life; it is vital, all-important, in fact. And to decide this question, Catholic doctrine was now moving toward the definitive formulation that Christ was a divine *Person with two natures*, a divine nature and a human nature.

In the development of this new terminology, the Greek words *hypostasis* and *prosopon* were increasingly being used to express what we today call "person" (from the Latin *persona,* originally meaning an actor's mask; Greek: *prosopon*). Indeed the very concept of a "person", as we understand that term today, was originally worked out in the course of the Church's search to explain who Jesus was and is. The definition the Church finally arrived at was confirmed by the Council of Chalcedon in the way that it treated Christ the divine Word and his position within the Holy Trinity.

The Greek word *physis* more often designated what we now call "nature". This usage caused a difficulty, since none other than St. Cyril of Alexandria himself, speaking of "the one nature of the incarnate *Logos*", used *physis* to mean the fusion of the human and the divine in Jesus, which later was expressed by the word *person*. In a negotiated theological settlement among the parties that had contended at Ephesus, St. Cyril agreed that the new terminology of "one person" and "two natures" really did express the belief that he professed about Christ.

Many of Cyril's followers in the Alexandrian theological school did not agree with the new formulation as willingly as did the bishop himself. After St. Cyril's death in 444, a new heresy emerged, Monophysitism, or "one-nature-ism", the opposite of Nestorianism. According to this way of thinking, Christ possessed only one nature, a divine nature, his divinity in effect absorbing his humanity. In advancing this view, the Monophysites obstinately and erroneously claimed to be championing the view of St. Cyril.

In trying to correct the new error, the Church was to witness at Chalcedon the condemnation, deposition, and exile of a bishop of Alexandria, Dioscoros—a successor of St. Athanasius and of St. Cyril, and traditionally the second bishop of Christendom—just as at Ephesus a bishop of Constantinople, Nestorius, had been condemned, deposed, and exiled. In both cases, tragically, splinter churches, the Nestorian and the Monophysite, broke away from the true Church of Christ. These fifth-century divisions in the body of Christ have endured to the present day in some Christian commun-ions of the East.

A leading monk in Constantinople, Eutyches, contended that Christ, being divine, was not of the same substance as we are (*homo-ousios*). According to this Monophysite view-point, Christ had no human soul; rather the divine in him functioned in place of a soul.

Eutyches was quickly denounced for preaching heresy. In 448 he was brought before a local synod for judgment by the patriarch of Constantinople, St. Flavian, who was in the see between 446 and 449. But the stubborn Eutyches refused to argue his case, telling the synod that subtle distinctions were beyond him; he was a simple monk, after all. Given that the monk did not cease to espouse his views, the synod had no choice but to condemn him.

But this "simple monk" had influential friends in high places, including Emperor Theodosius II himself. Another friend was the hot-tempered, high-handed bishop of Alex-andria, Dioscoros. To settle the controversy over Monophys-itism, the emperor resorted to the time-honored practice of calling a general council—at which he expected his imperial will to prevail.

Accordingly, again at Ephesus, in 449, a council was pre-sided over with imperial connivance by Dioscoros of Alex-andria. The unhappy results were a foregone conclusion: Eutyches was rehabilitated by this body, and St. Flavian of Constantinople, who had challenged him, was condemned and deposed. Literally dragged away from the altar by sol-diers, he died three days later as a prisoner. For the moment, Dioscoros of Alexandria ruled the ecclesiastical roost in the East. Such was the famous "Robber Council" (*Latrocinium*) of Ephesus of the year 449—it was decidedly *not* another general council of the Church!

Meanwhile, the bishop of Rome, Pope St. Leo the Great (440–461), had not been idle. St. Flavian had written to him earlier concerning the Eutyches affair, and the pope replied with a doctrinal letter to Constantinople, in which was set forth in clear but majestic Latin what has ever since been received as the essential teaching of the Catholic Church: Christ is a divine Person possessing both a divine nature and a human nature. The date of the great *Tome of St. Leo*, as this letter was called, was June 13, 449.

Pope St. Leo had also agreed to the emperor's idea of another ecumenical council and had sent legates to Ephesus in 449 with instructions to have his *Tome* read to the council and accepted by it as the definitive teaching of the Church. However, at the Robber Council the papal legates were not even allowed to speak by Dioscoros and his allies. Instead, the legates were obliged to flee from the violence that engulfed St. Flavian and the orthodox party.

When St. Leo learned of the disgraceful outcome at Ephesus, he wrote to the emperor demanding that a real council be held, characterizing what had taken place in the false council as *non iudicium sed latrocinium*—"not a council but a gathering of robbers", a name that has been applied to it ever since.

Since things had been decided to his satisfaction, Emperor Theodosius II simply ignored the pope's call for an authentic council. But Theodosius was killed shortly afterward in an accident with his horse (July 450). His successor, Emperor Marcian (451–457), an orthodox Catholic, promptly issued a summons for a council, as the pope had requested. The council was originally to have been held at Nicaea again, but was changed to Chalcedon (modern Kadiköy) on the Asiatic shore of the Bosphorus across from Constantinople, since Nicaea was more than forty miles away from the new capital.

The Council of Chalcedon opened on October 8, 451. Six hundred bishops, perhaps even more, attended this council, the largest in antiquity. Most, as usual, came from the East, but the bishop who presided, Paschasinus, was from Sicily; he headed the legation appointed by Pope St. Leo the Great to represent him.

The pope's instruction to this Roman legation was to have the *Tome*, the pope's letter to St. Flavian, read and adopted by this council. When the *Tome* was read aloud, the members of this predominantly Eastern gathering were reported to have cried out with virtually one voice: "It is Peter who says this through Leo. This is what we all of us believe. This is the faith of the apostles...."

When the truth was thus dramatically brought to their attention, the Eastern bishops spontaneously affirmed the primacy of the successors of Peter in the see of Rome, the popes. Moreover, such an impressive tribute to the position and actions of the bishop of Rome pronounced by the bishops of the Eastern Church at an ecumenical council was by no means confined to the Council of Chalcedon.

The same phenomenon was to occur at other ecumenical councils. More than two centuries later, at the Third General Council of Constantinople (680–681), when the heresy being dealt with was a variant of Monophysitism called Monothelitism, which affirmed that Christ had only "one will", Pope Agatho (678–681) sent a letter to the council similar to the *Tome* St. Leo had sent to Chalcedon. It was a clear, simple statement of the traditional Roman belief in Christ, specifically affirming, in continuity with the decisions of Chalcedon, that in Christ there were necessarily two wills, divine and human, just as there were two natures.

Constantinople III acclaimed Pope Agatho's statement as profusely as the Fathers at Chalcedon had acclaimed St. Leo's

Tome two centuries earlier. Agatho's statement, the council declared, was "written by the highest divine summit of the apostles." This seventh-century council then affirmed:

> The supreme prince of the apostles has struggled along with us; his emulator and the successor to his chair is on our side and has explained to us through a letter the mystery of the divine incarnation. The ancient city of Rome has brought forth a confession written by God and has caused day to dawn in the West for this dogma. It appeared in paper and ink and Peter spoke through Agatho. . . .

This council also declared that the gates of hell would never prevail against the "orthodox empire" (something Christ had never promised). Eastern acclaim for the words of the Western pope was nevertheless real and sincere.

The acclaim for Leo at Chalcedon in 451 was not at all exceptional. Praise for the pope was practically the rule for early ecumenical councils. And Chalcedon carried out its work in entire accord with the doctrinal principles laid down in Pope St. Leo's *Tome*.

Dioscoros of Alexandria was condemned at Chalcedon for his role in the Robber Council, then banished by the emperor, an action that occasioned keen humiliation among his followers and set the stage for the eventual separation of the Monophysite-leaning Coptic Churches of Egypt and Ethiopia from the Catholic Church. This was truly a tragic outcome, revolving around party spirit and misunderstandings of key words. Father Philip Hughes, in *The Church in Crisis*, has even characterized the whole affair as "the *misunderstanding* of Chalcedon" (p. 95)! Nevertheless, the separation that resulted from it has unfortunately lasted, with many vicissitudes, down to our own day.

The Council of Chalcedon did not issue a new creed, as Emperor Marcian had wanted. Rather, it validated the existing Niceno-Constantinopolitan Creed (and by doing so also validated the Council of Constantinople in 381 as an ecumenical council), thus placing the definitive seal of the Church's teaching authority upon the traditional four marks of the true Church: One, Holy, Catholic, and Apostolic.

More than that, Chalcedon also placed the definitive seal of the Church's teaching authority on the doctrine developed through the Catholic Church's first four great councils concerning who and what Jesus Christ the Savior was and is. Difficult as it was to formulate in exact words, it had always been understood that Jesus somehow had to be simultaneously true God and true man. Any other formulation of the fundamental truth contained in this paradoxical idea would not do justice to the truth about our salvation. If Jesus had not been God, he could not have saved us—he would not have had the divine power to save us—but if Jesus were not also man, a member of our race, he could not have saved us in the manner that he did.

To state this is to touch upon yet another ancient formulation of the Fathers of the Church to the effect that only what was "assumed" by Jesus was "saved" by him. The ancient Fathers were acute thinkers; in many respects no one since has been able to go beyond them. Pope St. Leo the Great wrote:

> The divine nature and the nature of a servant were ... united in one person so that the Creator of time might be born in time, and he through whom all things were made might be brought forth in their midst. For unless the new man, by being made in the likeness of sinful humanity, had taken on himself the nature of our first parents, unless he had stooped to be one in substance with his mother while

sharing the Father's substance and, being alone free from sin, united our nature to his, the whole human race would still be held captive under the dominion of Satan. The Conqueror's victory would have profited us nothing if the battle had been fought outside our human condition.... (*Epis.* 31, 3)

Such was the quality and the clarity of thought in these doctrinal questions at the time of Chalcedon. It is worth quoting in full the definition arrived at by the Council of Chalcedon, since it expresses the fullness of the truth about himself that Jesus Christ came into the world to reveal:

Following then the holy fathers, we all with one voice teach that it should be confessed that our Lord Jesus Christ is one and the same Son, the same perfect in Godhead, the same perfect in manhood, truly God and truly man, the same [consisting of] a rational soul and a body; *homo-ousios* [consubstantial] with the Father as to his Godhead, and the same *homo-ousios* with us as to his manhood; in all things like unto us, sin only excepted; begotten of the Father before ages as to his Godhead, and in the last days, the same, for us and for our salvation, of Mary, the virgin, *theotokos* [mother of God] as to his manhood; one and the same Christ, Son, Lord, only-begotten, made known in two natures [which exist] without confusion, without change, without division, without separation; the difference of the natures having been in no wise taken away by reason of the union, but rather the properties of each nature being preserved, and both concurring into one person [*prosopon*] and one hypostasis—not parted or divided into two persons [*prosopa*], but one and the same Son and only-begotten, the divine *Logos*, the Lord Jesus Christ: even as the prophets from of old have spoken concerning him....

This final formulation of the Council of Chalcedon fittingly draws upon and contains elements from each of the three principal ancient sees of the Church: Alexandria, Antioch, and Rome. After all of the conciliar vicissitudes reviewed here, the arrival at this basic definition that Jesus is a divine Person with both a divine and a human nature surely bears abundantly the marks of divine inspiration.

Thus, through all the varied and sometimes violent history of the first four great councils of the Catholic Church, we clearly see, in retrospect, how the Church's Magisterium, despite enormous difficulties, reached the only possible and unerring expression of the original revelation that does justice to all the revealed data. The Holy Spirit evidently always did remain with the teaching authority of the Church through all that happened in the century and a quarter between Nicaea and Chalcedon.

Pope St. Gregory the Great (590–604), writing to the patriarch of Constantinople in 594, declared: "I profess that as I receive and venerate the four books of the Gospels, so do I the four councils"—which he listed: Nicaea, 325; Constantinople, 381; Ephesus, 431; and Chalcedon, 451. He described these great councils of the Catholic Church as "the four squared stones on which the structure of the holy faith arises".

VII.

The attestation of Pope St. Gregory the Great to the importance of the Church's ecumenical councils points to the historical relationship between popes and councils. Seventeen more ecumenical councils were to follow the Council of Chalcedon, making a total of twenty-one by the end of the twentieth century.

The fifth through seventh councils also took place in the East: the Second General Council of Constantinople, in 553;

the Third General Council of Constantinople, 680–681; and the Second General Council of Nicaea in 787. These first seven general councils of the Church are accepted as authoritative by Catholics, by most Protestants, and by the Eastern Orthodox alike.

Yet another general council was to be held in Constantinople, in the years 869–870—the fourth to meet in that imperial city—but it was not subsequently recognized as ecumenical by the Greek Orthodox among others. Following this last gathering, more than two and a half centuries were to pass before the first of the general councils of the Lateran was convened in Rome in 1123. All subsequent councils have been held in the West. Eastern Orthodox Christians were often invited to participate in these councils, generally convened under the auspices of the popes. Except in special circumstances, such as the threat of conquest by the Muslim Turks, Eastern Orthodox Christians have generally chosen not to participate.

Similarly, when the Reformation came about, Protestants too were invited to participate in the Council of Trent (1545–1563), but they declined. As a result of successive schisms and heresies, sizable numbers of those who profess belief in Jesus Christ as Savior have not participated in the conciliar ordering of the Church's business or in the development and refinement of the Church's teachings.

For large numbers of professing Christians, it is almost as if the teaching authority that Jesus undeniably promised to his Church somehow became suspended following the end of the Second General Council of Nicaea in 787. It is not clear why anyone should think this authority ceased. It is an even more remarkable position for Christians to hold when it is remembered that the same believers who deny the authenticity of the these later councils also do not recognize the primacy and the special teaching authority of the successor of Peter, the pope.

Where, then, *is* the teaching authority Christ promised to the Church? What happened to the authority that most Christians agree characterized the early Church, at least through the first seven general councils?

The position of those who deny both the primacy of the pope and the validity of the Church's general councils that followed the first seven seems to entail the position that an authoritative Magisterium no longer exists. This position seems to call for a strictly Protestant-style private judgment on doctrinal questions from 787 on. And it would seem effectively to bar the Church from teaching *as the Church* anytime after the Second General Council of Nicaea. Yet Christ directed the apostles to "make disciples of all nations . . . teaching them to observe all that I have commanded you" (Mt 28:19–20).

In the opinion of many who separated from the Roman Catholic Church, once the "great undivided Church of antiquity" became "rent by schisms", no Church body has been able to carry out this command. This inability has persisted since the year 787 if, in order to be considered valid, a general council must be accepted by all of Christianity (and if the papal primacy and the special papal Magisterium are also denied on principle).

Jesus promised that the Church would always be able to speak for him (cf. Lk 10:16). He promised that the Holy Spirit would always guide his disciples in the Church "into all the truth" (Jn 16:13), and this Counselor would be with them "forever" (Jn 14:16). By continuing to convene general councils in spite of the refusal of other parts of Christianity to participate, the Catholic Church still relies on Christ's promises and utilizes an obvious means developed in her early days to help realize in practice Christ's solemn promises to the Church.

The Catholic Church alone continues to exhibit one of the very notable features of the early Church, namely, the convening of ecumenical councils. So much a part of the Church's nature has this institution of councils become that, from time to time, some have even invoked a "conciliar theory" to oppose what they consider the unwarranted claims to primacy in the Church by the bishop of Rome. According to this way of thinking, authoritative decisions in the Church should only be made after consultation with, and consent of, all relevant elements within the Church—as was the case with the first seven general councils.

More surprisingly, a theory still exists that the General Council of Florence in the fifteenth century actually endorsed the notion that no council can be ecumenical unless all five of the ancient patriarchs are present or represented (the Pope being considered the patriarch of the West).

It is true only in a manner of speaking that all five patriarchs were present at all of the first seven councils universally recognized as ecumenical. There was no patriarch of Constantinople at Nicaea, for the simple reason that Constantinople was not founded until the year 330, five years after the Council of Nicaea! It took even longer for Jerusalem to be considered a patriarchate, since, in those centuries, the ancient city of David, where Christ was crucified, was overshadowed by the Roman Caesarea.

The term *patriarch* did not come into general use until the fifth century, although the special status of the sees of Rome, Antioch, and Alexandria was universally recognized from very early times. The apostle Peter was considered the founder of the first two sees; his disciple Mark, the founder of the third. All three were, therefore, "apostolic sees" from the beginning, even if it was several centuries before their bishops finally came to be called patriarchs.

But how did Constantinople and Jerusalem get into the picture to make five patriarchates? Actually, the efforts exerted over a very long time to secure patriarchal status, especially in the case of Constantinople, provide a classic example of the harm that is sometimes done to the Church by excessive politicization and by too close an identification of the Church with the secular state. Already at the Council of Constantinople in 381—at which the pope was not represented—a canon was enacted, though never approved by the bishop of Rome, that read as follows: "The bishop of Constantinople shall have the primacy of honor after the bishop of Rome, because [Constantinople] is new Rome."

This canon seemed to assume that the pope's position in the Church was based, not on Christ's promise to Peter, but on the position of old Rome as the former capital of the empire. Some of the prestige of the popes did inevitably stem from the respect that was still accorded to the former capital of the empire. But it should still go without saying that the Roman claim to primacy in the Church, if valid, never depended upon the fact that the pope was bishop of the (former) imperial city; to think this is to view the pope's position from a mistaken, secular perspective.

The idea persisted that the importance of the see somehow stemmed from the secular importance of the city in which it was located. Some seventy years after the Council of Constantinople, the great Council of Chalcedon took up the matter of patriarchal precedence again—at a session at which the papal legates were not present—and enacted another canon, according to which Constantinople, "the city now honored with the presence of the emperor and the senate, and which enjoys the same [state] privileges as the old royal Rome, should be as great as she in what relates to the Church, and rank second to her (Hughes, *Church in Crisis*, p. 88)."

When the papal legates returned to the Council sessions, Sicilian Bishop Paschasinus, the principal papal legate, strongly objected to the enactment of this canon. Another papal legate, Bishop Lucentius of Ascoli, flatly declared that the canon violated Nicaea. But these Roman protests were somewhat vitiated by the fact that Bishop Paschasinus had given the first place after the legates at the Council to Bishop Anatolios of Constantinople—to the detriment of Alexandria and Antioch. This action was in accord with the pragmatic way in which Rome would in practice more than once accede to the claims of Constantinople in succeeding centuries regarding nondoctrinal questions. No doubt this was an effort to avoid the ultimate schism between East and West, which eventually came about.

As far as the principle was concerned at the time, though, Pope St. Leo I simply declined to ratify the canon of Chalcedon transforming Constantinople into the second see of the Church. He wrote to Bishop Anatolios, reproaching him for the harm done to Alexandria and Antioch by this move and declaring that the earlier canon of 381 had no force, since it had "never [been] notified to the Holy See by your predecessors". To Emperor Marcian, Leo wrote, saying that it was not possible for Anatolios to convert Constantinople into an apostolic see. Everything done in contravention to Nicaea, the pope declared, "we dismiss as without legal effect. . . . By the authority of the blessed apostle Peter, we quash it utterly by a general sentence."

This Roman judgment did not prevent the steady rise of Constantinople, which soon became the de facto second see of Christendom, mostly because of its political position as the city where the Roman emperors still resided. The popes were obliged to take this political fact of life into account and deal with Constantinople accordingly. They themselves were subjects of the emperor. Except for a period in the fifth and sixth centuries when barbarian kings ruled Italy, the popes, although elected by the Roman clergy, had to be confirmed by the emperor in Constantinople before they could be consecrated and installed in office. (This was the case until the eighth century.)

The position enunciated by the Council of Florence centuries later (requiring participation by all five patriarchates for an ecumenical council to be valid) seems to have been imposed on the Church as part of the price of being able to function within an imperial system. Nevertheless, this requirement of the Council of Florence was rendered unrealizable by the movement of history: for more than sixteen hundred years the incumbent of the ancient patriarchate of Alexandria, for example, has regularly been a Monophysite who has expressly rejected the Church's orthodox Christology decided at Chalcedon. The ancient patriarchal city of Antioch (Antakya in Syria) no longer exists as a city of importance, and several small oriental communions lay conflicting claims to the title "patriarch of Antioch".

Similarly, there are currently several "patriarchs of Jerusalem" representing different communions; it is hard to see how *the* patriarch of Jerusalem could be identified for purposes of an ecumenical council. The "Ecumenical Patriarch of Constantinople" himself, although rightly enjoying honor and prestige as titular head of the Greek Orthodox Churches, for several centuries has been obliged to "rule" from inside a small, walled enclave in the city of Istanbul. (Turkey, a Muslim nation, has a secular government.)

Considering how situations like this have been imposed on the Church by history, we can legitimately conclude that the Church has to carry on nevertheless to preserve and hand on what she received from Christ as transmitted by the apostles and their successors, the bishops.

The Catholic Church plausibly continues to claim that this is exactly what she has done over the centuries—in addition to being the only Christian body that continues to convene ecumenical councils to help order the life and teaching of the Church. She also holds that Christ's promise to Peter to be the "rock" on which the Church was to be built (Mt 16:18) continues in Peter's successors in the see of Rome, who are therefore obliged in a special way to feed Christ's sheep (cf. Jn 21:17) and strengthen his brethren, the successors of the apostles, the bishops (cf. Lk 22:32).

Through the supreme authority of the popes and the councils, the universal Church of Christ has been governed throughout her long history. In a subsequent chapter, we shall consider in detail the question of the primacy of Rome in the early Church. To conclude this chapter, it is important to show that the Church's ancient and valid custom of convening councils to decide important doctrinal and disciplinary questions in no way conflicts with the primacy given by Christ to Peter and passed on to his successors in the see of Rome. We need to view this question in relation to our present topic, the Church's first four great councils.

VIII.

The First General Council of Nicaea was convoked in 325, not by the bishop of Rome, but by the Roman emperor, as was the Second General Council of Constantinople in 381. No pope was present at either council. That Roman emperors, not popes, were responsible for convoking what have been universally understood afterward to be the formative general councils of the Church is sometimes used to argue (1) against the proposition—which the Catholic Church has always insisted upon—that papal consent and ratification are necessary in order for the acts of a general council to be considered authentic; and (2) against the very idea of Roman primacy in the Church.

It would be fairly accurate to say that Emperor Constantine *ignored* the Roman primacy when he decided to call the Council of Nicaea. Constantine's basic attitude, like that of many of his successors, was pragmatic, directed toward resolving Church problems that were causing turmoil in the empire.

Constantine was not hostile to the Church of Rome as such. Indeed he exhibited unusual generosity in endowing this Church. He donated his mother's Lateran palace to the popes as a residence, and he made provision for the construction of the first St. Peter's Vatican Basilica on the site of the tomb of the Prince of the Apostles, the present site of St. Peter's in Rome.

Constantine, however, often did not bother to consult the pope when making decisions affecting the Church. For an all-powerful Roman emperor to have acted in this way for what he considered the peace and good order of the empire, though, is not an argument against the Roman primacy. Constantine had his own idea of what the position of the Church should be in the empire, and while he recognized and respected a certain autonomy for the Church, as Nicaea proved, it also seems, as various documents he issued pertaining to the Church show, that he considered the Church, like everything else in the empire, to be under his authority.

As Roman emperor, Constantine was the *Pontifex Maximus*, that is, the chief custodian of all the recognized cults, with supervisory authority over all religious affairs. This, in his mind, surely included the Church. Until the imperial office of *Pontifex Maximus* was abolished in 379 in the East and 382 in the West, the Roman emperor ruled over pagans and Christians alike.

Nor is it greatly surprising that once Christianity became recognized by the empire, the emperor would consider the Church to be strictly under his authority. The work of convincing those in power that the Church must be independent of all secular authority—one of the great achievements of the papacy—has required a thousand years and more. We cannot expect to find at the time of Constantine anything like the principle of separation of Church and state, a concept that would have been unintelligible to a Roman ruler in the fourth century.

The primacy of the Roman Church over other Churches might even have seemed to Constantine a theological fine point. He was well aware in general of the position of the bishop of Rome and, while still in the West, Constantine had had a number of specific dealings with the pope. Very soon, however, Constantine removed himself to his new capital in the East.

Regarding the papal attitude toward the general council of the Church that the emperor decided to call in 325, ecclesiastical historian Eusebius of Caesarea wrote that "the bishop of the imperial city" failed to attend the Council of Nicaea because of his "advanced age" (*Vita Constantini*, III, 7). This statement is regularly repeated by historians, but we really do not know whether this was the only, or even the principal, reason Pope St. Silvester I (314–335) did not attend the Church's first ecumenical council at Nicaea.

However advanced Pope Silvester's age may have been in 325, he nevertheless reigned quite ably for a full decade after

Nicaea. We also know, from other evidence concerning imperial interventions in the affairs of the Church in the West, that this pope may well have considered Constantine highhanded in the way he typically decided Church questions without consulting anybody.

Pope Silvester did not openly oppose Constantine's plan to call a general meeting of the bishops, that might not have been very prudent. No bishop of Rome had any control over what a Roman emperor might decide. Pope Silvester simply did not attend the meeting of the bishops convened by Constantine; instead he sent two priests as representatives, or legates.

Silvester had similarly not attended a local council the same emperor had convoked in Arles in 314. Again, he sent legates in his place, stating that he was unable to leave the Eternal City. Sending legates to represent him at Church meetings enabled him to keep his distance and reserve judgment concerning actions taken at these meetings. Sending legates was already a practice of this pope a full decade before Nicaea— certainly well before his own age was all that "advanced".

It is not unlikely that it was a conscious policy of the early popes to keep their distance from all-powerful Roman emperors disposed to impose their wills upon the Church whenever they felt like it. If so, it was a wise policy; the popes thereby significantly lessened the number of times that they might be imposed upon or dictated to from the imperial throne. Absenting themselves from Church meetings initiated by an emperor may even have been a policy calculated to safeguard and preserve their real primacy in the Church, necessarily opposed, as it was, to any artificial primacy an emperor might try to exercise.

The popes, at this time and for many centuries into the future, lacked the power to enforce their claim of primacy against the emperor; they possessed only moral power.

In the absence of the pope, the Council of Nicaea was probably chaired by a Western bishop, Hosius of Cordova, flanked, as we have noted, by two Roman priests who, representing Silvester, signed the acts of the Council ahead of all the other bishops. This indicates some recognition of the moral power and preeminent position of the bishop of Rome in the Church at that time, even in the East, and even if we cannot conclusively prove that the Roman primacy was then accepted in the East and by the empire.

We should not forget that when the Council of Nicaea was originally called by the Emperor Constantine, nobody yet really knew what an "ecumenical council" was—or would become in the ongoing life of the Church. There never had been such an inclusive council; the rules for holding one had not yet been established. Nobody could know in advance what the force and authority of the decisions and enactments of such an assembly of Catholic bishops would be. Until that time there had never been any practical possibility that the Catholic bishops of the world could meet in a "general council". Nobody could have known in advance what the relationship would be between what the successors of Peter did and taught and what a "worldwide" gathering of Catholic bishops would collectively do and teach.

Similarly, more than a half century later, when the Second General Council of Constantinople was convoked—one more in a series of meetings and synods and councils called to deal with the continuing Arian troubles—nobody yet knew what an "ecumenical council" was or what weight to accord to its acts. This particular council only came to be considered ecumenical when the Creed it issued was ratified more than three quarters of a century later by the undeniably ecumenical Council of Chalcedon in 451. The popes themselves only later came to recognize this council of 381 and ratify most of its acts—again, as a result of how important these acts themselves turned out to be, not because anybody had planned for this council to be ecumenical.

By the time of the Council of Ephesus, in 431, however, the role of a general council in the life of the Church was finally beginning to be understood. By this time, too, it was no longer the Roman emperor who was the instigator and moving spirit of the Ephesus Council but the bishop of Rome, Pope St. Celestine I (422–432). Celestine inaugurated what would become the regular Roman practice of writing a letter of "instructions" to the Council. He also effectively dictated the outcome of the gathering, even though he did not attend it. And, of course, as we have seen, the most prominent and visible figure on the scene at Ephesus, St. Cyril of Alexandria, acted as the willing agent of the pope.

Recall that the incident leading to the calling of the Council of Ephesus was the accusation of heresy St. Cyril of Alexandria had lodged against Nestorius, the bishop of Constantinople. Cyril accused Nestorius by writing to him directly. He had also written to Pope Celestine in Rome, enclosing a dossier on Nestorius. The language employed by St. Cyril in his letter to the pope is indicative of the position of the latter. "Since the old custom of the Churches persuades that questions of this kind should be communicated to your Holiness," the bishop of Alexandria wrote to the bishop of Rome, "I write, driven by necessity" (*Inter Ep. Caelestinei* I, VIII). The year was 430.

Pope Celestine promptly convoked a synod in Rome that, just as promptly, declared the teaching of Nestorius to be unacceptable and called upon him to recant. The pope even imposed a time limit—ten days after the receipt of his letter. Otherwise Nestorius would be excommunicated. Celestine appointed Cyril to carry out this sentence. Clearly the bishop of Rome had the authority to excommunicate the bishop of Constantinople and employed the bishop of Alexandria as his agent.

In response, Nestorius, bishop of the emperor's own city, persuaded the latter to convoke another general council to gainsay the judgments of the pope and the bishop of Alexandria. Emperor Theodosius II readily acceded to the request of Nestorius—this, too, was by then an established imperial practice—setting June 431 as the date for the meeting. The emperor was, of course, well aware that the pope had already condemned Nestorius. Some historians cite the emperor's attitude and action here as evidence that, since he did not recognize the Roman primacy in this matter, there was no Roman primacy recognized by the emperor and the Church in the East.

But the emperor's attitude and action in calling a council in order to contradict the judgment already rendered by the pope is yet another in what would prove to be a very long series of documented instances of Christian emperors opposing Church judgments that did not please them and attempting to dictate to the Church on their own terms. Centuries later, when the Roman Empire itself was no more, it would prove to have been most providential that, mainly because of the principled and determined resistance of the popes, the Roman emperors never succeeded in establishing themselves as effective heads of the Church. It was certainly not for lack of trying. But Christ's promise was delivered to Peter, after all, not to Caesar; so things ultimately worked themselves out in history.

Once the Council of Ephesus was finally convened—after numerous delays already recounted—what this valid council did was to *ratify*, in effect, the judgment already made by Pope Celestine concerning Nestorius and his heretical teaching. The council did so, as we have seen, despite protests by the emperor's agents.

Also at Ephesus the Roman priest Philip, one of the papal legates, delivered one of the strongest and clearest statements in Church history regarding the claim of the bishop of Rome to primacy. The historical record does not show that Philip's statement was rejected or contradicted by anyone at the council, including the many Eastern bishops. On the contrary, the statement was at least indirectly supported by other contemporaneous statements and letters. Indeed, several sentences of this statement were destined to be quoted nearly a millennium and a half later in the Dogmatic Constitution *Pastor Aeternus,* in which the First Vatican Council, in 1870, solemnly defined the doctrines of the primacy and infallibility of the pope.

Here is what the Roman priest Philip said to the assembled Fathers at the Council of Ephesus in 431:

> There is no doubt, and, in fact, it has been known in all ages, that the holy and most blessed Peter, prince and head of the apostles, pillar of the faith and foundation of the Catholic Church, received the keys of the kingdom from our Lord Jesus Christ, the Savior and Redeemer of the human race, and that to him was given the power of loosing and binding sins: who, even to this time always lives and judges in his successors. Our holy and most blessed Pope Celestine the bishop is according to due order his [Peter's] successor and holds his place, and he sent us to supply his presence in this holy synod.

The Council of Ephesus, reporting on its own actions, addressed Pope Celestine in a way that the description of his position in the Church by Philip would lead us to expect. Celestine was described as one whose "zeal . . . for piety and

. . . care for right faith . . . [supports] the churches which you have made your own care. . . . All things which have taken place should be brought to the knowledge of your holiness." This was the testimony of the Council of Ephesus to the pope's position in the Church.

Even at the misbegotten Robber Council of 449, the papal legate, an Italian bishop, Julius of Puteoli, before he was obliged to flee along with the others, was seated ahead of all the other bishops, including the bishops of Antioch and Jerusalem. (Bishop Dioscoros of Alexandria chaired that false council.) Yet even Dioscoros, like Emperor Theodosius II, felt obliged at least to pay lip service to the Roman primacy. The Robber Council demonstrated, moreover, how far astray a council could go when acting without Rome's guiding hand.

For this unfortunate, false council claimed to be ecumenical—a claim that was very widely accepted, at least temporarily. The gathering, which included most of the bishops of the East, promptly deposed and sent into exile those bishops who were opposed to it. Moreover, all these actions were duly confirmed by the Christian emperor.

The Robber Council felt able to set aside the *Tome* of Pope St. Leo the Great, declaring that the Church's Christology was authoritatively to be found exclusively in the formulations of St. Cyril of Alexandria as interpreted by his tendentious successor Dioscoros. Writing in the nineteenth century about this situation, John Henry Cardinal Newman was to observe: "If the East could determine a matter of faith independently of the West, certainly the Monophysite heresy was established as apostolic truth in all its provinces from Macedonia to Egypt" (*An Essay on the Development of Christian Doctrine*, 6, III, 9).

This official establishment of Monophysitism as the faith of the Church by the Robber Council of 449 was reversed only by the decisive action of Pope St. Leo the Great. Scarcely did this disgraceful gathering end than the appeals to Rome began to come in from the losing side, including one from the by-then-dead bishop of Constantinople. Pope Leo's reaction was to brand the Robber Council with the name by which it is known in history and to insist, unconditionally, on the convening of another council to undo the damage it had done.

Yes, the greatest ecumenical council of antiquity, the Council of Chalcedon, which involved both East and West, did not involve the Roman emperor at all. In spite of what is sometimes said by historians who should know better, this council was called at the behest of the bishop of Rome. At first Theodosius studiously ignored the pope's demand for a new council—as so many Christian emperors did when it suited them.

But then Theodosius died in an accident, and his successor, Emperor Marcian, responded favorably to Leo, addressing him as the one who "held the supreme place [*principatus*] in the episcopate of the divine law". By then, since many Eastern bishops were returning to orthodoxy following the death of Theodosius, Leo himself had begun to wonder whether another council was really necessary. But the invitations had already been sent out.

When the Council of Chalcedon convened in the fall of 451, the legate of Pope Leo, the Sicilian bishop Paschasinus, was in the chair. We have already seen how, in formulating for the Church the true definition of Christ's divine Person and his divine and human natures, the Fathers of the Council of Chalcedon also acclaimed the words of Pope Leo as the voice of Peter himself.

Perhaps less understood is how this Council unmistakably reaffirmed the belief in the primacy of Rome as the belief of the whole Church. The Council characterized the deposition of Dioscoros from the see of Alexandria, for example, as an action of Leo's accomplished *through* the Council. The sentence pronounced by the papal legates at the Council read as follows:

> The most holy archbishop of Rome, Leo, *through us and the present Council*, with the apostle, St. Peter, who is the rock and foundation of the Catholic Church and of the orthodox faith, deprives him of the episcopal dignity and every sacerdotal ministry. (Emphasis added.)

In other words, the pope's claim to be able to remove bishops anywhere for cause was here *upheld* by the ecumenical Council of Chalcedon. In the course of the Council's proceedings, one of the papal legates, Lucentius, referring to the Robber Council at Ephesus, asserted that the crime of Dioscoros had been, precisely, that "he dared to hold a council without the authority of the apostolic see, something that had never happened before and should never happen."

Following Chalcedon, the Fathers of the Council addressed a letter to Pope St. Leo acknowledging him as the "constituted interpreter of the voice of Blessed Peter" and "the very one commissioned with the guardianship of the vine by the Savior".

In view of this kind of evidence found in the conciliar documents of the ancient Church, therefore, it will not do to speak of these ecumenical councils as independent of or somehow in competition with the popes. Still less, in light of material we have reviewed here pertaining mainly to the first four great councils, can these gatherings be cited in opposition to the primacy of the pope or as rivaling the authority claimed by the successors of Peter.

Conflicts there manifestly were, and will be as long as there are human beings interacting with one another. But in the solemn, defining moments of what centuries later would be called the extraordinary Magisterium of the Church speaking with the promised assistance of the Holy Spirit, the popes and the councils invariably ended up complementing one another: both spoke with the authority Christ had promised to the apostles; both demonstrated that this promise of Christ did not fail when the Church was in need.

Later, beginning around the twelfth century, Church canonists developed a useful maxim that holds to this day: a general council *with the pope* is greater than the pope by himself. This idea received definitive expression in the Second Vatican Council's great Dogmatic Constitution on the Church, *Lumen Gentium*. Probably no better illustration of it exists than that of the Council of Chalcedon, when Pope St. Leo the Great succeeded in getting the Church to adopt a formula which, in the words of Cardinal Newman written nearly fourteen hundred years later,

> the Creed did not contain, which the Fathers did not unanimously witness, and which some eminent saints had almost in set terms opposed, which the whole East had refused as a symbol not once, but twice, which patriarch by patriarch, metropolitan by metropolitan ... was refused upon the grounds of its being an addition to the Creed.... (*Essay*, 6, III, 15)

No council could have arrived at this definition without the prior formulation of the question by Pope St. Leo I, and probably no pope could have secured its acceptance by the Church except through its adoption by an ecumenical council. Thus it was that pope and council worked together at Chalcedon, as would be the case many more times in history to fulfil the original promises Christ made to the Church.

There is much else to learn from the first four great councils. One of the principal lessons is that in the development of the Church's doctrine, as of her various ecclesiastical practices, disciplines, and institutions, the always turbulent gatherings that the ecumenical councils were, were nevertheless guided as if "from elsewhere" to the authentic formulations and decisions required by the Church at each critical stage. The councils never failed in the end to verify the solemn promises Jesus Christ made to his apostles and, through them, to his One, Holy, Catholic, and Apostolic Church.

Chapter 4

THE PRIMACY OF ROME IN
THE EARLY CHURCH

I.

A few short years before the end of the first century, around
the year 96 or 97 A.D., an entity describing itself as "the
Church of God that is at Rome" addressed a letter to an
entity styled "the Church of God that is at Corinth"—in
Greece. It seems that some of the younger men in Corinth
had rebelled against the leadership of the local Church and
had even succeeded in removing some of the presbyters (or
"elders") of the Church there.

The Church in Corinth was one of the original Churches
founded in the apostolic age; it was a Pauline Church, as we
know from the two New Testament Letters of Paul to the
Corinthians addressed, precisely, to "the Church of God
which is at Corinth". We know from the tone and content
of Paul's letters that this Corinthian Church, never free of
troubles, was prone to such disturbances as factionalism and
schism, among other things. According to 2 Corinthians
12:20, "quarreling, jealousy, anger, selfishness, slander, gos-
sip, conceit, and disorder"were some of the things St. Paul
sought to correct.

Now, a little more than a generation later, another outbreak of factionalism and schism seems to have recurred. The

letter from the Church of Rome to the Church of Corinth
near the end of the first century was an attempt in the same
vein as the two Letters of St. Paul to admonish, exhort, and
encourage the Corinthian Christians to remain true to the
authentic spirit of Christ and to the apostolic teaching that
had been given to them, including submission to the duly
constituted authorities in the Church.

We do not know how this Roman letter was initially received in Corinth; nor do we know what effect it had with
regard to the immediate troubles besetting the Church there.
We do, however, have historical evidence concerning the
long-term effect of the letter, which was preserved and trea-
sured by the Church in Corinth and periodically read at services as if it were Scripture.

The writings of the apostles and other apostolic men that
were produced in the apostolic age, almost from the beginning of the Church, were publicly read as lessons in the
Churches. Eventually they were collected, authorized, and
after church approval, compiled to form what today we call
the New Testament.

The letter sent from Rome to Corinth around 96 A.D. was
in the end not included in the New Testament; but for a time
it was treated as Scripture, not only in Corinth, but in neighboring Churches as well, where it was read along with the Gospels and other writings. At that time the question of what would
finally be included in the Bible canon approved by the authority of the Church—the writings publicly read at Masses and
other liturgies—was still somewhat fluid, although the general idea that Scripture consisted of inspired writings authentically expressing and expounding the faith of Christ was clear
enough in most people's minds even then.

It is noteworthy that a contemporary letter from one
Church to another should have been placed, even tempo-

rarily, in the category of inspired Scripture. Yet an early Christian writer, Clement of Alexandria (d. ca. 215), explicitly quotes from this Roman letter as if it were Scripture, and it is included in some early Coptic and Syriac lists of the New Testament books as well.

Some seventy-five to eighty years after this letter from Rome to Corinth was sent, a bishop of Corinth named Dionysius, replying to a letter from his contemporary, the bishop of Rome, Pope St. Soter (ca. 166–ca. 174), remarked that the earlier letter that had been received from Rome was still being read virtually as Scripture in the Church of Corinth. This fact was confirmed by "the Father of Church History", Eusebius Pamphilus (ca. 263–339?), who wrote, "We know that this letter has been read publicly in many churches in the past and in our own day" (*Ecclesiastical History*, III, 16).

The later letter from Dionysius to Pope Soter, dating from around 170, contains the oldest explicit written statement we possess verifying the common belief of the early Church that the "founders" of the Roman Church were the apostles Peter and Paul. To describe these apostles as founders, as the early Church did, did not mean that there were no Christians in Rome before Peter or Paul arrived there. Before he arrived in Rome, Paul was already writing to the Roman Christians, complimenting them on the fact that their faith was "proclaimed in all the world" (Rom 1:8).

The foundation of the Roman Church by the two great apostles seemed to have meant that the teaching and structure with which they endowed the Church after coming to Rome were the teaching and structure handed down from then on in Rome. Also, in the minds of the early Christians, that both Peter and Paul were martyred in Rome definitively put the seal on the foundation of the Church of Rome by these two great apostles.

It is indubitable that successive bishops who headed the Church in Rome were ever afterward explicitly considered "the successors of Peter".

That the Church of Rome was considered to have such an apostolic foundation also helps explain the veneration with which a letter from this Church might be received by a sister Church, even one that was itself apostolic in origin, as Corinth was. And Bishop Dionysius of Corinth revealed yet another interesting fact in his letter to Pope Soter, naming Clement as the writer of the first-century letter from Rome to Corinth.

In the earliest lists of the bishops of Rome, the name of Clement figures as the third successor of St. Peter (after Linus and Cletus). Another ancient tradition has Clement succeeding Peter directly, but this may merely refer to the fact that it was Peter who ordained Clement to the priesthood. Most likely, Clement was the third occupant of the chair of Peter, after the martyrdom of the apostle under Nero (37–68), who reigned as emperor from 54 to 68.

We do not know exactly when Clement became head of the Church. The date of his accession is variously given as 88 or 91 A.D. Nevertheless, to this day, the Roman Canon of the Mass commemorates these ancient popes and martyrs, successors of Peter, when it refers to "Linus, Cletus, Clement ..."

In the letter he wrote around 96 A.D., Clement speaks of the twin martyrdoms in Rome of Peter and Paul as "very near to our own time" and refers to these apostles as belonging to "our own generation". Clement of Rome was thus certainly so not far removed from the apostles that he could not have known them personally. Almost certainly he knew others who had known them personally. His letter mentions that some of those ordained by the apostles were still around.

It is not evident from the text of Clement's letter that the established grades of ministerial orders of the Church of Rome of his day consisted of bishops; presbyters, or elders (later priests); and deacons. Clement refers to bishops and presbyters more or less synonymously. The traditional division into bishops, presbyters, and deacons is clear in the letters of St. Ignatius of Antioch (d. ca. 107), which were written only a little more than a decade later. Ignatius describes presbyters and deacons as being firmly under the authority of the bishop (*To the Magnesians* 13:1–2); in another letter Ignatius says that the presbyters should be "as closely tied to the bishop as the strings to a harp" (*To the Ephesians* 4:2).

The slightly earlier letter of Clement, however, does not clearly distinguish between bishops and presbyters. This is also the case in some New Testament texts (cf. Acts 20:17; 20:28; Phil 1:1; 1 Tim 3:1–2; 1 Tim 4:14). In 1 Peter 5:1, even the Prince of the Apostles refers to himself as a "co-elder", or "fellow elder" (Greek: *sumpresbyteros*). Terms describing ordained leaders of the Church were somewhat interchangeable for a period of time. Clement neither refers to himself as a bishop nor addresses his letter to any bishop in Corinth. He seems to be a presbyter writing to other presbyters. This can be interpreted in more than one way, though it is very clear from the New Testament that all the leaders of the Church were *ordained* by the laying on of hands (e.g., Acts 6:6; 8:17; 13:3; 1 Tim 5:22, etc.).

While the apostles were still alive, it was probably inevitable that the offices and structures in the Church would remain somewhat fluid, if only because of the special role played by the apostles in setting up new Churches and appointing bishops and elders (presbyters) to preside over them—meanwhile authorizing these new Churches to appoint bishops and elders in their turn (cf. Acts 14:23; I Tim 5:17–22; Tit 1:5–7).

However, the apparent lack of any clear distinction between *episkopoi* and *presbyteroi* in Clement's letter as in some other ancient documents, including the New Testament passages cited above, has led some modern historians to assert that what they call the "monarchical bishop" had not yet emerged in the Churches of Rome and Corinth by the end of the first century. The further implication of this position is that Clement was really not a bishop (hence, not really a pope either, in the line of succession from Peter?).

Some modern historians believe Clement merely "represented" the Church of Rome as a presbyter among presbyters when he wrote his letter—while the Church was presumably being governed by a committee, or college, of presbyters —or "presbyter-bishops".

The Oxford Dictionary of Popes describes Clement as the "leading presbyter and spokesman of the Christian community at Rome". Similarly, Eamon Duffy, in his generally sound, popular *Saints and Sinners: A History of the Popes,* uncritically adopts the view that still at the end of the first century "there was no 'pope,' no bishop as such, for the Church in Rome was slow to develop the office of chief presbyter, or bishop."

Some such account of the matter, whether or not intended to debunk the notion that there was a clear succession of bishops who succeeded Peter in the Roman see, appears in nearly every modern reference book that treats of Clement and his letter. A fair interpretation of the existing historical references is rarely honestly and explicitly made; rather, it is left to the reader to conclude on his own that apostolic succession of the popes descending from Peter may not really be a fact but simply a later invention of the Church.

But there is more than one way to interpret the data, scarce as they are, about all this. It should be noted that doubts about succession from Peter were never entertained in the early Church. When ancient Christian writers compiled their lists of the bishops of Rome, they believed that they really did represent a real apostolic succession of the popes. Clement, one of the earliest Christian writers, clearly makes the Church's traditional case for the doctrine of the apostolic succession, tracing it back to Jesus Christ, as is evident from the following passages from Clement's letter:

> The apostles received the Gospel for us from the Lord Jesus Christ; Jesus the Christ was sent from God. Thus Christ is from God and the apostles from Christ.... And so the apostles, after receiving their orders and being fully convinced by the resurrection of our Lord Jesus Christ and assured by God's Word, went out in the confidence of the Holy Spirit to preach the good news that God's kingdom was about to come. They preached in country and city and appointed their first converts, after testing them by the Spirit, to be bishops and deacons of future believers. (No. 42)

In a further passage, Clement seems almost to have uncannily anticipated modern writers who try to cast doubt upon whether there really was a single bishop at the head of the Church in Rome around the year 96:

> Now our apostles, thanks to our Lord Jesus Christ, knew that there was going to be strife over the title of bishop. It was for this reason and because they had been given an accurate knowledge of the future, that they appointed the officers we have mentioned. Furthermore, they later added a codicil to the effect that, should these die, other approved men should succeed to their ministry. (No. 44)

It would be hard to improve upon what Clement of Rome set down here concerning the Church's belief in the apostolic succession of bishops. The "evidence" modern historians cite that Clement himself was not really a bishop but only one of a number of presbyters in the Roman Church is extremely tenuous and speculative and wholly dependent upon interpreting in a certain way a document addressing very different questions than those that preoccupy historians today.

Furthermore, according to all the historical evidence that we possess—and quite apart from the separate question of the fluidity and even interchangeability of terms in the earliest times—the "monarchical bishop" undeniably, and very quickly, emerged everywhere in the Church, including Rome. Moreover, the bishops were believed by the Church—everywhere—to have descended from the apostles, on whom, according to the New Testament, Jesus Christ conferred the authority exercised by these bishops as successors of the apostles. What developed everywhere had to come from what was there earlier—everywhere.

More than that, no other alternative model of Church governance or authority besides that of the so-called monarchical bishop ever emerged or developed anywhere else in the Church. There is no solid evidence that the Church was ever ruled by boards or committees or colleges of presbyters—except temporarily, for example, during episcopal or papal interregnums. For all we know, both the Church of Rome and the Church of Corinth could simply have been temporarily without a bishop when Clement wrote. His letter would be entirely explicable on that hypothesis, without any necessity or, indeed, any justification for theorizing that no monarchical bishop had yet emerged in Rome.

Clement could well have written as a presbyter, even as a member of a college of presbyters temporarily administering the Church of Rome, and later have been elected bishop—in the line of succession from Peter.

To state these possibilities is in no way to assert that any of them happened. It merely reminds us that hypotheses such as these in no way contradict the existing evidence. We simply do not know. There is no evidence beyond the text of Clement's letter. And nothing in that letter forbids us from holding that Clement was the third bishop of Rome, as tradition universally attests. Modern historians interested in casting doubt on apostolic succession and the papal primacy have sometimes shown themselves too eager to rush to conclusions on the basis of very slender evidence.

In at least one case in ancient times when the Church of Rome was being temporarily administered by priests and deacons there, they affirmed the primacy of the Church of Rome! Around the year 251, the Roman clergy, "waiting for a bishop to be given us by God", following the martyrdom of Pope St. Fabian (236–250) in the great persecution of Emperor Decius, wrote to St. Cyprian of Carthage expressly quoting Romans 1:8 about how the faith of the Roman Church was "proclaimed in all the world", and declared that St. Paul would never have written in such a vein "if even at that time our vigor had not put strength into the roots of the faith" (St. Cyprian, *Epistolae*, XXX).

In view of the known facts, it is entirely legitimate to accept the Church's account of her origins and of the succession of her leaders. No existing evidence excludes or contradicts the Church's account of these things: that Christ conferred power and authority on Peter and all the apostles separately, and that Peter and the apostles in turn passed this power and authority on to their successors, the bishops. This is confirmed in the New Testament and is not invalidated by any available evidence from the first century, certainly not by anything contained in the Letter of Clement.

Of course, offices and structures in the Church may still have remained somewhat fluid for a certain period of time, even after the end of the apostolic age, just as they seem to have been somewhat fluid in New Testament times; but Peter's styling himself a co-elder or fellow elder (1 Pet 5:1) no more invalidates the fact that the popes at the head of the whole Church "descended" from him than a modern pope would compromise his office by addressing a group of priests as his "fellow priests". The pope *is* a priest; Peter *was* a "fellow elder"; so were Linus, Cletus, Clement, and the other popes.

When Clement wrote his letter to the Church in Corinth, he was fully conscious of speaking with authority on behalf of a firmly established, visible, institutional, sacerdotal, and hierarchical Church engaged in the business of dispensing the word and sacraments of Jesus Christ to her members, the faithful who had come to believe in Christ and had joined themselves to his body, the Church.

It is also clear from Clement's Letter that he was conscious of occupying a place in the Church of Christ that allowed—even obliged—him to adopt the didactic and hortatory tone toward a sister Church. Clement wrote "with authority" (Lk 4:32), in the New Testament sense.

Clement not only wrote to the Corinthians; we know from his letter that he also *sent envoys from Rome to Corinth* to be sure that matters there were set right. He wrote and acted as if he was conscious of bearing a definite responsibility for the faraway Church of Corinth. The whole proceeding bears the marks of an established and understood practice in the ancient Church. In taking note of such salient facts as these, we should also not forget that this was the situation before the end of the first century!

Clement notes further in his letter that he may have been somewhat remiss in not having written sooner concerning the troubles in Corinth. He failed to do so, he explains, because of "misfortunes and accidents" and "sudden and repeated calamities and afflictions" that had befallen the Church in Rome. He may be referring to the persecutions that took place under Emperor Domitian, who ruled from 81 to 96. Some historians even speculate that Clement himself was a Roman aristocrat, a cousin of Domitian, Titus Flavius Clemens, known to have incurred the displeasure of this emperor, who had him put to death for "atheism" (a charge frequently leveled by the pagan Romans against the early Christians).

Other historians, beginning in the fourth century, have speculated that Clement may have been the Clement mentioned by St. Paul in his Letter to the Philippians (4:3), which some think was written while Paul was imprisoned in Rome (1:7). More likely, though, Paul wrote this letter while imprisoned in Caesarea in Palestine. We do not know who Paul's Clement was.

Whoever Clement of Rome was, he certainly took it for granted that he needed to be concerned with the troubles and "quarrels" then going on in the Church in Corinth. That this concern arose from a perceived duty inherent in his position in the Church of Rome is compatible with the evidence of his letter; indeed, this is the best possible explanation for the letter's tone and content. It is true that other local Churches in ancient times frequently communicated with and even "corrected" one another by exchanges of letters. But in this case, Clement was intervening in a Church relatively distant from Rome, an apostolic Church that was not obviously subordinate to the Roman Church.

Yet there is no evidence that the Corinthians ignored or rejected Clement's intervention. It is even possible that one of the Corinthian factions had appealed to Rome, eliciting the letter in response. But examples of such appeals to Rome certainly occurred only a very short time later in the Church's history. There had to have been precedents for the growth of such a relatively early custom as appealing to Rome.

Also evident from Clement's letter is that, although quite gentle and ironic in tone, it does not fail to take the Corinthians to task for their lapses and failures, and for violations of established Church discipline. In the long run, as we know from the remarks of Bishop Dionysius of Corinth made three quarters of a century later, the letter was ultimately taken with the utmost seriousness in Corinth.

II.

The evidence from many sources in the early Church is virtually unanimous that the early Christians considered themselves part of one Church. There was frequent and regular contact between local Churches, including expressions of concern for one another's problems. As the Church grew and administrative divisions later to be called dioceses, provinces, and patriarchates developed, some Churches, usually in major cities, came to enjoy preeminence and, later, actual jurisdiction over others in the region. Often a local Church was the daughter of a mother Church in a larger city or metropolitan area. Eventually it became a settled thing for Churches to seek help for their problems from sister—or, indeed, mother—Churches, just as it became normal for the latter to intervene sometimes in the affairs of a daughter Church.

In Italy, for example, Churches from the time we have any record looked to the Church of Rome for leadership. With the passage of a century or two, this was true of all the Churches in the West. Within a couple of centuries after that, one of the titles the bishop of Rome would bear was "Patriarch of the West", a title the popes retain to this day.

But it was not just in the West that the leadership role of the Church of Rome was recognized. In addition to the territorial preeminence that came to be assigned to a number of major Churches, including especially the ancient apostolic sees of Alexandria, Antioch, and Rome, the Church of Rome from earliest times was also understood to enjoy a unique status in the whole Church.

Although at first the nature of this unique status was not clearly spelled out—spelling it out in concrete detail would take a long time—it nevertheless was universally recognized. From the first, it was based primarily on the common tradition that the apostles Peter and Paul had established the preeminence of the Church of Rome with the blood of their twin martyrdom there. It is also true that the Church of Rome derived prestige in the very early centuries from being located in the capital of the Roman Empire; but the Church of Rome herself never officially claimed the fact of her secular prominence as the basis of her preeminence among the Churches.

There are a number of tantalizing references in the works of the earliest Church writers and Fathers testifying to the special status enjoyed by the Church of Rome. In the salutation to his letter to the Romans, for example, St. Ignatius of Antioch, on his way to Rome, where he would suffer martyrdom, described the Roman Church in terms he accorded to no other Church: "preeminent in the land of the Romans, worthy of God, worthy of honor, worthy of blessing, worthy of praise, worthy of prosperity, worthy of her purity and foremost in love. . . ." We should not forget that these were the words of an Eastern bishop who was himself the occupant of an apostolic see.

For the words translated as "preeminent" and "foremost" in the sentence just quoted, Ignatius used the same Greek word, *prokathetai*, the word this bishop of Antioch and martyr in the Roman Coliseum also used to denote the headship of the bishop over the community of Christian believers (cf. *To the Magnesians*, 6). No ancient writer ever surpassed Ignatius in his belief in the authority of the bishop in his particular Church over all the faithful, including the presbyters and deacons, as all the letters of Ignatius testify.

In his Letter to the Romans, St. Ignatius of Antioch also referred to the apostles Peter and Paul. "I do not *command* you as Peter and Paul did", he wrote. "They were apostles. I am a convict. They were free. I am a slave to this very day" (4:3, emphasis added).

From such very early references to the "preeminence" of a Church whose apostolic "founders" issued "commands", we cannot conclude that the papacy as it is understood and operates today was already fully in place. Like all of the major features of the Church of Christ, the papacy developed over time as the life of the Church unfolded. Like the episcopacy—the headship of the Church's bishops—the papacy developed out of the original charge given by Christ to Peter and the other apostles.

Christ established the Church on the apostles and told them, "Whatever you bind on earth shall be bound in heaven and whatever you loose on earth shall be loosed in heaven" (Mt 18:18). And at Caesarea Philippi, Christ conferred the same power of binding and loosing on Peter individually, telling Peter that he was the "rock" on which he, Christ, would build his Church, "and the powers of death shall not prevail against it. I will give you the keys of the kingdom of heaven ..." (Mt 16:18–19).

To give someone "the keys" was to confer authority on him in a special way. To this day St. Peter is popularly visualized as guarding the doors of heaven for his divine Master— just as the successors of Peter continue to be accorded in the

Church's own authentic teaching what at least since the nineteenth century has been called a primacy of jurisdiction over the whole Church. (This has always meant also that communion with the successor of Peter is authentic communion with Jesus Christ.)

This actual primacy exercised by the successors of the apostle Peter in the see that has continued to bear his name existed only in germ in the period we are dealing with, but it did exist. Not a later invention of the Church, it went back to Christ himself, on the clear evidence of the New Testament. Those who hold that Christ had no interest in a "Church" to come after him, much less in offices or structures in that Church, have surely not meditated deeply on what Christ meant when he spoke of *building* his Church (Mt 16:18).

The witness of what St. Ignatius of Antioch understood the special status of the Church of Rome to be, like the earlier witness of what the Letter of Clement of Rome shows the Church of Rome unself-consciously engaged in *doing*, marks only the beginning of what would be a long and complex process of working out in history the implications of Christ's original charge to Peter.

As the outstanding early twentieth-century Church historian Pierre Batiffol remarked in his classic study *Primitive Catholicism* (1911), the primacy of the Church of Rome is found mainly in the facts; the Church of Rome did not so much *claim* the primacy—although we shall not fail to encounter an increasing number of instances of such claims on the part of this see as decades, then centuries proceed—so much as the Church of Rome *exercised* such a primacy, virtually from the beginning.

This is surely what St. Clement of Rome was doing around 96 A.D. in his Letter to the Corinthians about their quarrels; Clement was carrying out the commission of Jesus to Peter to "feed my sheep" (Jn 21:17). As we know from the Gospel, Jesus repeated these instructions to Peter no fewer than three times; it would have been surprising if a successor to Peter as near in time to the Fisherman as Clement had failed to remember it.

In the same way, by writing to the Church of Corinth, Clement was carrying out the commission Christ gave to Peter as reported by Luke. After explaining to his disciples that a leader in the Church must be "one who serves", Jesus went on to say this to Peter: "Simon, Simon, behold, Satan demanded to have you, that he might sift you like wheat, but I have prayed for you that your faith may not fail; and when you have turned again, strengthen your brethren" (Lk 22:31–32). St. Clement of Rome's intervention in the affairs of Corinth was surely a striking example in the early Church of strengthening one's brethren.

Interestingly, the very early popes did not generally cite as proof of their primacy the famous passage from Matthew 16:18 in which Christ promised to build his Church on Peter. The earliest known Roman citation of this particular passage in support of papal authority did not come until the reign of Pope St. Stephen I (254–257). If it seems surprising that the popes did not make use of this obvious citation for such a long time, we should reflect on the fact that it was not until 1870 that the Church *defined* the doctrine of papal primacy and infallibility.

Nevertheless, for almost two thousand years the popes have gone on *exercising* their primacy in the Church in the various ways required of them as the life of the Church unfolds. This is what Clement of Rome was doing when, before the end of the first century, he intervened in the affairs of the Church of Corinth in an effort to remedy the troubles that had overtaken that sister Church.

It is possible, even likely, that there were other early low-key Roman interventions of the kind we see in Clement's Letter. We will probably never know about them for the simple reason that the Church of that era, operating in secret and under persecution, did not pass on the evidence. Evidence from that period concerning the life, teachings, and practices of the Church is bound to be sparse, but the evidence that is available supports the Church's doctrines of the apostolic succession and the primacy of Rome.

III.

When modern historians attempt to trace the early history of such questions as the ministerial priesthood in the Church—or, more pertinent to our present inquiry, the history of the primacy of Rome in the early Church—they find themselves hampered by a lack of the kind of documentation on which the writing of history is customarily based. Many of the things we would like to know today about the early Church may not have been considered important by the early writers. Also, as an obscure, illegal body, the early Church was not likely to have left many traces of her activities or to have had much impact on what secular chroniclers considered the important events of the day.

As soon as the early Christians came to be noticed, they immediately became subject to persecution. The first references to the Christians in secular Roman writers such as Tacitus, Suetonius, or Pliny are in connection with measures taken against them.

The books of the New Testament dealing with events subsequent to the resurrection and ascension of Jesus similarly describe Christians as already subject to persecution. Other evidence of the existence of the Church in these early years that Christians themselves produced and that would be of the greatest interest to modern historians was lost or destroyed, given the conditions under which the Church was obliged to live and work. The result of all this is that there is little documentary evidence to use in chronicling the Church's very early years.

In particular, we have very little early documentary evidence from Rome itself concerning the early history of the Church of Rome. One of the principal reasons for this, in addition to those already enumerated, is that the library and archives of the Church of Rome are known to have been almost completely destroyed in the last great persecution of the early Church, launched in the year 303 under Diocletian. Therefore, much of the evidence concerning the early history of the Church of Rome comes from sources outside of Rome.

As soon as we examine documentary evidence of the existence and functioning of the Church anywhere, we find an institution everywhere headed by a leader called a bishop, who shared his powers with a class of appointed presbyters (later called priests) and was assisted in carrying out the work of the Church by a class of helpers called deacons. Thus, even if we cannot conclusively prove from historical evidence that Christ firmly did intend his Church to be led by ordained bishops, priests, and deacons, we can nevertheless legitimately conclude from the historical evidence we have that, very early, these offices grew organically out of the commission that Christ gave to Peter and the other apostles.

The presbyters seem to have assisted the bishops in carrying out Church activities, including the celebration of the liturgy (at first with the bishop, only later by themselves in separate "parishes"). The deacons, in the early centuries of the Church, were concerned mainly with the management of the Church's temporal affairs and with performing works of charity.

The establishment of the order of deacons is specifically described in the New Testament (see Acts 6:1–6). Because "the disciples were increasing in number", deacons were appointed to assist the bishops and enable them to devote themselves "to prayer and the ministry of the word".

The origin of the order of presbyters, or elders, is not so clear. We first hear of them in connection with the famine relief sent during 41–54, the reign of emperor Claudius, by Christians in Antioch to those back in Judea (cf. Acts 11:30). Sometime after the beheading of the apostle James, son of Zebedee and brother of John, by Herod Agrippa I, also in the early forties, there followed the imprisonment and subsequent miraculous escape from prison of Peter and his subsequent departure to "another place" (cf. Acts 12:1–17). The other apostles also seem to have left Jerusalem around the same time. And around the time of these momentous events, the order of presbyters seems to have been established; presbyters were ordained to help lead the infant Church in Jerusalem, from which the apostles were being forced to depart.

Shortly after this, we find Paul and Barnabas appointing as a matter of course *presbyteroi* for "every Church" they were founding (cf. Acts 14:23). By the time the primitive Council of Jerusalem recounted in Acts 15 convened, presbyters were participating along with the apostles. A little later, when Paul came to Jerusalem, he found a relative of Jesus, James, "the Lord's brother" (Gal 1:19), in charge of the Jerusalem Church as bishop, assisted by "elders", that is, by presbyters (Acts 21:18).

The existence of the three particular offices of bishop, presbyter, and deacon in the Church is entirely compatible with

Christ's original commission to the apostles, even if we are not always able to document every step in the development of these offices or state with precision all their duties or resolve satisfactorily some of the conflicts or inconsistencies found in the evidence.

There are not many such inconsistencies, as a matter of fact. Some of them are merely semantic. It is not difficult or illegitimate to conclude, therefore, that the early Church already possessed the threefold structure of ordained offices—bishops, priests, and deacons—that the whole Church would very soon exhibit everywhere.

Some modern skeptics, however, insist on interpreting any lack of documentation, or the uncertainty as to what the documentation that exists actually means, as a simple denial of the legitimacy of the development of this threefold structure of ordained officers. These ordained clergy, some skeptics maintain, were created by the Church at a later date. They hold that the Church then went beyond what they imagine was primitive Church "democracy".

Skeptics of this kind surely go too far. What emerged and was accepted by Christians everywhere can be affirmed as a legitimate development. If it cannot always be *shown* as going back to the apostles, neither can it be shown not to go back to them!

The same can be affirmed about the primacy of Rome in the early Church: if the earliest historical mentions of the Church of Rome point to a Church that was held in special esteem, particularly because of the universal ancient belief that the founders of the Roman Church were the two great apostles, Peter and Paul; if the earliest evidence we have of the actions of the bishops of Rome similarly shows them acting with the consciousness of the special status they believed they enjoyed; if, as the years and even decades passed, these same kinds of historical mentions and this same kind of evidence, though rather sparse, nevertheless continued to be completely consistent in according this special respect and status to the Church and to the bishops of Rome; if, meanwhile, the prestige of the See of Rome grew only because of the perception continually verified that, somehow, the bishops of Rome always ended up affirming the doctrine generally affirmed by the whole Church as orthodox; and if, at the same time, no tradition of any other Church was ever regarded in this same way—certainly not the "mother Church" in Jerusalem, which was in any case dispersed and destroyed when the city itself was razed by the Romans in 70 A.D.—if, then, all these conditions obtained, as they did, then we can legitimately conclude that what later ages came to call the primacy of Rome grew naturally and organically out of the primacy Christ expressly accorded to Peter as attested in the New Testament (cf. Mt 16:13–20; Lk 22:31–32; Jn 21:15–19).

Certainly the idea that the Church of the Prince of the Apostles should be the one to enjoy a preeminence and, indeed, a primacy, over other Churches, even those that were themselves apostolic in origin, is in no way incompatible with New Testament evidence. On the contrary, the New Testament abundantly confirms the special status and authority that Christ consistently accorded to Peter among all his disciples—and which Peter consistently *exhibited and exercised*, especially after Pentecost.

Over and over again, in addition to the three famous instances cited above, when Christ declared Peter to be the rock on which the Church would be built, when he expressly enjoined only Peter to strengthen his brethren, and when he instructed the Galilean fisherman to feed his sheep, the New Testament record invariably shows Peter as the first among the apostles.

No serious reader of the New Testament can doubt this fact. We need cite only a few of the many references: Peter is always mentioned first when the call of the apostles is described (Mt 4:18–22; Mk 1:16–20; Lk 5:1–11); or when the names of the apostles are listed (Mt 10:1–4; Mk 3:16–19; Lk 6:14–16; Acts 1:13). Peter is most often the one who speaks or reacts to Jesus, as when asking how many times we must forgive (Mt 18:21) or when pointing out how the apostles had left everything to follow Jesus (Mt 19:27)—and these are only two of the many examples found in the New Testament. Sometimes Jesus singled out James and John along with Peter, but Peter is, again, always mentioned first (e.g., Mt 26:37; Lk 8:51; 9:28; Mk 17:1), and Peter was the spokesman in the Transfiguration scene.

It was Peter to whom the Lord addressed himself in the Garden of Gethsemane (Mt 26:40–41; Mk 14:37–38)—just as Peter's threefold denial of Christ looms so large in all the accounts of the Passion, this incident was considered important precisely because of Peter's preeminence among the disciples. Peter was also the apostle to whom the risen Lord first appeared (Lk 24:34; 1 Cor 15:5).

John's Gospel certainly confirms the preeminence of Peter recorded in the synoptic Gospels: Peter was the one to whom Christ gave a new name (Jn 1:42); he was the one who confessed that the disciples could not leave Jesus because he had "the words of eternal life" (Jn 6:68); and he was the first to enter the empty tomb (Jn 20:6; also, Lk 24:12).

Further evidence from the New Testament is consistent in always affirming the position of Peter ahead of the other disciples. After the resurrection and ascension of Jesus, Peter remained the uncontested leader of the infant Church. He presided over the choice of a successor to Judas (Acts 1:15–26). He preached to the crowds assembled at the time of

Pentecost (Acts 2:14–40) and performed such miracles as the healing of the blind beggar at the Temple (Acts 3:1–10). It was revealed first to Peter that salvation was destined for the Gentiles as well as for the Jews (Acts 10:9–48). He was considered the leader of the Church, not only in Jerusalem, but also in Samaria and Caesarea—indeed, wherever he happened to be. He is explicitly depicted as having definite oversight responsibilities where evangelization had already been carried out by others (Acts 8:14 ff.).

Similarly, when "the apostles and elders were gathered together" at the primitive Council of Jerusalem, it was Peter who rose up "after there had been much debate" and summed up the meaning of the momentous decision the infant Church was about to make on that occasion, namely, to admit converts to the Church without subjecting them to the Jewish law (cf. Acts 15:6–11).

Finally, it was Peter to whom St. Paul had recourse, even though Paul himself had been the recipient of a special revelation from above when Jesus appeared to him on the road to Damascus. But even Paul thought it essential to go to Peter to confirm that the gospel he, Paul, was preaching was indeed the correct one—"lest somehow I should be running or had run in vain" (Gal 2:2), Paul noted, very significantly.

On the evidence of the New Testament, Peter enjoyed a primacy over the other apostles and, indeed, over the whole infant Church. Peter was always looked to as the unquestioned leader, and it was to him that the others always "appealed". Quite early in the history of the Church, the later bishops of Rome were exercising a similar primacy and, as time went on, claiming ever more explicitly that they did so on the basis of the mandate originally given by Christ to Peter.

The real question at issue is whether the authority exercised by the early popes as they continued to affirm ever more clearly their right and duty to exercise it as they did represented a continuous and legitimate development of the authority conferred on Peter by Christ. We shall see that the historical development of papal authority is entirely consistent with the original conferral of authority on Peter by Christ.

IV.

Those who deny the continuity and legitimacy of the development of what ultimately came to be the papacy out of the authority that Peter personally possessed and exercised in the Church of the Apostles must reckon with the incontestable fact that there was never a time in the history of the early Church following the expansion of the Church beyond Jerusalem and Palestine when the preeminence of the Church of Rome was not recognized, at least in some sense. As we have seen, the first century had not yet ended when we find Clement of Rome authoritatively intervening in Church affairs as far away as Corinth; and the first century scarcely had ended when an Eastern bishop, St. Ignatius of Antioch, was already clearly testifying to the special position of the Church of Rome.

There are other early mentions of the popes and the Church of Rome. Almost all of them support—and none of them calls into question or contradicts—the idea that the Church of Rome enjoyed a preeminence among all the Churches. Many of these mentions are found scattered through the pages of the *Ecclesiastical History* of Bishop Eusebius of Caesarea. Although this work was not written until the fourth century, Eusebius had access to documents going back much earlier, many of which are now lost. Eusebius thus remains an important and generally reliable source for certain aspects of Church history, sometimes our only source.

Nowhere in his *Ecclesiastical History* does Eusebius describe the Roman primacy clearly, although, by the fourth century, the popes had been exercising it for some time and, increasingly, claiming it explicitly. What explains this omission? For one thing, Eusebius lived in the East and thus tended to concentrate on events there. For another, he was dazzled by his contemporary, Emperor Constantine, who had brought the Church out of the catacombs into the full light of legal recognition by the empire. Eusebius thus framed his history more in terms of the coming to fruition of the legal Church within the empire rather than on the development of the Church in Rome as following the original commission given by Christ to Peter.

At this precise period Constantine was moving his capital from Rome to the East. Once this move was made, "old Rome" was bound to be seen as less important—along with its bishop!—to someone living in the East. All of these things tend to explain the Eastern focus of Eusebius' *Ecclesiastical History*. There is also abundant evidence from this period showing that events in the West—indeed, the West itself—came to seem less important and was even looked down on from the perspective of the newly eminent East.

On the other hand, nothing in Eusebius undermines the thesis of Rome's primacy in the early Church. On the contrary, Eusebius provides some tantalizing references to the early presence of Peter in Rome and to the early preeminence of the Church of Rome. Quoting from a work by Clement of Alexandria, Eusebius locates Peter in Rome, where his preaching inspired his listeners, "not satisfied with one audience only, nor with the unwritten teaching of the divine gospel ... [they] besought Mark, a follower of Peter and the one whose gospel is extant, that he would leave them a written record of the doctrine that had been communicated to them by word of mouth" (*Ecclesiastical History*, II, 15).

In this reference to the composition of the Gospel of Mark, Eusebius says that Peter "sanctioned the book for use in the churches", adding that Papias, an early second-century bishop of Hierapolis (fl. ca. 120), agrees with Clement that Peter had gone to Rome. This latter reference, then, is a testimony that, perhaps no more than a decade after the martyrdom of St. Ignatius of Antioch, yet another established historical source confirmed that Peter was established and exercising his apostolic-episcopal authority in Rome—"preaching".

There are many other references to Peter and his successors in Rome in Eusebius' *Ecclesiastical History*, especially those relating to the third century and later. A number of these will be quoted later. It is necessary to note, however, that working as Eusebius did with ancient sources, what he asserts or quotes cannot be taken as the final word without corroboration from other sources. For example, Eusebius records that Peter came to Rome during the reign of Emperor Claudius (41–54). He records further, as do all the ancient sources, that the apostle suffered martyrdom during the reign of Emperor Nero (54–68). This would have given Peter an enormously long reign, well over twenty years, if his stay in Rome was continuous.

We know that Peter "departed and went to another place" (Acts 12:17) somewhere outside of Jerusalem after the persecution launched by Herod Agrippa I, who ruled Palestine between the years 41 and 44, but we do not know whether Peter went directly to Rome or, if he did, whether he stayed there continuously.

The *Liberian Catalogue*, a document dating from 354, asserts that Peter's reign in Rome lasted "25 years, 1 month,

9 days; [he] was bishop . . . from the consulship of Minucius and Longinus to that of Nero and Verus. He suffered together with Paul, June 29, under the aforesaid consuls in the reign of Nero. . . ."

One problem with this account is that we know that Peter was back in Jerusalem for the primitive Council of Jerusalem described in Acts 15, a gathering that took place around 49 A.D. At some point, Peter was also in Antioch, where Paul speaks of being obliged "to oppose him to his face" (Gal 2:11) over whether Peter was being completely honest about the liberation of Jewish Christians from the demands of the Jewish law.

Peter's presence in Rome was, thus, not necessarily continuous. It was the common practice of the apostles to travel about founding new Churches. A number of sources, including Eusebius, identify Peter as being the founder of the ancient patriarchal see of Antioch as well as of that of Rome. And, in the New Testament, 1 Peter 1:1 is addressed "to the exiles of the Dispersion in Pontus, Galatia, Cappadocia, Asia, and Bithynia". The text of the Letter that follows this salutation suggests that Peter had some role in evangelizing those areas and was writing to them from Rome. Paul appears to confirm this impression by his reference to "Cephas" (Peter) in 1 Corinthians 1:12. At the very least, Paul confirms that Peter enjoyed "authority" in Corinth, regardless of where he was physically located.

It is significant that in his own First Letter, in the New Testament, Peter was writing from Rome, as is confirmed by his use, at the end of this letter, of the word "Babylon" (5:13), an obvious reference to pagan Rome, since Peter obviously was not writing from the actual, long-destroyed Babylon. This New Testament reference confirms Peter's presence in Rome, as do all the ancient sources. The very same reference, making mention of "my son Mark", provides corroboration of the account of the origins of the Gospel of Mark described above by Eusebius.

Eusebius, in his *Ecclesiastical History*, like Clement of Alexandria before him, did not fail to cite 1 Peter when speaking of Peter's being at Rome. In another work of Eusebius, the *Chronicon*—lost except for excerpts quoted by others—this "Father of Church history" notes that "Peter *presided* over the Church in Antioch and then over the Church in Rome until his death" (emphasis added). Eusebius also writes that Peter and Paul suffered martyrdom in Rome and that Peter was succeeded by Linus there. In *Ecclesiastical History*, he writes that Linus, whom he identifies with the Linus mentioned in 2 Timothy 4:21, "was the first after Peter to hold the bishopric of the Roman Church" (III, 2).

According to Eusebius, after Linus "had been bishop of the Church of Rome for twelve years, delivered up his office to [Ana]cletus. . . . Clement also . . . was appointed third bishop of the Roman Church . . ." (ibid. III, 9, 13). There was no doubt in Eusebius' mind concerning the apostolic succession or, especially, the existence of a monarchical bishop in Rome around the end of the first century or that St. Clement of Rome *was* a bishop!

These are only a few of the references in *Ecclesiastical History* to Peter and his successors in the Church of Rome. We should point out, however, the writing of history at the time did not always meet today's standards of historical verification.

We encounter some of the same problems in other ancient sources, including the fourth-century *Liberian Catalogue* already mentioned. The same is true of such documents as the *Liber Pontificalis*, a sixth-century document incorporating and updating some *Liberian Catalogue* material. These sources are necessary, indeed invaluable, for any history of the popes; but independent verification is always preferable. Although generally based on authentic though not wholly accurate sources, the historical standards sometimes range so far from what a modern historian would like to see that we must use them with caution. Almost all of the dates for the popes up to the middle of the second century, for example, are conjectural.

This is true, too, of Eusebius' *Ecclesiastical History*. No meaningful history of the Church can be written without him; nevertheless what he says must be weighed cautiously. Eusebius gives some credence, for example, to the legend that Peter while in Rome miraculously vanquished the sorceries of Simon Magus, the well-known Samaritan mentioned in Acts 8:9–24. As described in the Acts of the Apostles, when this Simon Magus saw that the Holy Spirit was given by means of the laying on of hands, he tried to purchase the gifts of the Spirit with money. (The sin of simony, or the buying and selling of ecclesiastical preferments, was thus named for Simon Magus.) Peter sternly rebuked Simon Magus, declaring, "Your silver perish with you, because you thought you could obtain the gift of God with money!" (Acts 8:20). This account reports that Simon Magus was properly contrite following Peter's rebuke (Acts 8:24)—and thereafter he disappears from recorded history.

A number of stories concerning one or more magicians or charlatans named Simon circulated in ancient times. These legends became conflated into a story about Simon Magus' going to Rome to traffic in sorceries and engage in other nefarious deeds. The story says that it was the very Peter who, in the Acts of the Apostles, had corrected the original Simon Magus, who also later in Rome went on to thwart and defeat this sorcerer through the power of God.

A vast apocryphal literature celebrating Peter grew up around the Simon Magus legends. Some of it was accepted by otherwise serious ancient writers. Although most of it must be discounted as lacking a factual basis, it testifies to the high regard in which Peter and the Church of Rome were held in ancient times.

Eusebius of Caesarea was not the only recognized Church historian to lend credence to at least some aspects of the legend of Simon Magus in Rome. So did the author of the *Liber Pontificalis*. Eusebius certainly dignified the story far beyond its worth in such passages as the following: "The evil that hates what is good and plots against man's salvation produced at that time Simon [Magus], the father and author of this great wickedness, as if to oppose him as a mighty antagonist against the noble and inspired apostles of our Savior." Eusebius seems to suggest that in some sense Peter came to Rome *in order* to combat Simon Magus: "Providence, that watches over all things, led Peter, the strongest and greatest of the apostles, who on account of his valor was spokesman for all the rest, to Rome against this base destroyer of life" (*Ecclesiastical History*, II, 14).

This mention of the legends and literature surrounding Simon Magus recall many ancient, fanciful, apocryphal writings about Christ, the apostles, and the early Church. In particular, apocryphal "gospels" and "epistles" proliferated in those years.

It was the Church herself, often the popes, that issued warnings against giving credence to these dubious writings. Contrary to the ideas sometimes expressed by those modern writers who regard all ancient Church sources, including the four Gospels themselves, as fanciful, there is a marked difference between the writings that serious modern investigators find themselves obliged to accept as authentic and fabrications that the Church herself was the first to reject.

Pope St. Innocent I (401–417), for example, denounced many of these legendary writings as spurious and unreliable. He issued specific condemnations of uncanonical works ascribed to Matthew, James, Peter, John, Andrew, and Thomas. The decretal attributed to Pope St. Gelasius I (492–496) also solemnly condemned a long list of these apocryphal-type works, along with their authors. The early Church had a healthy sense of what constituted truth and true history, and the early popes were the conscious guardians of both, for which later ages can only be grateful.

On the other hand, the careful sifting that began in ancient times also makes it possible for us to rely on some of the sources that passed the muster of credibility for people a lot closer to those sources than we are. Even though some of our sources are relatively sparse, some valid judgments based on them are nevertheless possible, especially when these judgments can be confirmed by later sources. What developed in the Church was obviously based on what was there when Christ established the Church. And what we can surely properly exclude are modern agnostic judgments that the available early sources for the history of the Church are mere speculations or even fabrications by ignorant or dishonest Christians.

Meanwhile, we can regard with our own skepticism the modern historical skepticism that doubts whether such pronounced features of the later Church as visible Church "structures", the sacramental system, the ministerial priesthood, the "monarchical bishops"—and the primacy of Rome in the early Church—actually go back to a commission of Jesus Christ.

Proceeding with our examination of the historical evidence for the primacy of Rome in the early Church, we should remember that this primacy, as well as the common understanding of it in the Church at large necessarily *developed over time*. To state this is in no way to invalidate either the legitimacy of such development or its results. The Church has not ceased to affirm that the revelation of Christ concerning our salvation, of which she is the guardian and exponent in the world, was fully delivered and complete at the time of the apostles.

The apostles did not enjoy a full and instant understanding of every aspect of Christ's revelation. Peter required a special vision before finally understanding that baptism and Church membership were destined for non-Jews as well as Jews (cf. Acts 10:9–48; 11:1–18). Similarly, the conferral of supreme authority in the Church on Peter the Rock was known to most Christians at least from the time of the appearance of Matthew's Gospel reporting Christ's solemn conferral of it on him. What this conferral meant in practice and what all the implications of it were, however, could only be understood progressively as the successors of Peter were obliged to act in particular situations on the basis of the authority that had been passed on to them.

Just as the Roman primacy could often be discerned on the basis of how the popes exercised it in particular cases, its real meaning and scope could sometimes be discerned in how others *reacted* to it. This at times proved to be the case even when others *opposed* it. It is a serious mistake to argue from verified historical instances of opposition to the Roman primacy, as do some modern historians, that this primacy did not really exist, was not legitimate, or had not really been conferred by Christ on Peter and handed down to his successors. Such historians typically argue or imply that the Roman primacy merely developed out of the ambitions and usurpations of the bishops of Rome; opposition to Rome by other elements in the Church is supposed to be one of the proofs of this.

On the contrary, nothing was perhaps more to be expected than sharp, negative reactions to the exercise of the Roman primacy when it went against preferred local practices or preferences. More than once in the course of our narrative, we shall encounter the phenomenon of an apparently ready acceptance of the Roman primacy—as long as it continued to serve local interests or preferences. But then, suddenly, this acceptance is replaced by a usually newly-minted "principled" opposition to Rome's primacy as soon as it is perceived as opposing a local interest or preference. This is the way any "central authority" is often treated: in many spheres of life, if authority rules against us, we are immediately tempted to deny its legitimacy.

There were many examples of this phenomenon in the history of the Church of Rome. Among those who denied the Roman primacy expressly was Tertullian (ca. 160–ca. 230), who believed that the authority to bind and loose—that he, too, affirmed had been given to Peter—did not include remitting sins deemed unpardonable by the rigorist Tertullian himself. Tertullian would have been glad enough if the pope had only ruled *for* him and his fellow Montanists; since he did not, the pope surely could not have been acting properly and legitimately.

St. Cyprian of Carthage (200?–258), who believed in the conferral of authority on Peter by Christ, was nevertheless quick to rail against a pope for *not* exercising his primacy in the way St. Cyprian wanted. He rebuked the pope for failing to move decisively against a bishop in Gaul who was refusing to reconcile lapsed Christians with the Church in accordance with the policy agreed upon by both Rome and Carthage.

There are many variations on this theme; the primacy did not arrive fully developed and understood by everybody. As a phenomenon of Church history, the development of the primacy, like the Church's full understanding of it, was necessarily a work of time. In the remainder of this chapter, we shall chart the gradual development of the primacy from the middle of the second century through its substantially full development, which was achieved by the beginning of the sixth century.

V.

From the middle of the second century on, references in ancient sources to the primacy of Rome slowly begin to multiply. So do references to various actions of the bishops of Rome that tend to illustrate what the primacy was all about and how it worked. By the third century, these references become more frequent still, and unmistakable in their meaning.

By all indications, second- and third-century popes understood that they had a special role and status in the Church of Christ, and they spoke and acted accordingly when the occasion required. But we should not forget that during this period *how* they were able to speak and act was often limited by the fact that the Church was still an illegal entity in the Roman empire and, hence, the popes themselves, like other Christians, were considered outlaws.

References to the position of Rome and the popes in the Christian literature of this early time are quite interesting. Around the year 150, for example, an apocalyptic work, *The Shepherd of Hermas*, written by an ex-slave, was widely circulated among other Churches, even those considerably distant from Rome. *The Shepherd of Hermas* was a visionary call to repentance at a time when Church discipline was growing somewhat lax in the relative freedom from active persecution temporarily obtained under Emperor Antoninius Pius (138–161). The work as a whole, highly symbolical and allegorical, would have provided little evidence to any Roman magistrate of "illegal" Christian activity.

Hermas was quite popular for a time and widely read at Church services, as if it were Scripture. Later the work fell into disuse and, finally, obscurity; it would certainly never have qualified permanently as Scripture.

From another ancient document, the Muratorian Fragment, dating from around 170 to 180, we learn that *The Shepherd of Hermas* "was written quite recently in our own time by Hermas, while his brother, Pius, was filling the chair of the Church of the city of Rome". Pope St. Pius I seems to have occupied the chair of Peter between the years 140 and 155, approximately; he was probably the pope who presided over the expulsion from the orthodox Roman community of the early heretic Marcion, founder of the Marcionites, an event that occurred in July 144.

That *The Shepherd of Hermas* may well have been written by the brother of a pope is of some interest to us because in the work it is stated that it was to be sent out to "the cities abroad" by the hand of one Clement; "for that is his duty", the document adds. That the Church of Rome was sending things out to "the cities abroad" is not without relevance to our thesis.

The reference to a Clement here, by the way, has led some historians to believe that Clement of Rome was some kind of corresponding secretary for the Roman Church; *Hermas*, too, refers generically to "the rulers" of the Church, not to "the bishop". Clement of Rome, however, wrote his Letter to Corinth more than fifty years before this particular document, which does not pretend to be history.

More pertinent than the reference to the name Clement is the suggestion that the wide circulation and popularity the document enjoyed arose from the fact that it was sent out by the Church of Rome, which employed someone whose "duty" it was to send it out. If so, this would indicate the existence of a rudimentary teaching office in the Church of Rome: it amounted to instructing the faithful on a scale far wider than the local Church of Rome—and by means of a widely distributed document apparently written by, in this particular case, the pope's own brother. That such a writing could be accepted, even for a while, as "Scripture", again points to a special status for teachings emanating from Rome.

The name Clement may even have been attached to the document to help identify its source and give it greater authority; or there may have been another Clement, a name not uncommon at that time.

Although *The Shepherd of Hermas* affords us an interesting glimpse of the religious mentality of the day, when Christians were still a despised, clandestine minority, it does not directly address the Roman primacy but merely provides indications of the regard in which the Church of Rome was held.

A much more dramatic instance testifying to the position of the Church and bishop of Rome in the second half of the second century comes from St. Irenaeus of Lyons (ca. 130–ca. 200).

In his great work *Adversus Haereses* (*Against the Heresies*), Irenaeus emphasized the role of the Church in handing down intact the authentic tradition of the apostles; he insisted that the Church could be trusted to teach and interpret the true Gospel of Christ with the help of the Holy Spirit. Preeminent among all the Churches, according to Irenaeus, was the Church of Rome, with an unbroken succession of bishops going back to apostolic times. Irenaeus speaks explicitly of Peter and Paul "preaching at Rome and establishing the Church". He states plainly the belief of the early Church that the two great apostles "founded and reared up this Church and afterward committed unto Linus the office of the episcopate" (III, 1, 3).

Firm believer in the apostolic succession that he was, St. Irenaeus' list of the bishops of Rome is one of the earliest we possess. It is completely consistent with another early list, the one compiled independently by another Easterner, Hegesippus of Syria (fl. ca. 160–175), who visited Rome during this period. His list includes Roman bishops up to Pope Anicetus (ca. 155–ca. 166). In the view of Hegesippus, the unbroken line of Roman bishops constituted a guarantee of the genuineness of the Roman tradition—an idea that Irenaeus also stressed.

Irenaeus' list of the popes went all the way to Pope Eleutherus (ca. 174–189), whom St. Irenaeus had been sent from Lyons to consult in person. His purpose in visiting Pope Eleutherus was to urge the latter to approve the condemnation of the heresy of Montanism that a local synod of bishops in the East had recently decided upon. That the pope's approval was sought for a decision of an Eastern synod tells us something about Rome's position in the early Church in both East and West. Irenaeus may well have been chosen as an envoy to go to the pope because he had special knowledge of Montanism from contacts in his native East. In any event, Pope Eleutherus, following the counsel given by Irenaeus, rejected the Montanist novelties, thus adhering strictly to tradition, which Irenaeus noted was the consistent hallmark of the Church of Rome.

Around the time of his own visit to Rome, Irenaeus seems to have written *Adversus Haereses*. It contains one of the clearest and strongest expositions of Catholic doctrine that have come down to us from the early Church. It is a key document from the late second century evidencing and supporting the primacy of Rome in the early Church.

As discussed, when he was young, Irenaeus had been personally instructed by St. Polycarp of Smyrna in Asia Minor, who had received instruction directly from St. John the Evangelist. Irenaeus emphasized how Polycarp had always abhorred heretics and false doctrine and never deviated from his affirmation of the true faith in one God, Creator and Father, and one Son of God, who had truly lived and suffered in the flesh.

Yet, in expounding the faith, Irenaeus does not rely on the words of his teacher so much as on the authentic, unbroken tradition of the Church of Rome. There could hardly be a clearer statement of the Church's claim to interpret revealed Scripture authentically to the faithful with the help of the Holy Spirit than the one found in Irenaeus. Similarly, there could hardly be a clearer testimony to the special authority and responsibility of the Roman pontiffs in the Church of Christ than the following passage from *Adversus Haereses*, which Irenaeus wrote around the year 180:

> Now it is within the power of anyone, who cares, to find out the truth and to know the tradition of the apostles, professed throughout the world in every Church. We are also able to name those who were appointed bishops by the apostles in the Churches and their successors down to our own times. . . .
>
> But inasmuch as it would be very tedious in a book such as this to rehearse the lines of succession in every Church, we will put to confusion all persons, who, whether from waywardness, or vainglory, or blindness, or perversity of mind, combine wrongfully together in any way, by pointing to the

tradition, derived from the apostles, of that great and illustrious Church founded and organized at Rome by the two glorious apostles, Peter and Paul, and to the faith declared to mankind and handed down to our own time through its bishops in their succession. For unto this Church, on account of its commanding position, every Church, that is to say, the faithful from everywhere, must needs resort, and in it the tradition that comes from the apostles has been continuously preserved by those who are from everywhere. (III, 3)

Irenaeus immediately goes on to list all the popes who occupied the chair of Peter up to his own time, beginning with Linus and going on with [Ana]cletus and Clement, whom he clearly designates as a bishop. He is also familiar with the Letter of Clement which he quotes in support of some of his own positions.

Irenaeus is an invaluable witness to the authentic early tradition of the Church of Rome. We should be aware, however, that the last sentence of the passage quoted above is quite controversial. Although the thrust of the sentence clearly supports the hypothesis of a Roman primacy, the exact meaning is not entirely clear. This may result in part because the original Greek text of *Adversus Haereses* has been lost. We possess the text of this work only in a rough, literal Latin translation, although this translation is almost as early as the original, since Tertullian quoted from it only a few years later.

In view of the controversy surrounding this passage, we shall provide here the Latin of the last sentence quoted above, along with another translation of it that Catholic scholars have defended: *ad hanc enim ecclesiam propter potentiorem principalitatem necesse est omnem convenire ecclesiam, hoc est, eos qui sunt undique fideles in qua semper ab his qui sunt undique conservata est ea quae est ab apostolis traditio.* A standard Catholic translation of this reads: "With this Church, on account of its pre-eminent authority, every Church *must be in agreement*, that is, the faithful everywhere, among whom the tradition of the apostles has been continuously preserved by those everywhere" (emphasis added).

We sometimes find "standard" translations of ancient texts that mean somewhat different things, perhaps depending upon what the translator wishes to prove. Nevertheless, ambiguities in the historical record do not forbid our making the best case we honestly can from what is before us. In the present case, the second translation supports the hypothesis of the Roman primacy more clearly than the first; the first translation, far from excluding it, also points toward it, even if not quite as clearly as the second.

Another possible translation of the Latin verb *convenire* in this passage is simply "to come or go to". Does it strengthen the case for the Roman primacy to hold that Irenaeus thought that "every Church" must "come to" or "go to" the Church of Rome? It certainly does not weaken it.

Modern Catholics cannot fail to be reassured when they recall that the Dogmatic Constitution *Pastor Aeternus*, of 1870, by which Vatican Council I defined the doctrine of the primacy and infallibility of the pope, itself quotes from and adopts as an integral part of its definition the very sentence from Irenaeus that we have been considering, thus adopting it as part of the Church's irreformable patrimony.

The dispute, hindered as it is by ambiguous or inconclusive evidence, may never be finally resolved by scholars. How important the whole thing is can be questioned; perhaps the whole dispute really illustrates how slender the straws are at which some scholars are willing to grasp.

We could cite other modern translations of Irenaeus, for instance, in which the idea that other churches might have to be in agreement with the Roman Church is carefully and studiously avoided—not disputed or refuted, just avoided. We can scarcely admire this way of proceeding. Abundantly clear from the overall testimony of Irenaeus is that the Roman primacy is powerfully supported by this ancient writer—one of the most significant of all the ancient Christian writers.

VI.

When considering the primacy of Rome in the early Church, we should remind ourselves that no other ancient Church ever had the notion of primacy attached to it. All the other great Churches of antiquity with any degree of authority over surrounding Churches achieved their positions not entirely because of their apostolic foundation—if they boasted that—but also because of the importance of the cities in which they were located. The Church of Rome, which admittedly *began* in what was still the greatest city of the empire, actually got demoted in terms of secular importance by the movement of the capital of the empire to the East. Nevertheless the Church of Rome did not lose the primacy just because the city where she was located declined in secular importance.

The importance of the Church of Rome derived, not from the secular importance of that city, but from the conferral of special authority on the apostle Peter by Christ. As we shall further document, the Roman primacy can be verified from many sources: thus, *if* Christ truly intended there to be a primacy in his Church, it could certainly not have been located anywhere but in the Church of Rome, given the link between the Church of Rome and the apostle Peter.

At this point we briefly review some further pertinent references to the primacy of Rome in early Christian literature dating roughly from 150 to 250 A.D.

A certain Caius, who lived in Rome under Pope Zephyrinus (ca. 199–217), defended the superior authority of the Roman doctrine against the Montanists on the ground that the Roman Church was a creation of the apostles and still served as the repository of their bones. "I can show you the trophies of the apostles", Caius wrote, according to Eusebius (*Ecclesiastical History*, II, 25). Caius employed the Greek word *tropaios*, probably making reference to the still visible inscriptions that marked the Roman tombs of the apostles.

The African Tertullian, perhaps the most important theologian in the Latin West prior to Saints Cyprian and Augustine, lived and wrote between around 160 and 230. Among other testimonials that he supplied, Tertullian, with characteristic bluntness, wrote that "there is no difference between those whom John baptized in the Jordan and those whom Peter baptized in the Tiber" (*De Baptismo*, 4), thus locating Peter's primary mission in Rome. Speaking of the lists of the bishops of the various apostolic Churches, Tertullian notes, "in this form the apostolic churches do present their registers, such as the Church of Smyrna, which shows that Polycarp was appointed there by John, and the Church of Rome, which states that Clement was ordained by Peter" (*De Praescriptione Haereticorum*, 32). And, writing as he did from Carthage in Africa, Tertullian does not hesitate to describe the Church of Rome as the source "whence also our authority is derived", adding, "Where Peter endured a passion like his Lord's" and "where Paul won his crown in a death like John's" (ibid. 36).

Tertullian was one of the first ecclesiastical writers to quote the famous passage from Matthew 16:18–19 about Peter as the rock on whom the Church was to be built and to whom the keys of the kingdom of heaven were given. He did this in the context of his discussion of the apostolicity of the Churches. Perhaps curiously, he did not quote this passage as an argument for the primacy.

Tertullian was a gifted Latin writer whose testimony concerning the belief and practice of the early Church is rightly considered invaluable. His own writings, however, show that Tertullian was also a very rigid and opinionated man who eventually fell into heresy, adopting the overly strict moral views of the Montanists. He seems to have been moved to this position by his disgust and contempt for what he considered the undue leniency of the bishops of Rome, for this African lawyer was a fierce partisan of the ancient view that certain sins committed after baptism were unforgivable.

The popes of that era, especially Pope St. Callistus (217–222), relaxed somewhat the severe ancient penitential discipline of the Church. The more lenient discipline adopted by Pope Callistus seems to have angered Tertullian, particularly the idea that widows were allowed to remarry (or noble women were allowed to marry freed slaves). Also Tertullian could not abide what he saw as an undue relaxation of the Church's penitential discipline for confessed sinners. Nevertheless, even after he went over to Montanism, some of his writings still provide at least indirect evidence for the primacy of Rome.

In his Montanist writing *On Modesty*, for example, Tertullian refers sarcastically to the pope, mentioning that "the *Pontifex Maximus*, that is, the bishop of bishops, has issued a decree" (*De Pudicitia*, V) remitting the sins of adultery and fornication for some who had done a prescribed penance for them. It was Tertullian's belief that such sins could not be remitted at all, so he naturally attacked the pope for pretending to be able to remit them.

But to refer to Pope Callistus, even sarcastically, as "the bishop of bishops" indicates how the pope was regarded in Tertullian's day. Similarly, his ironic reference to the pope as "*Pontifex Maximus*" anticipated by many centuries the adoption of this ancient Roman title by the popes. In Tertullian's day, the Roman emperor was the *Pontifex Maximus*, that is, the head of all the pagan cults in Rome. Applying the term to the pope only underlines the pope's perceived headship.

In *De Pudicitia*, Tertullian argued strenuously *against* the use of Matthew 16:18–19 as proof of the papal primacy. As far as he was concerned, any authority conferred by Christ could have been conferred only for purposes other than remitting sins; and, as many who denied the papal primacy would continue to argue over almost the next eighteen centuries, the African firebrand argued that whatever authority Christ may have conferred on Peter did not descend to Peter's successors. (The fact that Tertullian judged some of Peter's successors to be unworthy of such a charge affected his viewpoint on this.)

Tertullian was not the only ancient writer who, having separated himself from Catholic orthodoxy, turned around and argued vigorously against the primacy of Rome. This phenomenon would be encountered in many cases in the later history of the Church. Nevertheless, Tertullian must have seen the primacy as a salient, stubborn fact if it had to be argued against so fiercely.

Origen of Alexandria (ca. 185–ca. 254) possessed perhaps the most powerful intellect of all the early Fathers; he was an exegete, a theologian, an indefatigable preacher, and the long-time head of the famous catechetical school in Alexandria. He was also one of the most prolific of ancient Christian authors.

Origen was also another early witness to the universal belief of the early Church that Peter, "having come to Rome . . .

was crucified head downward, for he had asked that he might suffer in this way" (quoted by Eusebius, *Ecclesiastical History*, III, 1). Origen had come to Rome as a young man. Like Tertullian, he eventually fell into a number of errors in the course of his life and voluminous writing. He also defied his bishop in a particular case: in 231 or 232, he was tried and condemned by a synod of Eastern bishops under the presidency of Bishop Demetrius of Alexandria for insubordination, self-mutilation, and heterodoxy.

Of interest about Origen's trial, as far as our present subject is concerned, is this: because not all the bishops from Palestine, Phoenicia, Arabia, and parts of Greece accepted the verdict of the Alexandrian tribunal, the bishop of Rome, Pope Pontian (230–235), convoked a Roman synod to review the matter. We do not know whether or not Pope Pontian was asked to do this, that is, whether or not there had been "an appeal to Rome". But we will not fail to encounter examples of such appeals, some of them dramatic, as we follow the history of the popes.

The mere fact that the bishop of Rome did convene a synod to review the Alexandrian decision in the case of Origen is significant. The conditions under which Pope Pontian carried out this task may perhaps be gauged by the fact that a little later he was arrested and deported to the mines in Sardinia, where he died under cruel conditions (ca. 235). He is the first pope known to have abdicated and voluntarily resigned his office, probably to allow a successor to be elected following his deportation (an action that availed little, since his immediate successor, Pope St. Anterus (235–236), reigned for only about two months.

The Roman synod convened by Pontian in the matter of Origen confirmed the judgment of the Alexandrian tribunal, according to St. Jerome (*Epistolae*, XXXIII, *Ad Paulam*).

Quite significant in this regard is the apparently routine assumption of a kind of appellate jurisdiction by Rome over a case from another apostolic see, the second see of Christianity. It was evidently accepted on all sides that Rome did have such jurisdiction in a case such as this. It was accepted without dispute—so long as Rome ended up confirming the Alexandrian judgment rather than quashing it.

Origen himself, although another of the ancient Christian writers who specifically argued against the use of Matthew 16:18–19 to justify the Roman primacy, nevertheless seems to have made some kind of appeal to Rome against the judgment lodged against him. According to St. Jerome, he expressly wrote to a successor of Pontian, Pope Fabian (236–250), defending his orthodoxy and professing to regret certain things he had written, stating that they had been published by others. It seems significant that this famous Eastern theologian, who continued to enjoy important episcopal patronage in the East even after his trial and conviction in Alexandria, still thought it necessary or at least helpful to write to the faraway Roman bishop about his case.

Pope Fabian is known to have intervened in yet another far-flung doctrinal case. A local council in Carthage under Bishop Donatus condemned for doctrinal errors one Privatus, a bishop of Lambaesis (modern Tazoult in northeast Algeria), and Fabian wrote a confirmation of this sentence—another instance of appellate jurisdiction of a sort from the same early period.

These are some of the major references in the works of ancient Christian writers bearing upon the question of the Roman primacy from the end of the second century through the beginning years of the third. These references are unfortunately rather exiguous, indeed, maddeningly sparse. Much more is needed to fill out the picture.

Nevertheless, it can be affirmed that the Church of Rome was definitely seen in this early period as occupying a special position in the Church. This position was surely due to the reverence in which the legacy of Peter and Paul was held. Further, the Roman Church they left behind them definitely exercised, with what seems from evidence to have been general acquiescence of the Church at large, what we can legitimately call a primacy, at least on certain important issues. This primacy was not as highly developed as it would one day become—with the applicable principles and procedures laid out and codified—but it was there, and it functioned.

As time passed, instances of the same kind would turn up in an increasing number of writings and documents pertaining to the Church of Rome. In no way was this accidental; the Roman primacy was destined to develop over time as the Church herself developed.

VII.

Perhaps the most convincing evidence for the primacy of Rome in the second and third centuries comes not so much from the testimony of early Church writers as from actions taken by some of the bishops of Rome. When Pope Pontian convened a Roman synod to review the decision of the Alexandrian tribunal that had condemned Origen, he was exercising the authority to "bind and loose" that Christ had given to all the apostles (Mt 18:18) but to Peter in a special way (Mt 16:18–19). Probably the faithful of the day understood his action in precisely these terms.

The divergent views of some who had departed from Catholic orthodoxy and then argued that the special authority conferred on Peter did not devolve on his successors would logically seem to have to lead to a denial that Catholic bishops in general also inherited the authority given by Christ to their predecessors, the apostles.

No ancient Christian writer—not Tertullian, Origen, or any other—ever denied the apostolic succession or the authority inherited by the bishops. That the Church had been established on the apostles was a truth that no professing Christian would attempt to deny for at least another thousand years, when the mistaken idea that the faith of Christ could somehow be based on "Scripture alone" was launched by the Protestant Reformation. For the Christians of antiquity, the fact that the Church was headed by bishops as successors of the apostles was as plain as the fact that the Church existed.

That the successors of Peter occupied a position in the Church analogous to the position Peter had occupied in the apostolic Church was widely if not universally believed, even if this primacy was not always understood as the strict, legal "primacy of jurisdiction" that Rome would later claim and exercise. The acts of the popes of the second and third centuries provide a number of instances that testify both to the way they thought and acted and to the very definite sense they possessed that their decisions had universal application in the Church.

The story of one of the most interesting incidents concerning the attitudes and actions of an early second-century pope comes from the pen of St. Irenaeus of Lyons, whom we have already encountered. Writing to Pope St. Victor (189–198) about another matter, which we shall consider later, Irenaeus recounts how his own revered teacher, St. Polycarp of Smyrna, had found it necessary to come to Rome around the year 154 or 155—only a year or so before St. Polycarp's celebrated martyrdom in Asia Minor.

In Rome Polycarp, then nearly ninety, was graciously received by the bishop, Pope St. Anicetus (ca. 155–ca. 166). We are not told the purpose of what must have been his rather arduous journey. From the brief account given by Irenaeus, the bishops of Smyrna and of Rome conferred about the calculation of the date of Easter.

In the East, many of the Churches had maintained the tradition of tying the celebration of the Lord's resurrection to the time of the Jewish Passover. Easter was accordingly celebrated on the fourteenth day of the Jewish month Nisan, regardless of the day of the week it fell upon.

In the West—in the Churches of the tradition of Peter and Paul—the connection between the resurrection and Sunday was maintained, and Easter was accordingly celebrated as a distinct Christian festival no longer related to the Jewish Passover; it was celebrated on the Sunday after the first full moon of the vernal equinox. By the time of Pope Anicetus and Bishop Polycarp, this divergence in the celebration of Easter by different Churches was widely deplored, and St. Polycarp may even have come to Rome for the express purpose of straightening the matter out.

Irenaeus informs us, however, that in spite of their discussions, which he emphasizes were conducted in a spirit of mutual charity, Pope Anicetus was unable to "persuade Bishop Polycarp not to observe what he had always observed in company with John, the disciple of the Lord, and other apostles he had known. Nor could Polycarp prevail upon Anicetus to adopt that observance, since he said that he ought to observe the custom of the presbyters who had preceded him" (quoted in Eusebius, *Ecclesiastical History*, V, 24). The use of the term *presbyters* by St. Irenaeus is interesting in the light of our earlier discussion about how the use of the same word by Clement of Rome has been taken by some modern historians to mean that this earlier writer was not a bishop but *only* a presbyter. Clearly this word also had a generic meaning in the early Church and could simply refer to an officer of the Church, as it does here in this text of Irenaeus.

We should make no mistake about identifying one of the most notable things about this meeting between Polycarp and Anicetus, as reported by Irenaeus: Anicetus, much younger than the venerable bishop from Smyrna and far removed from any direct apostolic connection, nevertheless declined to yield to his guest's promoting a tradition that stemmed directly from "John, the disciple of the Lord". Instead, Anicetus insisted on continuing the tradition handed down to him in the Church of Rome regarding the celebration of Easter.

The Roman tradition would come to prevail throughout the Church, just as the Roman tradition would prevail in the matter of remitting after penance certain sins earlier thought by some not to be remittable. Eventually the variant practice found in parts of the East linking the celebration of Easter with Passover would fall into desuetude—though not without strenuous intervention by a later pope, as we shall see, and, finally, a canon passed by the Council of Nicaea.

At the meeting between St. Polycarp and St. Anicetus, the matter failed to get resolved. As St. Irenaeus informs us, "Anicetus yielded the administration of the Eucharist to Polycarp as a mark of respect." This Eastern bishop and future martyr was thus allowed by the pope to go on celebrating Mass according to his own tradition. Anicetus insisted on maintaining intact the tradition of the Church of Rome even in the face of urgings from an "apostolic man" in person, St. Polycarp.

Other references from this period to actions of contemporary popes tell us something about their status and role. In the time of Pope Anicetus, Hegesippus came from Syria to Rome to compile an independent list of popes from the founding apostle to his own time. This list was to be part of a much more extensive work, now lost, concerning several apostolic Churches he visited. Among the few sentences from it reproduced by Eusebius is the important observation that this early Syrian "received the same doctrine from all" the apostolic Churches (*Ecclesiastical History*, IV, 22).

Pope St. Anicetus was succeeded by Pope St. Soter (ca. 166–ca. 174). Bishop Dionysius of Corinth, whom we have already encountered, was a copious letter writer, and his letter to Pope Soter includes an eloquent paragraph on the preeminence of the see of Rome in his time, and at least one reason for this preeminence:

> [T]his practice has prevailed with you [Rome] from the very beginning, to do good to all the brethren in every way, and to send contributions to many churches *in every city*—thus refreshing the needy in their want, and furnishing to the brethren condemned to the mines what was necessary, by these contributions *which you have been accustomed to send from the beginning*, you preserve, as Romans, the practices of your ancestors, the Romans. [This] was not only observed by your bishop, Soter, but also increased, as he not only furnished great supplies to the saints, but also encouraged *the brethren that came from abroad*, as a loving father his children, with consolatory words. (Quoted by Eusebius, *Ecclesiastical History*, IV, 23; emphases added)

It is hard not to relate these typical activities and practices of the Roman see with the consciousness of its incumbents of their own *universal* responsibilities within the Church.

Pope St. Soter was succeeded by Pope St. Eleutherus (ca. 174–189), the last pope St. Irenaeus included in his *Adversus*

Haereses. This was the pope to whom the rigid Montanists in Phrygia in Asia Minor had appealed to support their views, which they claimed had the direct sanction of the Holy Spirit. Soter was the pope to whom St. Irenaeus had also been sent by the Church of Lyons to lobby against the Montanists' appeal to Rome. Probably the Church of Lyons maintained close contacts with the East, if only through Irenaeus, who, therefore, had special knowledge of the true nature of Montanism.

It was not that Montanism did not have its attractions. It may have been tempting to believe that each Christian could receive directly into his own soul the full truth of Christ. Unfortunately, a rigid, literal adherence to this viewpoint was inevitably sectarian and undermined the basis of the visible, sacramental, sacerdotal, and hierarchical Church, the kind of Church Christ had in fact established: the One, Holy, Catholic, and Apostolic Church.

We do not know what influence Irenaeus had on the decision of Pope Eleutherus to hold fast against the Montanist innovations. It could be that the firsthand knowledge acquired by Irenaeus of how Eleutherus handled the Montanist situation was one of the factors that helped establish in his mind the lofty view of the Roman primacy expressed in *Adversus Haereses.*

It was the ill-natured, waspish Tertullian who reported in one of his Montanist works that Eleutherus, initially favorable to the Montanists, was turned against them by one Praxeas:

> For after the bishop of Rome had admitted the genuineness of the prophecies of Montanus ... , [Praxeas], by importunately urging false charges against these prophets and their Churches, and by *insisting upon the authority that belonged to*

bishop's predecessors in the see, forced him [Eleutherus] to recall the conciliatory letter which he had sent out and to desist from his purpose.... *(Adversus Praxeam*, I, emphasis added)

It is doubtful that Pope Eleutherus was "forced" to hold fast to the traditions handed down in the Church of Rome. According to the evidence, the popes had been doing this right along. Eleutherus had been a deacon under hold-to-the-tradition Pope Anicetus, who had adopted the same stance in the matter of the date of Easter.

The typical stance of the bishops of Rome was to hold fast to the tradition handed down to them. St. Irenaeus, writing from firsthand experience, had singled out this characteristic for particular praise. Holding fast to the tradition has been typical of popes throughout the history of the Church. *Intransigence* is the word normally employed by enemies of the Church to describe it, and the popes have very often been reproached for it, including in our own time.

We must note yet another salient thing about this whole case: the Montanists, whom Tertullian favored, were themselves appealing to Rome for approval and vindication, while others (Praxeas, as well as Irenaeus himself) were also appealing to Rome to rule against the Montanists. This is a very strong indication that Rome was recognized by all sides as possessing the authority to arbitrate the issue and issue a final decision.

Tertullian would have been quite happy if Pope Eleutherus had *not* followed the advice of Praxeas and had issued a decision in favor of the Montanists. The pope's disapproval of the Montanists was a significant setback to their quest for legitimacy. Those on the receiving end of the decisions of authority are seldom strong defenders of that authority afterward. We have encountered and shall encounter other instances of this kind.

VIII.

One of the most dramatic of all instances of the exercise of the primacy of Rome in the early Church occurred near the end of the second century. Of African origin, Pope St. Victor I (189–198), who had succeeded Eleutherus, was, according to the *Liber Pontificalis*, the first pope to write in Latin. He was also the first known to have had direct dealings with the Roman imperial household. Through the influence of Marcia, favorite mistress of Emperor Commodus (180–192), who may have had Christian relatives, he secured the release of some Christians condemned to hard labor in the mines of Sardinia.

With Victor what had hitherto been the typical kind of Roman intervention, reaching decisions after convening Roman synods and communicating them by means of rather low-key letters, seems rather suddenly to have been transformed into a policy of bluntly issuing orders and expecting them to be carried out. Accounts of Pope Victor depict him as almost resembling one of the masterful pontiffs at the height of the medieval papacy; his attitude seems to have been that it was for him to issue orders from on high and for those subject to him to obey without question.

He did not hesitate to excommunicate Theodotus of Byzantium, a proponent of the Adoptionist heresy. Adoptionists believed that Jesus was not God but merely a man to whom special graces had been given at his baptism in the Jordan, a view Victor could not tolerate. Victor imposed discipline in other ways as well, for example, defrocking the former priest and Gnostic writer Florinus.

This pope did not fail to arouse opposition to some of his actions, but that fact itself indicates that he must have understood himself to possess special authority, which he certainly did not hesitate to exercise.

The most prominent example of this during his pontificate concerned the date of Easter. In parts of the East, the Quartodecimanians, as they were called, still linked the celebration of Easter with Passover, but there was considerable and growing sentiment in the Church to standardize the Sunday celebration of Easter. Local synods were convened in a number of places at the suggestion of the bishop of Rome, most of which decided to adopt the Roman custom of celebrating Easter on Sunday. Eusebius informs us that local synods in Palestine, Pontus, Mesopotamia, Gaul, Greece, and elsewhere, as well as in Rome, issued statements to this effect.

The Church in Asia (eastern Asia Minor), however, preserving her own memories of the apostles John and Philip, announced, exactly as St. Polycarp had done a generation earlier, that she could not depart from the venerable tradition of celebrating Easter on 15 Nisan in conjunction with the Jewish Passover.

Pope Victor's reaction was vigorous—indeed, unprecedented. He not only declared that the Church in Asia Minor was mistaken, along with any other Churches taking the same position; he severed communion with them, flatly declaring them to be excommunicated, not merely as far as Rome was concerned but as far as the whole Church was concerned. "Thereupon Victor," Eusebius reports, "who was head of the Church at Rome, immediately undertook to cut off from the common unity the parishes of all Asia and such Churches as agreed with them as heterodox; and he wrote letters pronouncing all the brethren there totally excommunicate" (*Ecclesiastical History*, V, 23–25).

Up to this time individuals had been excommunicated for cause but never entire Churches. Pope Victor was confronted with a storm of protests. Even some of those who favored the Roman discipline concerning the celebration of

Easter and disagreed with the Quartodecimanian practice were concerned about the manner in which Pope Victor had exercised his authority. With Victor, the previous custom of employing exhortation and persuasion in letters exchanged between Churches suddenly acquired a sharper and even peremptory new tone.

Some perceived Victor's resorting to excommunication as too drastic. Since the dispute was seen as disciplinary rather than doctrinal, they thought that some allowance should be made for variations in practice.

Among those who wrote to remonstrate with Victor and counsel greater moderation was St. Irenaeus, who recounted the story of the meeting between Pope St. Anicetus and St. Polycarp described above. Anicetus had certainly taken a more relaxed view of the divergence of practices in the various Churches than Victor was now taking. Irenaeus, too, was of the opinion that, while the Roman practice of celebrating Easter was correct, the whole business did not justify a break between the Churches.

Irenaeus took for granted Victor's authority to act; he simply thought Victor should have acted with more restraint, exhibiting the toleration and charity that Pope Anicetus had earlier exhibited toward St. Polycarp.

Though Victor's action was unprecedented at that time, it was implicit in the papal possession of the primacy that a case could someday arise in which entire churches, obstinately holding to local usages and traditions, would refuse to go along with the teaching and practice of the universal Church. As long as local synods amicably agreed with each other, no further action was necessary. But what if they disagreed?

In such a case, the possessor of the supreme authority in the Church—the primacy—might be obliged to uphold the authenticity and integrity of the universal Church's teaching and practice. And as it happened, this particular case arose at the close of the second century in the matter of the Eastern Quartodecimanians. As the incumbent of the chair of Peter, Pope Victor was obliged to act for the universal Church in a case in which the system of calling local synods of bishops had failed to resolve the problem. Whether Victor's action was necessary or even helpful in this particular case is arguable. Inherent in the nature of authority, however, is the possibility that cases necessitating drastic action can arise; in Victor's judgment, his action was necessary.

In one very important sense, Victor was drawing out the logic of the position he held on the primacy, whatever might be said of the manner in which he acted. Victor was reacting to a fact: the system of convening local synods to make decisions coordinating and regulating the Church's life and worship had not worked; the synods had met and made their decisions, but the case remained unresolved, all because one local synod declined to go along with the rest. Higher authority was therefore needed to resolve such a case, as Victor clearly saw, and he acted accordingly.

Other similar—and often more serious—cases would arise in which Victor's successors would similarly be obliged to act. If Christ truly gave to Peter and his successors ultimate authority to decide and act when disputed questions arose, they were obliged to act as best they knew how in such cases. That is what Victor did, however his action may be judged with hindsight.

Even though the Roman discipline concerning the celebration of Easter on Sunday would eventually come to prevail throughout the entire Church, the issue was not definitively settled by Pope Victor's action. His immediate successors did not press the case after Victor's death. A century and a half later, the Council of Nicaea would still be grappling with the same question—although it ultimately took the same position on it that Pope Victor had.

IX.

The important insight that the early popes did not so much claim a position of primacy in the Church as exercise it is confirmed by consideration of the rather complicated history of the relationships between the Church of Rome and the Churches of Africa and Asia in the third century. In dealing with problems that arose in these relationships, the popes were increasingly moved to articulate explicitly their claim to primacy in the whole Church.

Considering these relationships between Churches in different areas, we should remind ourselves that, two full centuries and more after her founding and after she had spread throughout the whole Roman Empire and beyond, the Church still remained a *religio illicita*, an illegal religion. At any time, emperors, magistrates, or mobs—perhaps all three together—might move against her and, during persecutions, did.

By the third century, though, Christians had acquired a considerable degree of de facto acceptance. Between persecutions, they worshipped openly in church buildings. Emperor Alexander Severus (222–235), without according Christians legal recognition, allowed them to assemble for worship. The Church was allowed to possess property in the same de facto way. Pope Zephyrinus (199–217), for example, placed his deacon, the future Pope Callistus, in charge of "the cemetery" in Rome—almost certainly Church property.

These new rights to assemble publicly and own property, were not very firm—as the two great persecutions to come would demonstrate. The Church of Rome never entirely abandoned the catacombs until the full legalization of Christianity in the fourth century. During persecutions, she quickly retreated into them. But there were also long periods of toleration when Christians could apparently coexist peacefully with the empire in spite of the laws still on the books against them.

The first half of the third century was relatively peaceful nearly everywhere. But active persecution was again renewed and intensified under Emperor Decius, who acceded to the imperial purple in 249. The Decian persecution, a particularly serious one, began in 250, and continued on and off through the next decade under his successors, Gallus (251–253) and Valerian (253–260).

The edict launching the Decian persecution has not been preserved, but apparently every citizen of the empire was required to sacrifice or perform some act of homage to the pagan gods at one of the public altars. In order to undermine the leadership of the Church, bishops who refused could be put to death immediately. To break down their resolution, ordinary Christians could be imprisoned, tortured, or deprived of food.

Those who satisfied the magistrates concerning their compliance with the law received a certificate (*libellus*) to that effect. Although history records that many Christians gladly suffered persecution and martyrdom, many did not. Defections were sometimes massive. A half century of peace and relative toleration had moderated the fervor of many. This would create great problems for the Church. After the persecution was over, many Christians who had lapsed, the *lapsi*, clamored to come back to the Church. The question of what the conditions of their readmission should be, especially if they had been clergy or bishops, then came to the fore.

The contemporary bishop of Alexandria, St. Dionysius (247–ca. 264), describes the panic brought about by the Decian persecutions and some of the varied reactions to it:

> The decree ... arrived, very much like that which was foretold by our Lord, exhibiting the most dreadful aspect, so that, if it were possible, the very elect would stumble. All indeed were greatly alarmed and many of the more eminent immediately gave way.... Others who were in public offices were led forth by their acts; others were brought by their acquaintances, and when called by name approached the impure and unholy sacrifices.... Pale and trembling, as if they were not to sacrifice, but themselves to be the victims and the sacrifices to the idols, they were jeered by many of the surrounding multitude, and were obviously equally afraid to die and to offer the sacrifice. But some advanced with greater readiness to the altars, and boldly asserted that they had never before been Christians—concerning whom the declaration of our Lord is most true, that they will scarcely be saved.
>
> Of the rest, some followed the one or the other of the preceding; some fled, others were taken, and of these some held out as far as the prison and bonds, and some [only] after a few days imprisonment abjured.... But some also, after enduring the torture for a time, at last renounced.
>
> Others, however, firm and blessed pillars of the Lord, confirmed by the Lord himself, and receiving in themselves strength and power, suited and proportioned to their faith, became admirable witnesses of his kingdom.... (Quoted by Eusebius, *Ecclesiastical History*, VI, 41)

One of the first victims of the great Decian persecution was the bishop of Rome, Pope St. Fabian (236–250), who went to his death as a martyr on January 20, 250. It was said that Decius intended his edict to apply to the bishop of Rome in particular. Decius is supposed to have said that he would rather hear of the appearance of a rival claimant to the empire than of the election of a new bishop in the capital—thus providing a confirmation from a pagan source of the growing prominence of the bishops of Rome.

The bishop of Antioch also died in prison under the Decian persecution. The bishop of Alexandria, rescued from imperial soldiers by a crowd of his own people, went into hiding. The bishop of Carthage in North Africa, St. Cyprian (ca. 200–258), whose letters describe the condition of the Church during this period better than any other source, also went into hiding.

At the height of the Decian persecution, it proved to be impossible—and would have been foolhardy—to elect a pope to replace St. Fabian. For more than a year, the Roman clergy under the leadership of the priest Novatian maintained the administration of the Church of Rome and carried on correspondence with other Churches. During this extremely difficult and confused period, with the bishop of Rome dead and the bishop of Carthage in hiding, factions grew up in both Churches that would later cause considerable grief and, eventually, schisms—particularly in connection with the readmittance to the Church of penitents who had lapsed during the persecution.

Then, in the spring of 251, while Emperor Decius was fighting the Goths in the Balkans, Pope St. Cornelius (251–253) was elected bishop of Rome. His was a short but very significant reign. He had been a pious priest of fairly lenient views on the question of readmitting *lapsi* to communion. For that reason his election immediately proved unacceptable to a party of hard-liners among the Roman clergy, who viewed his leniency as a repudiation of ancient Church tradition. Members of this faction promptly and illicitly elected a bishop of their own, the antipope Novatian (251–258), who had been the principal leader of the Roman clergy during the papal interregnum.

Novatian had expected to become pope himself, almost automatically, but his leadership of the party that held that the sin of renouncing Christ, even under persecution, could not be forgiven had probably militated against his being elected. Meanwhile, in Carthage, the lax, or indulgent, party was busy contesting the position of the rightful bishop, St. Cyprian.

All of these developments brought about exchanges of correspondence between Rome and Carthage—especially between Pope Cornelius and the bishop, Cyprian—that are too complicated to be recounted in any detail here; but these provide a fascinating and unforgettable picture of how questions of doctrine and discipline were handled by the leaders of the Church in the middle of the third century, a time of either threatened or actual persecution. These exchanges of correspondence also afford us more than a glimpse of how the Churches of the day normally related to one another.

Included in the extensive collection of the Letters (*Epistolae*) of St. Cyprian for this period are two from the hand of Pope St. Cornelius. In these documents we possess the first actual words of a bishop of Rome since those in the Letter of Clement nearly a century and a half earlier.

One of the letters from Cornelius that is quoted by Eusebius contains the earliest extant description of the ranks (and numbers) of the Roman clergy; it demonstrates that the Church of Rome by the middle of the third century, although still illegal, had largely emerged from the catacombs and was a fairly substantial operation. In his letter, Cornelius, after reproaching his rival, the antipope Novatian, with not understanding that there should be only "one bishop in the Catholic Church", goes on to relate that "in our Church there are forty-six priests, seven deacons, seven subdeacons, forty-two acolytes, fifty-two exorcists, readers, and door-keepers, and fifteen hundred widows and needy persons, all of whom are fed through the Master's grace and loving kindness" (*Ecclesiastical History*, VI, 43).

Most of the letters exchanged between the Churches concerned the ongoing doctrinal and disciplinary crises stemming from the Decian persecution. We can provide only a bare summary of the results of some of this extensive correspondence by noting that Cornelius was recognized as the legitimate bishop of Rome against the challenge of the Novatianist schism by St. Cyprian of Carthage, who was able to bring the whole Church in Africa along with him. Cyprian, meanwhile, was recognized and confirmed by Cornelius as the legitimate bishop of Carthage against the faction there that had risen up to challenge *him*.

Perhaps more important, the Roman position on readmission of those who had lapsed under persecution was endorsed and adopted by Cyprian and by the Church in Africa as a whole.

This same position on the readmission of the *lapsi* was accepted and adopted in Alexandria and Antioch as well. Pope Cornelius had written to both of these Churches, urging adoption of the policy. After convening their own local synods to consider the matter, these Churches, too, accepted and confirmed it. This discipline was a development of the position taken a generation earlier by Pope St. Callistus when he decided, much to Tertullian's disgust, that sins of the flesh earlier held by some to be unforgivable when committed after baptism could be remitted by the Church.

Now the same Church with the power "to bind and loose" was holding that even the grave sin of denying Jesus Christ in the face of persecution was forgivable in the case of those who sincerely proved their repentance by doing the prescribed penance. This was a momentous decision, and the drama of how it was arrived at in the give–and–take between the Churches—and between the factions within the Churches—can barely be conveyed by the summary we have given here.

It remains very significant that the Church's substantive decision on the remission of grave sins after baptism was the traditional position of the Church of Rome. It was now being reiterated by a pope who was being challenged by a considerable faction of his own clergy. These men had contested the validity of his election and now continued to work against him. Meanwhile, intermittently, the fierce persecution by the Roman state continued.

This kind of situation was not unusual in the history of the Church of Rome up to this time. It was in response to successive crises such as this that the primacy was actively exercised in practice and would increasingly be articulated by successive popes.

An important question remains: Did the third-century prelates involved in this controversy over the remission of grave sins committed after baptism explicitly recognize the special authority of the bishop of Rome in the Church's decision making concerning this matter? Specifically, did the bishops of Alexandria, Antioch, and Carthage, who ended up accepting the Roman discipline in the matter, recognize that their colleague Pope Cornelius occupied a position superior to theirs within the Church?

The question was not formulated in these terms at the time. Judging from the language employed in the correspondence among the Churches, the other bishops recognized and accorded a clear precedence to the successor of Peter.

He enjoyed special respect as their "elder brother". Thus, in at least one important sense, they did recognize his primacy.

It seems to have been quite clearly recognized by them that, if only as head of the Church in the seat of the imperial power, he had a natural responsibility beyond his special status as the successor of Peter to maintain contact with the Churches everywhere, especially in view of the continuing persecution by the state.

It is, nevertheless, not entirely clear from these mid-third-century exchanges among the bishops of the major cities that the other bishops recognized in their Roman colleague what many centuries later would be defined as a legal "primacy of jurisdiction". We who know how the primacy of Rome ultimately did develop and come to be defined should not attempt to read into the source documents more significance than they can bear in an effort to "prove" the Roman primacy.

The proof of the primacy of Rome in the early Church is not to be found primarily in instances of other bishops overtly showing their acceptance of primacy. Rather, this proof is to be found in the cumulative effect of many diverse instances over time and in different regions and diverse circumstances where the Church of Rome is seen to exercise special authority. Meanwhile, there is no other method or candidate or claimant for exercising the same higher authority when it is necessary for resolving disputed questions concerning the Church's life and teachings.

Rome then steps in to decide because, quite simply, somebody has to. Rome's authority is accepted in such cases because it is seen that intervention by higher authority is necessary. Christ gave ultimate authority to Peter; the testimony of the New Testament is clear about that. What remained to be worked out by his successors were the details of how this authority would actually be applied in various cases—and how it would be recognized by the rest of the Church.

However, it would be a serious mistake to conclude that merely because in specific cases there did not seem to be clear acknowledgment by other bishops of the Roman primacy as we now understand it, no such primacy existed. No, it would be both simpler and more accurate to conclude that all the implications of the conferral of special authority on Peter by Christ to be handed down to his successors had not yet been fully worked out in practice and were, therefore, not always fully understood within the Church until after the fact.

Not even the popes who exercised it understood all the implications of their authority until cases arose requiring that it be tested. It was probably impossible to know before the fact whether a pope had the authority to excommunicate entire Churches, as Pope Victor did on the Easter question; it was impossible to know this until the case arose of a local Church refusing to go along with the considered judgment of the rest of the Church. Only through experiencing such situations did the Church—and the popes—gradually learn what was fully involved in the power to "bind and loose" and in the commission to "confirm the brethren".

What is clear from the correspondence between the major Churches in the middle of the third century on the matter of readmitting lapsed Christians to communion is that the bishops of Alexandria, Antioch, and Carthage—the major sees—acknowledged the special position of the bishop of Rome and conceded greater authority to him.

At the same time, they did not see this greater authority as binding on them in the sense of legal jurisdiction. Rather, they seemed to consider themselves the pope's roughly equal partners as bishops and heads of individual Churches. All ended up adopting the Roman position, but they did so only after conducting their own synods on the issue and independently reaching their own decisions.

Another interesting fact about these exchanges between the principal bishops of the day is that Pope Cornelius proved to be no Pope Victor. His letters urge and persuade, even cajole and complain—especially about the thorn in his side, the antipope Novatian and his party. There is little suggestion in Cornelius of trying to lay down the law from above. This should not surprise us: each pope has his own style and fills the shoes of the Fisherman to the best of his ability. Cornelius had been a "compromise candidate" for the papal office to begin with, one of the Roman priests less in view; he did not by nature possess the confidence of a Victor.

St. Cyprian of Carthage *was* a very confident individual and a dominant figure in the whole affair. His writings are very important for our understanding of the Church in this whole era. Yet St. Cyprian did *not* concede a clear primacy, as he understood the idea, to his Roman colleague. The evidence is mixed, but Cyprian generally emphasized a strong belief in the collegiality of the episcopate. He respected the Roman see in particular and lavished unusual respect and praise on Cornelius personally, writing at the time of that pope's election that "all our colleagues ... firmly approve and maintain you and your communion, that is, the unity and also the charity of the Catholic Church" (*Epistolae*, XLVIII).

But in his important work *On the Unity of the Church*, Cyprian outlines his own ecclesiological theory, in which the authority conferred on Peter by Christ is shared equally by the other apostles and their successors. Quoting not only Matthew 16:18–19 about the rock but John 21:16–17 about feeding the sheep, Cyprian writes:

> Upon one man he builds the Church, and, although he grants to all the apostles after his resurrection an equal power and says: "As the Father has sent me, even so send I you.... Receive the Holy Spirit. If you forgive the sins of any, they are forgiven; if you retain the sins of any, they are retained" (Jn 20:22–23)—yet that he might make clear their unity, he established by his authority that unity at the beginning as if it originated in one man. Assuredly the rest of the apostles were equal to Peter, endowed with the same partnership in honor and power, but the beginning was made in unity, that the Church of Christ might manifestly be one. (*De Catholicae Ecclesiae Unitate*, 4)

Cyprian's idea seems to be that Christ first entrusted authority to Peter primarily to show that the bishops should act as one, not that the successors of Peter inherited his special authority. The evidence of *unity* is not entirely consistent about this however. Two versions of the text have come down to us. In one of them, specific language is found that does appear to accord a special primacy to Rome (although this is not consistent with the passage just quoted); in the other version this language is missing.

Some scholars believe the language in favor of the primacy was interpolated later by partisans of Rome; others believe it was Cyprian's original language, which he then decided to drop after a falling out with a successor of Cornelius that we shall presently describe. This is another scholarly question that will probably never be settled on purely academic grounds, for the simple reason that we lack the evidence needed to resolve the question.

Neither can the matter be resolved from Cyprian's letters, since in one of them (XXVII) he repeats the idea expressed above, namely, that "You are Peter" referred to the whole episcopate. In another (LIX) he speaks of the Church of Rome as the *Ecclesia principalis unde unitas sacertotalis exorta est*, "the principal Church from which priestly unity has sprung".

St. Cyprian certainly took the question of Church unity very seriously because he considered the Church herself essential for our salvation. Elsewhere in this treatise, he declares:

> Whoever is separated from the Church and joined to an adulteress is separated from the promises of the Church, nor shall he who forsakes Christ's Church attain Christ's rewards. He is a stranger, a blasphemer, an enemy. He who has not the Church for his mother has God no more for his Father. If a man could escape who was outside the ark of Noah, then he also may escape who is outside the Church. . . . (Ibid., 6)

Cyprian's view of the Church's unity is a lofty one, but his theory of the equality of bishops in the Church is less than compelling, especially as it seems to ground the authority of all the bishops in the commission given to Peter alone; but Christ gave authority both to Peter alone (cf. Mt 16:17–19) and separately to the apostles (including Peter) (cf. Mt 18:18–19; *passim*).

It is little short of amazing that Cyprian could ever have held such a view, considering the very superior and unequal role that the bishop of Carthage always played among the bishops of Africa. The bishop of Carthage automatically chaired all the African synods and was otherwise the uncontested leader in everything connected with the African Church; the question of equality never entered in. From these considerations alone, Cyprian should have been able to appreciate the inevitability of the Roman primacy in the Church as a whole. After all, the bishop of Carthage was equally inevitably the primate over the Church of Africa!

As respected as St. Cyprian of Carthage was among the ancient Christian Fathers and writers, the Church did not accept his view of the equality of all bishops in the way that he probably formulated it. What would turn out to be the Church's definitive view of the matter was already quite clear even before the death of Cyprian, even though the great bishop of Carthage had only a few more years to live. He would be martyred in the year 258 under Emperor Valerian. Yet even before then, a bishop of Rome would expressly invoke Christ's commission to Peter as the justification for the papal primacy in the whole Church.

X.

Pope Cornelius died in exile in June 252, not long after the smoldering Decian persecution had been rekindled by Emperor Gallus. Cornelius was succeeded by Pope St. Lucius I, who was in office less than a year (June 253–March 254) when he was succeeded by Pope St. Stephen I (254–257). Stephen, while Cyprian was still alive, seems to have been the first pope to cite Matthew 16:18–19 explicitly in support of the doctrine that the popes enjoyed supreme authority in the whole Church by virtue of Christ's original commission to Peter.

That Stephen was apparently first to cite this famous passage does not mean that the popes who preceded him did not know about the passage or think of it as a source of their authority; it merely means that we do not possess any citations made of it by a pope prior to Stephen. We have already noted that we have no actual words from any pope on any subject between the Letter of Clement at the end of the first century and the two letters of Pope St. Cornelius included in the collection of St. Cyprian's Letters (*Epistolae*) in the middle of the third.

We possess no document in which Pope Stephen I expressly claimed the primacy. That he did make such a claim we can infer from reading the vigorous reactions against him, notably in letters from St. Cyprian and from Firmilian, the bishop of Caesarea in Cappadocia (Kayseri in what is today central Turkey). Firmilian's letter to Cyprian refers to Pope Stephen as one "who brags so loudly of the seat of his episcopate and who insists that he holds his succession from Peter, on whom the foundations of the Church were laid" (*Epistolae* LXXV, 17). This is an unmistakable reference to an earlier use by Stephen of Matthew 16:18–19, asserting papal authority.

The principal issue in dispute at that point was whether those who had been baptized by heretics outside the Church needed to be rebaptized when they sought entry into the Catholic communion. On this subject, Roman tradition was clear: when properly performed in the name of the holy Trinity—Father, Son, and Holy Spirit—the sacrament of baptism was objectively valid, regardless of the possible erroneous beliefs or moral failure of the one performing it. To repeat the sacrament would be sacrilegious.

It is possible that, just as Pope Victor, some sixty years before, had attempted to secure conformity in the matter of Easter observance, Pope Stephen may have intensified this later dispute by demanding that the Eastern Churches either bring their practice into conformity with that of Rome or place themselves outside of communion with Rome. This was the position Pope Stephen took. Eusebius reports that Stephen "thought that no innovations should be made contrary to traditions that had prevailed from ancient times", and that he was "greatly offended" that Cyprian thought that rebaptism was called for.

Quoting St. Dionysius of Alexandria, Eusebius records that Stephen "had written before respecting Helenus [bishop of Tarsus] and Firmilian, and all those from Cilicia and Cappadocia and Galatia, and all the nations adjoining, that he would not have communion with them on this account, because, he said, they rebaptized heretics" (*Ecclesiastical History*, VII, 3 and 5).

The bishop of Alexandria, St. Dionysius, seems to have been the one who consulted Stephen regarding rebaptism in the first place because "no little controversy" concerning it had arisen (ibid., 2). This is yet another early example of referring a disputed question to Rome. Stephen then wrote to all the Churches in the East to set them straight. In style, this pope resembled Pope Victor, who had followed the same procedure two generations earlier.

After the controversy became transformed by reactions against Stephen's position, St. Dionysius of Alexandria again wrote to Stephen counseling peace and a more moderate approach—even though, once again, Alexandria firmly agreed with the Roman discipline in the matter. It should have been clear to all that this question involved more than mere discipline; it involved doctrine; it was a matter about which the Churches really did have to agree; therefore, it was a matter on which Rome was bound to be "intransigent".

Pope Stephen encountered particularly vigorous opposition to his position in North Africa, where he was already engaged in disputes over appeals from two bishops in Spain who had lapsed and about whose depositions Rome and Carthage had disagreed; and also over what Cyprian considered to be Pope Stephen's dilatoriness in dealing with the bishop of Arles in Gaul, one Marcianus, who had adopted rigid Novatianist views and was refusing to grant even deathbed reconciliation to formerly lapsed but now repentant Christians.

For a bishop who apparently did not accept the Roman primacy in the full sense, Cyprian was certainly ready enough to grant virtual plenary authority to the pope as soon as it was a question of getting the latter to act in the way Cyprian wanted him to act! He wrote to Stephen as follows, granting thereby that the pope had authority over the Gallic episcopate: "You should write very plainly to our colleagues in the episcopate in Gaul, that they no longer allow the obstinate and proud Marcianus to insult our college [of bishops]" (*Epistolae* LXVIII).

The business of rebaptism was something else again. Cyprian vigorously contested Pope Stephen's position that those baptized by heretics should not be rebaptized if their original baptism had been valid. The bishop of Carthage even convoked two African synods, in 255 and 256, which dutifully confirmed his and the African Church's variant position that rebaptism was necessary for those who had been baptized by heretics. Clearly Cyprian was prepared to act on his theory that the pope did not enjoy full primacy in the Church, at least on what Cyprian considered to be a disciplinary matter.

Pope Stephen was not impressed and even refused to receive the envoys sent to Rome by the African prelate to argue further about a matter the pope considered settled. Rebaptism was an innovation that violated the Church's authentic tradition. Rome had spoken. In a manner made familiar by heretics and dissenters of all eras, St. Cyprian of Carthage went on treating a firm decision of legitimate Church authority as an invitation to further debate and discussion.

On this issue the great St. Cyprian was clearly in the wrong. His own letters reflect his pain and perplexity—he who had so often and so effectively fought for orthodoxy, few more effectively in the Church's long history—at suddenly finding himself part of a condemned and outlawed faction in the Church by virtue of a decision rendered by the bishop of Rome.

St. Cyprian redeemed himself by his glorious martyrdom in the year 258. The account of the martyrdom of St. Cyprian of Carthage is one of the most moving of all the *acta* that have come down to us from the Church of the early martyrs. We can quote only this climax of the ancient account:

> Galerius Maximus the proconsul ordered that Cyprian the bishop should be brought before him on the morrow where he sat in the Hall Sauciolum. When he had been brought before him, Galerius Maximus the proconsul said to Cyprian the bishop, "Are you Thascius Cyprianus?"
>
> Cyprian the bishop answered: "I am."
>
> Galerius Maximus the proconsul said: "Have you taken on yourself to be pope of persons holding sacrilegious opinions?"
>
> Cyprian the bishop answered: "Yes."
>
> Galerius Maximus the proconsul said: "The most sacred emperors have commanded you to perform the rite."
>
> Cyprian the bishop answered: "I refuse."
>
> Galerius Maximus the proconsul said: "Consider your own interest."
>
> Cyprian the bishop answered: "Do as you are bid. In so clear a case there is no need for consideration."
>
> Galerius Maximus, having conferred with the council, gave sentence hardly and reluctantly in these terms: "You have long lived in the holding of sacrilegious opinions, and have joined with yourself very many members of an abominable conspiracy, and have set yourself up as an enemy of the gods of Rome and religious ordinances; nor have the pious and most sacred emperors, Valerian and Gallienus, the Augusti, and Valerian, the most noble Caesar, been able to recall you to the observance of their rites. And therefore since you have been convicted as the contriver and standard-bearer in most atrocious crimes, you shall be an example to those whom by

your wickedness you have joined with you: discipline shall be vindicated in your blood." With these words he read from his tablets the sentence: "It is our pleasure that Thascius Cyprianus should be executed by the sword."

Cyprian the bishop said: "Thanks be to God...."

So did the blessed Cyprian suffer, and his body was laid out hard by to content the curiosity of the heathen. Thence it was removed by night, and, accompanied by tapers and torches, was conducted with prayers in great triumph to the burial-ground.... A few days later Galerius the proconsul died. The most blessed martyr Cyprian suffered on the fourteenth day of September under the emperors Valerian and Gallienus, [but] in the reign of our Lord Jesus Christ, to whom belong honor and glory forever and ever. Amen.

The date was September 14, 258. St. Augustine, another great African bishop, would remark more than a century later that "if in this fruitful vine there was anything to prune away, the heavenly Father performed this cleansing action by his death." The Church today commemorates Saints Cornelius and Cyprian together on the same day, September 16.

Pope St. Stephen I had died the year before. Stephen was succeeded by Pope St. Sixtus II (257–258), who, in his short reign, apparently achieved a reconciliation with the Church in Africa on the rebaptism question while nevertheless holding fast to his predecessor's strong position on the matter. No doubt some of these controversies suddenly seemed of considerably less moment once active persecution was rekindled under Valerian. Widespread executions helped concentrate people's minds on what was important.

It is of some importance to our thesis, though, that in all of these ancient ecclesiastical disputes—the celebration of Easter, the readmittance to communion of lapsed penitents, and the acceptance into the Church without rebaptism of those validly baptized by heretics—it was the teaching and practice of the Church of Rome that came to prevail throughout the Catholic Church.

Pope St. Sixtus II himself died a martyr in the same persecution of 258 that claimed St. Cyprian. Emperor Valerian, in 257, had issued a severe edict flatly prohibiting any religious assemblies and calling for the summary execution of all Christian bishops, priests, and deacons. This renewal of the Decian persecution by Valerian was expressly aimed at the bishops. Its intent was to destroy the leadership of the Church as the most effective way to destroy the Church herself.

Pope Sixtus was surprised by the authorities while celebrating the Eucharist and preaching to a congregation in a cemetery where he had taken refuge with some of his little flock. He was beheaded on the spot, along with four of his deacons. Another of his deacons was the famous St. Lawrence, who when ordered by the prefect of the city to hand over the Church's valuables, assembled the poor and sick and presented them to the prefect. "Here", he said, "is the Church's treasure." St. Lawrence was roasted on a gridiron, according to various accounts which have come down to us, including one by St. Ambrose of Milan.

A century later, after the end of the active persecutions, Pope Damasus (366–384) erected a plaque commemorating the martyrdom of Pope Sixtus in a Christian cemetery for the crime of celebrating Mass. The legend of Pope St. Sixtus II grew, and he became one of the most beloved martyrs of Christian antiquity. Fittingly, the Roman Canon of the Mass to this day commemorates him along with Pope Cornelius and Bishop Cyprian, following the names of the first three successors of St. Peter: "Linus, Cletus, Clement, Sixtus, Cornelius, Cyprian ..."

XI.

The persecution of the Church by emperors Decius, Gallus, and Valerian through the decade of the 250s lasted until the year 261, when Emperor Gallienus (260–268), the son of Valerian, issued a rescript not only ending the persecution but actually ordering the return to the Church of church buildings, cemeteries, and other confiscated properties. This action constituted the empire's first official recognition of Christianity as a quasi-legal, property-owning entity.

There would be yet one more major effort by the Roman Empire to destroy Christianity: the great persecution by Emperor Diocletian more than forty years later, in 303. For the moment, however, the Church was at peace. The second half of the third century witnessed the consolidation and regularization of the Church's life in more ways than one. Membership in the Church is said to have doubled during this period and, by the beginning of the fourth century, amounted to ten percent or more of the empire's population.

Succeeding the martyred Pope St. Sixtus II was Pope St. Dionysius (260–268). He was not elected for nearly two years after the death of his predecessor, owing to the severity of the ongoing persecution. Yet his time in the chair of Peter was destined to be relatively peaceful, as would also be true of the next three popes, bringing the Church into the fourth century, when so many developments of enduring importance in her life and history would come about.

Fourth-century developments would include the legalization of Christianity and its later adoption as the official religion of the Roman Empire; the convoking of the Church's first two ecumenical councils, which would produce the Creed the Church professes to this day; the fixing of the canon of inspired writings of apostles and apostolic men that comprise the twenty-seven books of the New Testament; and, not least, the consolidation of the primacy of the see of Rome in the Catholic Church.

Pope St. Dionysius seems to have been the first bishop to divide the capital city—still predominantly pagan—into areas that would later become "parishes", assigning to each the care of a Christian cemetery, some of which were located outside the city walls. Dionysius also continued the long-established tradition of the Church of Rome of providing generous help and support to distressed Christians everywhere. So notable was his activity that more than a century later the Eastern Father St. Basil the Great (d. 379) recalled in one of his letters the help and encouragement provided by Pope Dionysius to the then beleaguered Church in Cappadocia, which included funds for ransoming Christians in captivity.

The pontificate of St. Dionysius witnessed at least two significant recorded incidents strongly supporting our thesis that the Church of Rome already enjoyed a recognized primacy. Even though not yet defined as it eventually would be, it was nevertheless very real. It was also a primacy that was increasingly recognized in the Church in both the East and the West.

The first of these incidents from the pontificate of Pope St. Dionysius had to do with an ongoing controversy over two heresies, Sabellianism and Adoptionism, earlier forms of Arianism, Nestorianism, and Monophysitism, which would convulse the Church in the fourth and fifth centuries and beyond. As we have seen, these heresies would call forth the great Trinitarian and Christological definitions of the Church's first four great councils.

The Sabellians believed that Jesus Christ represented merely a temporary manifestation in the flesh of the eternal God.

The Adoptionists believed very nearly the opposite: that Jesus Christ was a mere man who had, through love and suffering, achieved a kind of divine status. Around this time the Sabellians were actively promoting their views in the Pentapolis region west of Egypt (modern Cyrenaica in Eastern Libya). The bishop of Alexandria, also named Dionysius, exercised a degree of authority over the Churches of this area that, like the Roman primacy over the whole Church, though not strictly defined as a legal jurisdiction, was no less real.

Just as the bishops of Rome considered it a duty to insist upon correct doctrine even in distant Churches, Bishop Dionysius of Alexandria considered it his duty to admonish the bishops of the Pentapolis region concerning the dangers of Sabellianism. His authority to do this may not have been spelled out clearly in juridical terms, but he nevertheless felt the responsibility to do it. In his zeal to persuade them of the error of the heresy of Sabellianism, however, he employed in his letter some phrases that seemed to say there was a difference in substance between the Father and the Son, thus reducing the divine Son to the status of a creature and falling into Adoptionism, the error opposite from Sabellianism.

Some of the clergy in Alexandria, concerned about what seemed to be doctrinal error on the part of their own bishop, decided that something needed to be done. These Egyptian priests decided that any question of doctrinal error on the part of the bishop of Alexandria needed to be referred to the bishop of Rome. And this is what they did.

Pope St. Dionysius had already had some experience of his namesake in Alexandria. As a priest, he had been involved in the efforts of Pope Stephen to establish a uniform Church practice regarding the readmission of validly baptized heretics without rebaptism. As we have said, during that particular controversy, Dionysius of Alexandria, while agreeing with Pope Stephen that there was no necessity for rebaptism, had nevertheless written to the pope, counseling restraint and moderation while attempting to impose uniformity on the Church. Now this moderate peacemaker, occupying the second see of Christendom, Alexandria, was himself being accused of heresy by some of his own priests—a heresy involving a fundamental doctrine, the nature of Jesus Christ himself. How was the pope to handle such a case?

Pope St. Dionysius showed himself to be both wise and tactful. Though he was conscious that he had the right and the duty to act in the case, he refrained from issuing any hasty correction or condemnation of his Alexandrian colleague. The action he did take proved to be a precedent and even a model for similar actions that would be taken in similar cases by his successors, notably Pope St. Leo the Great, when he prepared his famous *Tome* on Christology for the instruction of the bishops at the Council of Chalcedon in the fifth century.

Pope Dionysius drew up a document carefully laying out the elements of the Church's understanding of what would become known as Christology, carefully avoiding the extremes of overemphasizing Christ's divinity, as the Sabellians (and later the Monophysites) did, and of overemphasizing his humanity, as the Adoptionists (and later the Arians and Nestorians) did. Christ was both fully divine and fully human. This truth represented the authentic faith that had been handed down in the Church, and now it was being authoritatively recalled and restated by the bishop of Rome.

Pope Dionysius also convened in Rome what St. Athanasius of Alexandria in the following century would describe as a "great synod" to consider the whole question. According to Athanasius, this Roman synod convened by

Pope Dionysius "declared that the Word of God was not a thing made nor a creature, but his own inseparable and begotten Son, of the substance of the Father" (*De Decretis Nicaenae Synodi*, 21).

The results of Dionysius' Roman synod were distributed throughout the Church. In his reply to the pope, Bishop Dionysius of Alexandria protested that his words had been misinterpreted as tending toward Adoptionism. "I have proved that their charge against me is false," he wrote to the pope, "namely, that I deny that Christ is of the same substance as God. For although I do say that I have not found the word [*homo-ousios*] anywhere in Holy Scripture, still my argument . . . is in harmony with this idea" (ibid., 26).

We have here a bishop of Rome, Pope St. Dionysius, along with a Roman synod expressly convened by him to consider the question, officially teaching that Jesus Christ is "of the same substance [*homo-ousios*]" as God the Father. This was some sixty years before the Council of Nicaea adopted and enshrined forever in the Creed of the Church this same term *homo-ousios*. From the context, the pope evidently was already insisting upon the use of this term as a test of orthodox Christology.

Moreover, this same pope and his Roman synod taught that Jesus Christ was necessarily "true God and true man"—more than a hundred and eighty years before the Council of Chalcedon would enshrine this phrase forever as an unchangeable article of the faith. Here is surely a classic and prototypical instance from the second half of the third century of how the popes have acted throughout the history of the Church to strengthen the brethren (cf. Lk 22:32), including especially the bishops of the Church.

We also have a bishop of Alexandria, another Dionysius, hastening to dispel any possible doubts that his own doctrinal position was ever anything but entirely in conformity with the position now carefully spelled out by the bishop of Rome and his Roman synod. All this took place in the 260s, well before the Church made clear in her formal documents that the doctrine of *all* her Churches *must* be in conformity with that of the Roman Church. This bishop of Alexandria nevertheless showed himself to be very conscious of the need for this conformity.

On the basis of facts about this affair—an affair that originated with the clergy in Alexandria appealing to Rome—we cannot definitely assert that all parties clearly understood that Rome had a strict and well-defined juridical right to call to account another metropolitan bishop, the bishop of the second see of Christendom. We can affirm that Pope St. Dionysius was conscious of having a *responsibility* to act as he did and to lay out the correct doctrine about Christ that had been handed down in the Church.

At the same time, Bishop Dionysius of Alexandria was equally conscious that his Church needed to teach in harmony with the bishop of Rome—even if this meant that he had to back away from positions perhaps hastily taken while attempting to address a somewhat different problem. Furthermore, the priests of Alexandria seem to have been conscious that if their own bishop ever fell into error, they still had recourse to the bishop of Rome.

This whole incident constituted an important precedent for what would eventually become a juridical relationship, with Rome exercising jurisdiction even over the metropolitans of the ancient apostolic Churches, which themselves exercised jurisdiction over the Churches in their respective regions.

Nearly a century later, in 341, Pope Julius I (337–352) would insist that St. Athanasius was entitled to another trial after that great bishop of Alexandria had been tried and deposed by kangaroo-type court proceedings organized by some of his Arianizing bishop–enemies in the East. At that time Pope Julius intervened to remind the Eastern bishops that it was the "custom" for such cases to be referred first to Rome, and for "a just decision to be rendered from this spot". By that time, the bishops of Rome rarely failed to describe incidents supporting their primacy as established Church "customs" in this fashion!

St. Athanasius recorded for posterity the essential facts about this important Roman intervention by Pope Julius I on his behalf (*Apologia contra Arianos*, 35). Nevertheless, this intervention was entirely consistent with the earlier one by Pope Dionysius, which aimed to insure the doctrinal orthodoxy of Bishop Dionysius of Alexandria—and the Church as a whole in the process. This was a task that devolved upon the bishops of Rome because it was a task given to Peter by Christ.

XII.

Another incident from the second half of the third century indicating that a Roman primacy was recognized, even in the East, took place at the end of the 260s. This incident involved the third apostolic see of the ancient Church, the see of Antioch (Syria).

The bishop of Antioch, a certain Paul from the Syrian village of Samosata, enjoyed the protection of a local ruler, the Arabian Queen Zenobia of Palmyra, who controlled a part of the eastern Roman Empire with the consent of Emperor Gallienus. The father of Gallienus, Valerian, had been disastrously defeated by the Persians in the year 260, and the Roman Empire had not yet recovered its full strength in that part of the world. Queen Zenobia held local sway for the moment; so, consequently, did her protege, Paul of Samosata, in the bishopric of Antioch.

As bishop of Antioch, Paul was a frank Adoptionist heretic. He even went so far as to forbid the singing of hymns to Christ as God, and he expressly taught that Christ the man had become holy and united to the Father only through his human effort and suffering. In addition to Paul's false teaching, his luxurious style of living dismayed and scandalized the bishops of the East, and at least two local Eastern synods of bishops were held in an attempt to bring him to heel. These were presided over by Firmilian, the Cappadocian bishop we have already encountered in connection with the rebaptism question.

As a result of these synodal efforts to unseat him, Paul of Samosata made repeated promises to his fellow Eastern bishops to reform both his doctrine and his life, but he never got around to fulfilling them. His case illustrates how cumbersome it could sometimes be to attempt to enforce the legitimate doctrinal and disciplinary decisions of the Church through the method of calling local synods or councils. The difficulties encountered in this case would be compounded and intensified in the following century, when the full fury of the Arian heresy would strike the whole Church and alienate many of the bishops from the authentic faith and practice of the Church.

Earlier efforts having failed, in the year 268 or 269, another synod consisting of some seventy bishops, priests, and deacons met again in Antioch, its constituents determined to deal once and for all with the heretical and loose-living bishop Paul of Samosata. This synod solemnly decreed the deposition of the unworthy bishop and elected Domnus to replace him.

Significant for our purposes here is what this Antiochian synod decided needed to be done in order to secure the approval of the whole Church for the solemn decision it had reached. The legality of such a synod deposing a bishop had not been established. Of course the provocation provided by Paul of Samosata had been very great, and the bishops at the synod were confident that they had done the right and necessary thing. Nevertheless, the need for the approval of the whole Church for what they had done was still keenly felt.

As Eusebius of Caesarea recounts, the bishops of this Antiochian synod decided to do the following:

> They drew up by common consent a letter addressed to *Dionysius, bishop of the Romans*, and to Maximus, bishop at Alexandria, and . . . all the provinces. In it they made clear their own fidelity and the perverted heterodoxy of Paul and the arguments and debates which they had held with him and they depicted besides the whole life and character of the man. . . ." (*Ecclesiastical History*, VII, 30, emphasis added)

This letter from a late third-century synod in Antioch, addressed to the two principal apostolic sees of Christendom—Rome in the first place—was also addressed in general to what the synodal bishops styled "the whole Catholic Church under heaven". From the context, it is clear that the approval of the bishop of Rome was the first and most necessary thing thought to be required in order to legitimize the synod's action.

The judgment against Paul of Samosata seems to have been accepted in Rome, either by Pope St. Dionysius himself—who died in 268—or by his successor, Pope St. Felix I (269–274). But there was a problem: Paul of Samosata, still protected by Queen Zenobia, refused to step down. Only when the new Roman emperor, Aurelian (270–275), striving to repair the empire's sagging fortunes in the East, defeated the proud queen's forces—in the year 272—and brought her back a prisoner to Rome did it become possible actually to depose him from the see of Antioch.

In what was probably the first recorded instance of Christians at odds with one another appealing directly to Caesar, the orthodox Catholics of Antioch petitioned Emperor Aurelian, asking that state power be employed to compel Paul and his followers to withdraw from the churches of Antioch and allow the rightful bishop, Domnus, in accordance with the decisions of the Antiochian synod, to take charge of them. Eusebius tells us about this petition and its results:

> Since Paul refused to surrender the church house, a petition was sent to the emperor Aurelian and he decided the question with great justice, ordering that the buildings should be given to that party to whom *the bishops of Italy and the city of Rome should award it.* . . . (*Ecclesiastical History*, VII, 30, emphasis added)

Perhaps for convenience, Emperor Aurelian decided to place the matter of the Church's properties of Antioch in the hands of the bishops in or closest to the empire's capital city. Aurelian's decision provides yet another piece of evidence concerning the preeminence of the Church of Rome. The bishop of Rome was by then recognized without question as the head of the bishops of Italy. Even the emperor cannot have been ignorant of the position of the bishop of Rome within the Church—his decision demonstrates that he understood perfectly well that Church property in Antioch should go to the bishop designated by Rome as being in communion with Rome. All this took place more than forty years before the formal legalization of Christianity within the empire.

Pope Felix I continued to act along the same lines as his immediate predecessor, Pope Dionysius. Besides taking charge of executing the judgment against Paul of Samosata, Felix demonstrated his leadership in other ways. More than a hundred and eighty years later, at the Council of Chalcedon in 451, a letter written by Felix was read and entered into the record. This letter, addressed to the bishop and clergy of Alexandria in Egypt, explained the orthodox view of Christ in contrast to the heretical view of the Adoptionists. Apparently this pope, too, considered it his duty to formulate correct doctrine and instruct other Churches concerning it. St. Cyril of Alexandria had quoted approvingly from this letter at the Council of Ephesus in 431.

Thus, in the 270s, Pope St. Felix I was writing to instruct the Churches of the East that Christ, "being perfect God . . . became at the same time also perfect man, incarnate from the virgin. . . ." Of even greater significance, in the matter of Paul of Samosata, the seventy Eastern bishops of the Antiochian synod and Emperor Aurelian spontaneously turned "first" to Rome as the proper place to insure the appropriate final settlement of the matter.

XIII.

The fourth century, destined to be one of the most momentous in the Church's entire history, began with the unleashing in 303 of the Roman Empire's last great persecution under Diocletian (284–305).

Diocletian's persecution was devastating. Churches were ordered destroyed, sacred books were to be surrendered, and sacrifices were to be offered to the emperor on pain of torture or death. A further edict forbade Christians to assemble for worship. The persecution was carried out more zealously in the East than in the West. The fury of this Diocletian persecution even affects our ability today to trace the early history of the popes, since the library and archives of the Church of Rome were destroyed. This alone would account for the paucity of Roman documentation of the early popes. We can gauge how serious the loss has been when we consider just two such important documents for our purposes as the letter of Pope Cornelius describing the condition of the Church of Rome in the middle of the third century, and the letter of Bishop Firmilian of Cappadocia attesting to the earliest documented citation of Matthew 16:18–19 in support of papal authority from a pope, Stephen I. Both of these letters were preserved and handed down from a non-Roman source—as it happens, they were included among the letters of St. Cyprian of Carthage.

There is a tradition that at the outbreak of the Diocletian persecution, Pope Marcellinus (296–304), apostatized. We have no details. Eusebius simply says that Pope Marcellinus was "overtaken by the persecution" (*Ecclesiastical History*, VII, 32); But later, in Emperor Constantine's reign, the name of this pope was omitted from the Roman calendar. Three quarters of a century later, Pope Damasus I (366–384), when composing verse tributes and inscribing them on plaques dedicated to the popes of the period, also omitted Marcellinus.

More than a century after that, the Donatist heretics of North Africa brought forward a series of accusations against Marcellinus. The Donatist case against him was vitiated, however, by the fact that these sectarians included with their accusations the names of three Roman priests who later became popes and served honorably: Marcellus, Miltiades, and Sylvester. The Donatists considered the Roman see itself polluted, so they thought that this pollution extended to all of the incumbents of the see.

On the basis of other evidence, it seems that none of the Donatist accusations against Marcellus, Miltiades, or Sylvester was true. Thus it is hard to assess what the truth may have been concerning the unfortunate Pope Marcellinus. St. Augustine, more than a century later, considered all of the Donatist accusations to have been slanders based on "palpable distortion of the documents" (*De Unico Baptismo*).

The Diocletian persecution, fierce as it was, failed to destroy the Church. It finally ended in 311, and Christianity became formally legalized in 313. Since the empire had been unable to defeat the Christians, it was getting ready to join them! The stage was being set for a century of great developments in the history of the Church.

The new era was inaugurated, not by actions initiated by the Church herself, but by those of Emperor Constantine (306–337), the moving spirit behind the legal recognition of Christianity. More than a quarter of a century later, this emperor would himself be baptized; meanwhile, the legal disabilities under which the Church had labored from the beginning were being removed.

By the time of Constantine, the empire's center of gravity was shifting to the East. In 286, Emperor Diocletian had moved his capital from Rome to Nicomedia, a city in northwest Asia Minor on the Bosphorus. Constantine would eventually erect his new capital, Constantinople, in the same area, at Byzantium. This imperial shift to the East meant that the popes, like the city of Rome itself, were no longer at the center of many important events of the day.

Some have even adduced the relative decline of the city of Rome as an argument against the primacy of Rome in the early Church: if such important developments as the fashioning of the Church's basic Creed took place so far away from Rome, in and through the great ecumenical councils convoked in the early centuries by the Christian emperors, then how can it be maintained that the popes really were in charge of what was going on in the Church? This flawed argument is still frequently heard today, but it can be refuted.

First of all, possessing a primacy in the Church in no way means that the popes were always in charge of whatever was happening in the Church or that they themselves had to carry out developments in the Church's life. On the contrary, such eminently legitimate developments as the rise of monasticism and the establishment of rules for the consecrated religious life almost invariably came, not only from outside of the orbit of the papacy, but as often as not even from outside the orbit of the episcopacy. The same was often true of the development of Christian art and architecture, Christian schools, Christian charities, hospitals, universities—of Christian culture in general.

The role of the papacy and the episcopacy in many of these things was usually to put the Church's stamp of approval on them after the fact. Neither the pope nor the bishops were necessarily the primary actors in some of the most significant developments in the life of the Church; rather, they oversaw them, retaining the power of decision when official Church actions became necessary. From the time of Peter and the other apostles, the role of Church leaders was to oversee, not to monopolize, the development of the Church's life and teaching, and to provide key doctrinal and disciplinary decisions when required.

Papal primacy always meant a kind of oversight over the whole life and teaching of the Church, including the activities of the other bishops. The primacy of the pope always meant confirming the brethren, exactly as Jesus had told Peter (cf. Lk 22:32), not superseding the brethren. (Of course, special problems always arose for the popes if and when the brethren failed to do their jobs; some of the most notable of alleged papal usurpations in history have arisen because the popes have usually been determined to carry out their Christ-commissioned task, even when the other bishops were not carrying out theirs.) It is a misunderstanding of the Roman primacy to imagine that the popes were always directly involved in whatever was legitimately going on in the Church.

As far as the primacy itself was concerned, when Christianity finally was legalized and the power of the Roman Empire began to enter forcefully into the life and activities of the Church, it probably was a special favor of Providence that the supreme authority in the Church found itself somewhat removed from the new center of secular power. The Roman Empire, after all, was not destined to survive for the ages; the Church was. There were clashes enough between popes and emperors as things turned out; if the Roman emperors had remained in Rome with the popes right there under their thumbs, the result might well have been a reduction to subservience of the papacy. History has witnessed, instead, the slow working out over time in the development of the papacy of the consequences of Christ's original promise and charge to Simon Peter at Caesarea Philippi.

Even so, there were still not a few times the popes were reduced by the secular power to the lot of the "court bishops" of the East. The malady, later called Caesaropapism, afflicted the East more severely than the West, precisely because the Christian emperor was there. The papacy managed to survive, not only the Roman and Byzantine Empires, but also all the later power centers that succeeded these empires, whether monarchical, republican, or totalitarian.

With respect to our present subject, evidence for the Roman primacy continued to develop and multiply despite the shift of the center of gravity in imperial affairs, and even Church affairs, toward the East, where it remained for many centuries as a result of the location there of the Christian Roman emperors.

The first four great ecumenical councils of the Church show evidence of important Roman input, as we have seen in chapter 3. The same is true of some of the other actions of the fourth- and early fifth-century popes acting apart from the intense conciliar activity of this period. It is this papal activity, independent of the great councils with a bearing on the Roman primacy, that we shall now review.

Among the first actions concerning the Church taken by Constantine after his victory at the Battle of the Milvian Bridge in 312 were a series of very generous imperial benefactions made to the Church of Rome. To Pope St. Miltiades (311–314) Constantine presented the Lateran Palace, which had been the property of his wife Fausta. The popes had definitely emerged from underground at this point! Henceforth their residence was to be a royal palace given by the emperor himself.

The popes would maintain their primary residence in the Lateran for nearly a thousand years, and on the same site arose the great Roman Basilica of St. John Lateran, "the Mother Church of Christendom", *Mater et caput omnium ecclesiarum*—one of the four great Roman basilicas today and an architectural treasure of the Eternal City.

Either at that time or on a subsequent visit to Rome in 315, Constantine ordered the construction of a large basilica on the spot traditionally believed to be the tomb of St. Peter. Perhaps the most famous and most photographed church in the world, St. Peter's Vatican Basilica, with its magnificent dome completed by Michelangelo, as well as the great columns by Bernini that enclose the square in front of it, was later constructed on the same site as the fourth-century Constantinian basilica.

The emperor's mother, St. Helena, resided periodically at another palace near the Lateran. It was she who imported from Jerusalem a fragment believed to be from the True Cross, as well as other relics; over these treasures arose the present-day Roman Church of Santa Croce in Gerusalemme.

Although Constantine and his family were generous benefactors of the Church and the bishops of Rome, there is little evidence that the emperor interacted much with either Pope Miltiades or his successors. Legends crediting Miltiades' successor, Pope St. Sylvester I (314–335), with curing the emperor of leprosy and baptizing him at the font of the Lateran are fables indicative of what people believed about both the imperial power and papal authority. No doubt it was hard for people to imagine that the imperial power and papal authority would not somehow go together.

The same thing was surely also true of the so-called "Donation of Constantine", a document fabricated in the eighth century. According to this document, the first Christian emperor is supposed to have granted direct sovereignty over the city of Rome, as well as authority over the bishops, to Pope Sylvester I—and to have removed himself and his capital to the East precisely in order to leave the pope unrivaled in Rome.

While there may have been a happy Providence in the removal of the seat of imperial power from the locus of the apostolic see of Peter, it is unlikely that this was ever consciously intended by Constantine. All the evidence concerning Constantine's policies toward the Church tends to underline the aptness of the judgment of the modern Catholic historian Fr. Philip Hughes, that "the most serious flaw in all [Constantine's] ecclesiastical policy [was] practical neglect

of the Roman primacy, which he treated as non-existent"
(*A History of the Church*).

XIV.

Although Constantine removed the seat of his imperial government far from Rome and never accorded official recognition to the Roman primacy, it is not the case that this first
of Christian emperors had no dealings with the popes. Those
he did have illustrate his attitude toward the growing Church
he had legalized and, thereby, allied with the cause of the
Roman Empire, which was increasingly beset by troubles both
from within and without.

Shortly after Constantine's victory at the Milvian Bridge,
the Church in Africa petitioned him to help restore to his
see a bishop of Carthage who had been challenged. A large
number of African bishops had convened a schismatic synod
and voted to depose the rightful bishop, Caecilian, on grounds
that he had been ordained by Bishop Felix of Aptunga, who
had lapsed during Diocletian's persecution and turned over
the sacred books to the authorities without protest. Felix
was therefore considered a traitor, incapable of performing a
valid ordination. The African schismatics held that any of
the ordained who had lapsed thereby nullified their own ordinations. This was the beginning of the Donatist schism.

Both sides in this dispute in the Church of Africa appealed to the victorious general-emperor, apparently newly
turned Christian. Constantine was in Roman Gaul when
these appeals from Africa reached him. He decided to summon ten African bishops from each side in the dispute to
appear at a hearing and argue their respective cases; and he
appointed three bishops from Gaul to judge the case. Note

that the Africans *asked* for bishops from Gaul to judge their case, perhaps to keep the matter from falling into the hands of the bishop of Rome.

The emperor nevertheless specified that the hearing should take place in Rome. He forwarded all the documents in the case to Pope Miltiades and told him to settle the case justly after a thorough airing so that peace could be restored to the Church.

We do not know whether Constantine was following the precedent of his predecessor Aurelian in referring such a matter to the bishop of Rome or whether he was influenced by his principal ecclesiastical advisor, Bishop Hosius of Cordova, Spain, that this was the proper procedure to follow.

It is interesting that Pope Miltiades promptly turned the charge to him from the Roman emperor into a more ecclesiastically conventional Roman synod. Miltiades, apparently with the consent of the emperor, appointed fifteen more Italian bishops as judges. The hearing convened in a hall of the Lateran Palace on October 2, 313.

The leader of the African schismatics was Donatus. The members of his party would come to be called Donatists. Those of the African Catholic party led by Bishop Caecilian were referred to as the Caecilianists. Pope Miltiades tried to steer the tribunal toward a just and statesmanlike resolution of all the outstanding disputes between the parties.

In the end, Caecilian was upheld as the rightful bishop of Carthage, and it was further decided that the bishop first ordained in each of the cities where there was a disputed incumbent should be confirmed as the rightful occupant of the see. The results of this Roman tribunal were then duly communicated to Constantine and circulated among the other Churches.

As in the cases of some other deep-seated schisms and heresies, the solution arrived at by this Roman tribunal did not succeed in restoring peace to the Church as the Roman emperor had desired. The Donatists simply treated the judgment of the tribunal as null and void, appealing the judgment to the emperor even more vociferously than before. The heresy of Donatism was destined to have a lengthy history; St. Augustine would still be combatting the Donatists more than a century later.

Emperor Constantine, annoyed that the Roman tribunal had failed to secure the agreement of all the parties to the dispute, sent two more bishops to Carthage in an attempt to settle the issue on the spot. This action constituted an instance in which Constantine paid no attention to the fact that Rome had already ruled in the matter; he simply tried to settle it in his own way.

The mission carried out by Constantine's two emissary bishops also failed, as was probably inevitable. Presently both Caecilian and Donatus slipped back to Africa, placing themselves at the heads of their respective parties, and the Donatist schism raged on until the Vandals overran North Africa more than a century later, in 428, wreaking havoc among Donatists and Catholics alike.

As far as we know, Constantine never again referred a case to the bishop of Rome for judgment. From the Church's own standpoint, by working through a duly constituted tribunal for the restoration of Caecilian as the rightful bishop, Pope Miltiades *had* upheld the teaching and discipline of the Church, as far as lay within his power.

Moreover, he and his successors carried on in the same vein by constantly insisting on the correct teaching about the sacraments in the face of continuing Donatist denials and rejections. Through ongoing actions of this kind against the Donatists, the Church eventually formulated and promulgated what remains her unshakable conviction: the validity and efficaciousness of a sacrament are independent of the moral state of the minister of that sacrament.

In 314 Pope St. Miltiades was succeeded by Pope St. Silvester I (314–335), who was destined to occupy the see of Peter for more than twenty years, almost up to the time of Emperor Constantine's death. It does not appear from historical documents that Silvester had much contact with the emperor, regardless of legends that grew up concerning the two of them. An imperial document dating from some fifty years later states that "Bishop Silvester, when accused by sacrilegious men, carried his case to the emperor." We do not know what the event referred to here was all about.

If Pope Silvester did appeal any case to the emperor, this would not have affected his primacy within the Church. The popes at this time, like the bishops—as would remain true for centuries—were still subjects of the emperor, and therefore an appeal to him concerning accusations made against them would have been both natural and logical.

No sooner had Silvester become pope, though, than Emperor Constantine convened another synod, this time in Roman Gaul, in an attempt to deal yet one more time with the stubborn Donatists, who had never ceased agitating against the decision of the Roman tribunal of Pope Miltiades and against Bishop Caecilian. This subsequent gathering, the provincial Council of Arles, proved to be a kind of dress rehearsal for the first ecumenical Council of Nicaea, which would take place a decade later.

One way in which this provincial council in Gaul created a precedent for Nicaea was that Pope Silvester declined to attend. Stating that it was impossible for him to leave the seat of the apostles Peter and Paul, he instead sent two of his priests to represent him at Arles.

This was exactly what Pope Silvester would do a decade later in the Council of Nicaea in 325. Regarding that, the historian Eusebius of Caesarea recorded that "the bishop of the imperial city failed to attend because of his advanced age, but his priests were there and filled his place" (*Vita Constantini*, III, 7). Yet after Nicea, Silvester was to remain pope for ten more years, during which there is no evidence that he was ever constrained to limit his activities because of his age.

He may well have declined to go to Nicaea for reasons of papal policy. This seems to have been the case with respect to the earlier gathering in Arles. By the time Nicaea came along, Silvester had already established a precedent for not attending a gathering of bishops convoked by the Roman emperor; there was at least the possibility that the all-powerful emperor just might attempt to dictate the results of such a gathering. His record up to that point certainly could not have been reassuring for the pope.

What sort of papal-policy reasons might have prevented the bishop of Rome from attending convocations of bishops ordered by the Roman emperor? In the case of Arles, Silvester was being invited to participate as just another bishop in judging a case that from the Church's point of view had already been decided by the tribunal of Pope Miltiades. The emperor was simply ignoring the Church's judgment and trying to settle the case as he thought best.

Silvester would not have needed a great deal of acumen to perceive that in this case the primacy of Rome was hardly being respected by the emperor. It was surely better for Silvester to draw back (while not failing to remind the emperor that he occupied the chair of Peter and Paul), await the outcome of the Council of Arles, and then be in a position to exercise responsibilities as the Roman bishop. As set up by the emperor, neither the provincial Council of Arles nor the later ecumenical Council of Nicaea offered an ideal situation for the exercise of papal authority or oversight—far from it!

Another reason for declining to attend both councils might have been to demonstrate, even to the emperor, that the bishop of Rome was not at the beck and call of the secular power. Emperor Constantine took it for granted that the Church's bishops were at his disposal.

Yet another policy reason for Pope Silvester's absenting himself from both councils may well have been the early popes' need to *establish* the precedence and preeminence they were conscious of possessing. Neither the empire nor the emperor had more than a rudimentary appreciation of the Roman primacy at this point. One way to reenforce the idea of the Roman primacy was to make clear that if anyone wanted to confer with the bishop of Rome, it was necessary to go to *him*. This would have been a common, time-honored way of establishing precedence or authority.

There would have been nothing illegitimate or surprising in the employment of such methods by the popes as an assertion of the primacy they were conscious of possessing. It is not at all to be excluded that the early popes, needing to demonstrate their position within the Church, as well as of the independence they were trying to claim from an absolutist state, may well have decided to avoid attending councils convoked by the Roman emperor and, thus, at least potentially subject to his control.

The early popes were certainly obliged to try to find effective ways of exercising their power to decide, which had been handed down to them from Peter. At the same time, the popes did not normally mount open opposition to the councils called by the emperor; they even showed themselves ready enough on most occasions to send instructions to these councils (another indication of their basic attitude

toward them). They also regularly commented on and ratified the acts of such councils after the fact—or, in some cru-
cially important cases, *declined* to ratify certain acts or councils.

The development of local or provincial synods or councils
in the Church then, and, later, of general or ecumenical councils in no way undermined the nature and structure of the
Church as established by Christ. In fact, the councils proved
to be important decision-making bodies in the Church's history. The primacy conferred by Christ on Peter and transmitted to his successors, however, required from them a
different stance—that adopted by Pope St. Silvester in declining to attend either the provincial Council of Arles or
the ecumenical Council of Nicaea convoked by the Roman
emperor, sending legates instead to represent him and report
to him so that he could make his own independent judgments on the actions taken by these bodies.

The stance taken by Pope Silvester in this matter is further
evidence for the primacy of Rome in the early Church: the
possessor of this primacy never allowed himself to be classi-
fied as just another bishop among bishops. The bishop of
Rome was always special, as the early popes made clear in
ways that were available to them.

Constantine's provincial Council of Arles was not able to
reach any other judgment about the African Church than
had already been reached by the earlier Roman tribunal of
Pope Miltiades. Bishop Caecilian was reconfirmed in the see
of Carthage, and the Churches in communion with him were
recognized as belonging to the Catholic Church in North
Africa. The Council of Arles also issued canons recognizing
as valid the ordinations that had been made by those accused
of having been *traditores*; another canon from Arles forbade
the deposition of such accused traitors without strict evidence against them. These were typical Roman positions.

The Council of Arles also decreed that the custom of the Church of Rome in the matter of celebrating Easter should be followed everywhere. This important measure would be confirmed by the Council of Nicaea a decade later. Arles also abolished the African custom of rebaptizing converts from the sects, again upholding the Roman insistence that baptisms performed in the name of the Holy Trinity were valid. The bishops gathered at Arles thus did not fail to recognize the Roman primacy in certain important respects, even if Emperor Constantine continued to be rather myopic about it.

After completing its work, the Council of Arles addressed a profoundly respectful letter to Pope Silvester regretting that he had been unable to attend the gathering and transmitting its decisions to him, which he was then asked by the council to transmit to the Church at large.

Constantine realized, following the Council of Arles, that peace with the Donatists was not to be achieved in the manner he had originally hoped. The Donatists rejected the judgment of Arles as stubbornly as they had rejected the judgment of the Roman tribunal of Pope Miltiades. Constantine interviewed both Caecilian and Donatus and then, after the confirmation of the former in his bishopric, ordered African provincial officials to eject the Donatists forcibly from their churches in North Africa.

Not only was this imperial action—the use of state power to enforce a judgment of the Church's bishops—an ominous precedent for the future; it was ultimately unsuccessful as well, since by this time the Donatist heresy had become a broad social movement that no longer could be suppressed by force.

Constantine, meanwhile, moved East, where he soon became occupied with matters far removed from schisms and heresies in Africa. He wished to be nearer to the strategic borders threatened by the barbarians. Defense of these borders was the first task of the emperor. One of the principal ecclesiastical matters in which Constantine would nevertheless continue to be involved was the ecumenical Council of Nicaea (discussed in chapter 3), which he would convene in 325. Pope Silvester, for his part, reigned quietly for another ten years in a Rome that was no longer the seat of the empire. He died in 335. Constantine followed him to the grave in 337.

XV.

However much the early papacy may have seemed to be in eclipse during the pontificates of Miltiades and Silvester on account of the new phenomenon of a Roman emperor who was a Christian, the pope elected in 337, the year of Constantine's death, demonstrated amply during the fifteen years of his pontificate that the see of Peter had in no way been diminished; nor had it abandoned its claim to possess a primacy descending from Peter. On the contrary, the middle years of the fourth century would witness a clearer articulation of the nature of the Roman primacy and a greater consolidation of it than at any previous time in the history of the Church.

The new bishop of Rome was Pope St. Julius I (337–352), a forceful native Roman whose election followed the brief pontificate of Pope St. Marcus, or Mark (Jan.–Oct., 336). As we shall see, Julius did not hesitate to intervene confidently in doctrinal and disciplinary matters concerning the Church in both the East and the West. Since his pontificate coincided with the period when the Arianizing party in the Church was attempting to recover from its defeat at the Council of Nicaea, there were a number of occasions when the interventions of Julius proved necessary.

Pope Julius explicitly claimed the primacy in the Church and consistently showed by his actions that he really possessed it. Moreover, the special papal authority to which he laid claim was immediately and universally accepted in the West in his time; it was accepted with gratitude by more than a few bishops in the East as well, especially by those who were deposed or exiled by the actions of the Arianizing party and who, consequently, often appealed to Rome.

Pope Julius also saw his primacy articulated and upheld by a major Church provincial council held in 343 at Sardica (modern Sofia, Bulgaria)—as it was upheld and enforced by the imperial power itself through the decade of the 340s because of the sincere convictions of the Catholic co-emperor, Constans, one of Constantine's sons. This imperial patronage, however, would be dramatically reversed in the following decade for Julius' successor, Pope Liberius (352–366), under the frankly Arian sole emperor, Constantius II, another of Constantine's sons.

After the death of Constantine, the empire was divided among his three sons, Constantine II (337–340), Constans (337–350), and Constantius II (337–361). Constantine II and Constans very soon fell out with one another and, in a brief civil war, Constantine II was killed. For a full decade thereafter, Constans was the sole ruler of some two-thirds of the empire, including Italy, North Africa, Spain, Gaul, Britain, and the Balkan peninsula. As long as Constans lived and ruled, he expressly upheld the primacy of Pope Julius out of Catholic conviction.

The principal problem afflicting the Church in the late 330s and the 340s, and for a considerable period afterward, was the continuing drive of the Arianizing bishops, particularly in the East, to gain control of the Church. These bishops no longer espoused the simple and frank Arianism decisively condemned by the Council of Nicaea in 325; they often tried to protest that they were not Arians at all. Nevertheless, one of the things most of them agreed upon was that they did not accept the Creed of Nicaea, with its famous term *homo-ousios*, meaning "one in being", or "consubstantial". They also generally accepted communion with Arianizers of different shades, sometimes even with outright Arians as well.

The Arianizing party was at first led by Eusebius of Nicomedia, an astute ecclesiastical politician who had proved to be an evil genius for Constantine. The Council of Nicaea was hardly over before Eusebius had begun to rehabilitate some of the Arians and even Arius himself. Since Eusebius was the bishop of Nicomedia, Constantine's capital before the construction of Constantinople, he was in a position to exert influence on the emperor. (Eusebius of Nicomedia should not be confused with the historian Eusebius, whom we have quoted frequently in these pages. The latter was bishop of Caesarea in Palestine; he too turned out to be somewhat soft on the question of the *homo-ousios*, but he was not a leader of the Arianizing party in the way Eusebius of Nicomedia was.)

With the advent of the co-emperor Constantius II in the East after the death of Constantine, Eusebius of Nicomedia successfully ingratiated himself with the new ruler, who had strong Arian sympathies. Eusebius even got himself transferred out of Nicomedia and made bishop of Constantinople, the new imperial capital. From this commanding position, which he held until his death in 341, he was able to lead the Arianizing party quite effectively; sometimes the members of the party were styled "the Eusebians" after him.

The greatest obstacle to the triumph of the Eusebians in the East was the presence in the see of Alexandria of the great St. Athanasius (d. 373), the unyielding defender of the Council of Nicaea. Even before Constantine's death, the Eusebians had engineered a trumped-up trial, condemnation, and deposition of Athanasius by a synod held in 335 in Tyre (modern Lebanon). Athanasius had nevertheless been able to return to Alexandria in 337 after the death of Constantine and the accession of his three sons.

The return of Athanasius from what would prove to be only one of several periods of exile in no way meant that the efforts of the Arianizers to unseat him had ceased. On the contrary, they redoubled their efforts, compiling a condemnatory dossier on Athanasius that was sent to all three co-emperors, as well as to Pope Julius. Even this action of the Arianizing party attested to the special position of the bishop of Rome. Their letter, sent in 338, specifically asked Pope Julius to call a council to judge the case of Athanasius. The implication was that Athanasius should be condemned.

This was an unusual but significant instance of an appeal to Rome. The Eusebian-Arianizers would surely have been very glad to have the authority of the pope and a Roman council placed behind their own determination to "get" St. Athanasius, the defender of the *homo-ousios*.

At least in part because of the unusual situation of an imperial triumvirate instead of a single emperor being in power, the empire stood aside in this particular ecclesiastical quarrel. So Pope St. Julius I, in 339, on his own authority, called a council. He invited, not only the bishops of Italy and the West, but bishops from far away in the East as well, especially those who had been involved in the original condemnation of St. Athanasius at Tyre.

It was the first time in the history of the Church that any Catholic bishop—and, as it happened, it was the bishop of Rome—had ever summoned a council of virtually the whole

Church to judge the case of other Catholic bishops, St. Athanasius of Alexandria and a number of other Eastern bishops who had been deposed through the machinations of the Eusebian-Arianizers. The other deposed bishops included Marcellus of Ancyra (modern Ankara, Turkey) and Paul of Constantinople. (Paul had been displaced and banished by Eusebius of Nicomedia himself, when the latter had taken over the see of Constantinople.) These deposed Eastern bishops had not only appealed to Rome, most of them had *fled* to Rome, where they found refuge with Pope Julius.

While Julius was preparing his council to judge all these outstanding controversies, the Eusebians were not idle. In a blatantly illegal fashion, they ordained a new (Arian) bishop of Alexandria, Gregory of Cappadocia, and had him installed there by force of arms provided by the co-emperor Constantius II. The rightful bishop, St. Athanasius, remained in Egypt only long enough to denounce this usurpation in a circular letter. He then promptly repaired to Rome, mentioning in one of his writings that he had been "summoned" by Pope Julius.

By this time the Eusebians were confident of the support of Constantius II. Instead of proceeding to the council that they had requested Pope Julius to convene, they wrote Julius a sarcastic and even insulting letter wondering why the bishop of Rome could not be satisfied simply to accept the judgment of a synod held in the East (the pseudocouncil of Tyre in 335). Their forefathers, the letter noted, had been willing to accept the judgment of the Roman synod condemning Novatian in 251. They even went so far as to assert that *they* would break communion with the pope if *he* would not accept the decision of the [pseudo-] council held in Tyre.

Catholic historian Fr. Philip Hughes characterized the threat by these Eastern Arianizing bishops backed by the Arian co-emperor Constantius II as "the first open denial" of the Roman primacy in the history of the Church. We could equally well characterize it as a remarkably insolent imitation of the way the Roman bishops, possessing the primacy, were themselves sometimes obliged to act in order to uphold the integrity of the doctrine or discipline of the Church—the difference being that the Eusebians were *not* upholding the authentic positions of the Church.

The letter sent by the Eusebians to Julius also argued that while the Romans were famous for their orthodoxy, they had originally received their faith from the East. So why should the East now be expected to take second place?

Why indeed? With the perspective of history, the rejoinder to this question could justly have been that those leaders of the Church in the East were leading the Church *astray*; they were leading the Church *into heresy*. The bishops of Rome, however, had never led the Church down the wrong path in this way. That, essentially, was the answer Pope Julius gave, judging by the actions he took after receiving the letter.

In the summer or autumn of 340, Pope Julius convened a Roman synod without the Eusebian-Arianizers. It was held in the Roman church of Vitus, who had been one of the papal legates at Nicaea. One after another, the cases of Athanasius, Marcellus of Ancyra, Paul of Constantinople, and the others were heard and judged. Most of these deposed bishops were found to have been victims of the Arianizing zeal and machinations of their enemies and were vindicated. After the completion of this Roman synod, the pope wrote a long, dignified letter setting forth the results of his synod's labors. This letter of Pope St. Julius I, reproduced in full by St. Athanasius in his *Apology against the Arians*, represents one of the clearest and most cogent examples from the ancient

Church of how the bishops of Rome understood and exercised their primacy.

Pope Julius wrote first of his concern for the state of the Church and reminded the Eusebian-Arianizers that they should have provided convincing proofs of the guilt of Athanasius and the others—if they had any. The pope would never condemn anyone in the absence of proof. Julius further declared that he would convoke yet another synod to go over the whole matter again if they would attend and state their cases honestly and against the orthodox bishops who had been deposed by them. "Their cases should have been tried according to the rule to the Church," Pope Julius wrote to the Eusebians, "not in this way." The pope continued:

> You should have written to us all, that a just sentence might be issued by us all. For the sufferers were bishops of no ordinary sort but those which the apostles themselves once governed in their own persons.
>
> And why was no word sent to us [Rome], particularly concerning the Church of the Alexandrians? Are you ignorant that the *custom* has been for word to be sent to us *first* and then *for a just decision to be proclaimed from this spot*? So if any grave suspicion rested upon the bishop there, notice of it should have been despatched to the Church here.... Not like this were the instructions of Paul, not like this the traditions of the Fathers. This is another mode of procedure, a novel practice. (Quoted by St. Athanasius, *Apologia contra Arianos*, emphases added)

Pope Julius declared further that what he wrote in his letter concerning the Roman primacy, he had "learned from blessed Peter the apostle ... and I should not have written it, for *I supposed you all understood it*, had not these events so distressed us all" (ibid., emphasis added).

The Arianizing party replied the following year, in 341. Assembled in Antioch for the dedication of a new basilica, the principal Eusebian-Arianizers sent a joint letter implicitly denying the papal claims and reaffirming their support of the usurper Gregory of Cappadocia as bishop of Alexandria. They also denied that they were Arians but still refused to profess the Nicene Creed, substituting for it a creed of their own devising. They recognized Arian bishops and counterattacked on other fronts. Among other things, they explicitly accused Marcellus of Ancyra of being a Sabellian.

At this point, with opposing parties of the Church's bishops at loggerheads, the two co-emperors, surviving sons of Constantine, Constans and Constantius II, decided to take action by calling a council to deal with the Church's continuing troubles. The place they selected was Sardica, a city in the territory of Constans but immediately over the border from the territory of Constantius. It seemed to be a good, relatively neutral place for the opposing parties to iron out their differences.

The Council of Sardica, though, would not rubber-stamp any easy imperial solutions to the Church's troubles; if anything, this new emperor-convoked council only complicated matters further.

XVI.

The Council of Sardica convened in the autumn of either 342 or 343. Pope Julius had acceded to the calling of this council by the two co-emperors, and he immediately reverted to the well-established Roman custom of sending two priests and a deacon to represent him. A veteran bishop, Hosius of Cordova, who had been close to Constantine and in all probability had chaired the Council of Nicaea in 325, was deputed by Constans to lead the Western bishops to this gathering and to preside over it.

The Council of Sardica was not destined to become another ecumenical council of the Church. Most of the Eastern bishops who came were Eusebians and Arianizers. When they arrived, they found to their disgust that Athanasius of Alexandria and Marcellus of Ancyra, among others, were seated at the council as legitimate bishops.

Even though these bishops had been cleared of wrongdoing and confirmed in their positions by the Roman synod of Pope Julius, they were nevertheless considered to have been condemned in the East, however unjustly (and by a pseudocouncil). In the opinion of these Easterners, they had been deposed and nobody had any business seating them again at a Church council.

The upshot was that the Eusebian bishops refused to join the Council of Sardica, blaming the resulting schism on the West. They produced their own statement, reaffirming their condemnations of Athanasius, Marcellus, and the others. In addition, they "excommunicated" Bishop Hosius of Cordova and Pope Julius for good measure.

The Council of Sardica went on with its work without the participation of the Eusebian-Arianizers. The council again exonerated Athanasius, Marcellus, and some other bishops as well. It then examined and condemned several Eastern bishops belonging to the Arianizing party. The council even considered issuing a new creed but was persuaded by St. Athanasius himself to be content with the Creed of Nicaea; too many competing creeds were already being promoted by various parties.

This Sardican gathering, although not ecumenical, also issued a number of canons that became a permanent part of the Church's patrimony. Pope Julius had the canons of Sardica inscribed on the Roman registers immediately following the canons of Nicaea. They have sometimes even been confused with the canons of Nicaea. These canons concerned such matters as forbidding the transfer of bishops and requiring bishops to eschew lengthy sojourns outside of their bishoprics. Another canon forbade bishops from receiving priests who had been excommunicated by other bishops. The tenor of this legislation indicates what some of the abuses in the Church were considered to be at that time.

From our point of view, the most important canons enacted by the Council of Sardica were those explicitly recognizing what we may call the appellate jurisdiction of the see of Rome in cases involving bishops. Such jurisdiction already existed and was recognized in practice, but Sardica put a conciliar stamp of approval on it. The custom of having erring bishops tried by other bishops from the same province was generally retained, but if either a condemned bishop or his judges were dissatisfied with the result, the Council of Sardica decreed, either side could honor "the memory of the apostle Peter", and appeal to the bishop of Rome.

In recognizing the right of appeal to Rome, however, the Council of Sardica attempted to provide a rather too detailed procedure to be followed, which the popes subsequently more or less ignored. Nevertheless, the principle was established: a major council of the Church had recognized and attempted to codify the primacy of the see of Rome in the Church. It is worth quoting from several of the canons enacted at Sardica, since the principles they embody were destined to find a permanent place in canon law:

CANON III: If a bishop is condemned [that is, deposed, as appears from the fourth canon] but thinks his case is a good one, so that a fresh sentence ought to be pronounced, then out of respect to the memory of the apostle Peter, a letter shall be addressed to Rome to Pope Julius, so that, if necessary, he may appoint a new court composed of the bishops near the province in question, and may himself appoint the judges. If it is not proved, however, that the affair requires a fresh inquiry, then the first sentence [of the provincial synod] shall not be annulled, but shall be confirmed by the pope.

CANON IV: ... If a bishop has been deposed by sentence of those bishops who are in the neighborhood, and he desires to defend himself, no other shall be appointed to his see until the bishop of Rome has judged and decided thereupon.

CANON V: If a bishop deposed by his comprovincials [the bishops of the same region] has appealed to Rome, and the pope considers a fresh examination necessary, then he shall write to the bishops living nearest the province in question, that they may thoroughly investigate the matter, and give sentence in accordance with the truth. But if the appellant can induce the bishop of Rome to send priests of his own to constitute, with the appointed bishops, the court of second instance, and thereby to enjoy the authority belonging to himself [the pope], it shall be open to the pope to do so. . . .

Thus was recognized the principle of appealing to Rome in cases involving bishops everywhere. Upon completion of its work, the Council of Sardica, significantly, drew up a respectful report officially communicating its actions to what it called the "head, that is, to the see of Peter the apostle".

The Council of Sardica had been called by the two co-emperor brothers with the intention of bringing peace to the Church. The result, however, was that the Arianizing and Catholic parties, each sponsored and protected by one of the co-emperors, were now more at loggerheads than ever before. The lines had been drawn. Nevertheless, as long as the Catholic co-emperor Constans lived, St. Athanasius was able to remain in his see and carry on as the rightful bishop. He returned to Alexandria from his Roman refuge bearing an eloquent letter from the one who had been his protector, Pope St. Julius I.

This situation was destined to change in the following decade, when Constantius II would become sole emperor. Constantius, by this time a convinced Arian, required no prodding from Eusebius of Nicomedia (who had died in 341) to dispose him favorably toward the Arianizing party and give support to its enterprises. After the death of Eusebius of Nicomedia, Constantius continued to rely on other Arianizing advisors, such as the devious and cowardly Bishop Valens of Mursa and, later, Basil of Ancyra. With the advice and consent of such bishops, Constantius would come close to imposing Arianism on the whole Church during the decade of the 350s; never before or since would the authentic teaching of the Church handed down from the apostles be in greater danger than under this son of Constantine, who effectively muzzled (if only for a short period) virtually the entire hierarchy of the Church.

In the year 350, the Catholic co-emperor, Constans, was assassinated at the foot of the Pyrenees. His brother Constantius hastened to put down the military conspiracy that had been behind his brother's assassination. Then, having quelled this rebellion, Constantius, now sole emperor as his father had been, turned his attention to other matters. Imposing the Arian heresy on the whole Church of Christ seems to have been one of his major projects.

By the time Constantius was in a position to attempt to carry out his project, however, the very successful Pope Julius was dead (352). His unfortunate successor, Pope Liberius (352–366), had to bear the brunt of the fearsome oppression that would be unleashed by this Arian emperor.

XVII.

Pope Liberius occupied the chair of Peter during a period when the Arian heresy was tearing the Church apart. The battle for Catholic orthodoxy would not be effectively won until the time of the ecumenical Council of Constantinople in 381. The fight against Arianism thus overshadowed the entire pontificate of Pope Liberius, who became one of its major casualties.

This pope would be abducted by the forces of the Arian emperor, imprisoned, and exiled. When he returned, he had to contend with an antipope, Felix II (355–365), who had been installed in Rome by Constantius in his absence. Liberius seems to have been by then a cowed and perhaps broken man who remained silent while the Arian emperor went on imposing an alien faith on almost the entire Church. Constantius took a giant step torward accomplishing this aim at the councils he convoked at Rimini and Seleucia in the year 359.

Only after the unexpected death of Constantius in 361 was Pope Liberius able to recover a measure of the authority and prestige of the Roman see in defense of Nicene orthodoxy.

Liberius started out bravely enough. He seemed to have been aware of what was at stake. While Constantius was still engaged in putting down the military conspirators who had been responsible for murdering his brother, Pope Liberius received letters from Arianizing Eastern bishops urging him to reverse the position of his predecessor, Julius, and condemn the stalwart symbol of Nicene orthodoxy, St. Athanasius of Alexandria, who was still precariously hanging on to his see. Only with the towering figure of the bishop of Alexandria removed from the scene could the Arianizing bishops hope to prevail.

Liberius was determined not to abandon Athanasius, however. He not only convened a Roman synod to reaffirm the Roman stand confirming Athanasius in his bishopric; he also received and responded favorably to a delegation Athanasius sent to Rome. Meanwhile, Constantius, who was in Gaul around that time, was convening a synod of his own in Arles, where he had no trouble getting the local bishops to vote for the condemnation of Athanasius. Those Gallic bishops knew little about the Alexandrian or about the Arian controversy that had been raging in the East for a generation.

Even St. Hilary of Poitiers, destined to become perhaps the greatest defender of Nicene orthodoxy after Athanasius himself, was to write that he had never even heard of the Creed of Nicaea before the winter of 353. At the time, the Gallic bishops still employed only a simple baptismal creed similar to the Apostles' Creed. So when the Christian emperor, son of the great Constantine, came to the bishops and asked them to condemn an Eastern prelate who was virtually unknown to them, who were they to question the Christian emperor's motives? They were happy to oblige.

Alarmed at this outcome so near at hand, Pope Liberius appointed two Italian bishops—one was Vincent of Capua, who as a priest had been one of the papal legates at Nicaea—to bear a letter urging the emperor to call another council so that all questions concerning Nicaea and Athanasius could be properly weighed by the Church's bishops in a suitable forum. Liberius probably realized that only a consensus of the Church's bishops could deflect the emperor from imposing his Arianizing views upon the whole Church.

Constantius' determination to proceed with his project may not have been completely appreciated, even by Liberius. It is hard to fathom what was driving this son of Constantine so relentlessly. In the atmosphere of the imperial court at Arles, even the pope's two bishop-representatives ended up subscribing to the excommunication of Athanasius demanded by Constantius. Incensed, Pope Liberius wrote that his representative Vincent "was lured into treachery". But the pressures the emperor brought to bear on the bishops must have been intense.

Constantius did not even deign to reply to the pope's letter. Liberius then appointed another bishop as his representative, Lucifer of Cagliari in Sardinia. Accompanied by a Roman priest and a deacon, Lucifer was instructed to proceed to Milan, where the emperor had moved, with yet another papal appeal for a general council to decide according to Church procedures Church questions including the status of the Creed of Nicaea and that of the bishop of Alexandria.

Constantius convened yet another local synod of bishops in Milan (355), to which he summoned all the bishops of Italy to condemn "the sacrilegious Athanasius". The Italian bishops were compelled to sign or face exile. This was the famous occasion when Constantius, hand on his sword, declared that canon law was his will. At one point in the proceedings, when some pro-Nicene bishops were attempting to get signatures subscribing to the Creed of Nicaea, the list was literally snatched out of their hands by the Arian bishop Valens of Mursa, who was close to Constantius.

Only the pope's representative, Lucifer of Cagliari, along with the bishops of Milan and Vercellae in Piedmont, held out—and for their defiance they were promptly despatched into exile by Constantius. An Eastern Arian priest in the emperor's retinue, Auxentius, a man ignorant even of Latin, was consecrated as the bishop of Milan.

Then came the turn of Pope Liberius. Certainly the way the Roman emperor ran these local synods amply justified the papal policy of not attending them in person. Even so, Liberius could not remain beyond the reach of the determined Constantius. Liberius was personally popular in the city of Rome, however, and Constantius evidently did not dare attack him openly there. Imperial officers were first sent to try to bribe or otherwise induce the pope to do the emperor's bidding. When these efforts failed and after Liberius had indignantly had the emperor's eunuch put out into the street, imperial orders were issued that the pope was to be abducted by night and taken to Milan, where the pope was a prisoner.

We possess a record of the tense dialogue Liberius had with Constantius in Milan. The pope still courageously refused to condemn Athanasius in the absence of convincing evidence against him. As far as Liberius was concerned, Athanasius had already been acquitted by a competent Church tribunal on the basis of convincing evidence—at the Roman synod of Pope St. Julius I in 340. Liberius felt obliged to uphold that judgment. As a result, shortly afterward he was exiled by the Emperor to Beroea in Thrace (Greece), where he came under the control of the Arian bishop of that place, Demophilus.

Back in Rome Liberius was hailed as a hero, and the Roman clergy bravely took an oath to accept nobody else as bishop. Constantius, however, moved immediately to counter this latest show of defiance by having an antipope, Felix, ordained bishop at a ceremony inside the Lateran with three palace eunuchs representing the Catholic laity. Imperial officers then saw to it that the Roman clergy had to agree at least outwardly to the imposition on the Church of the antipope Felix; no open opposition was allowed.

Shortly after the banishment of Liberius, Bishop Hosius of Cordova, then well over ninety, was summoned to Milan to face Constantius. Hosius had been Emperor Constantine's first ecclesiastical advisor; he had also been one of the major figures at the Councils of Nicaea and Sardica. Hardly anyone among the orthodox enjoyed greater personal prestige than this Spanish bishop, with the possible exception of Athanasius himself. But now Hosius was being asked to join in condemning Athanasius.

The aged prelate refused to submit. Whether because of his age, the position of trust he had held under the emperor's father, or for some other reason, Constantius allowed him to return to Spain unhindered.

Afterward Hosius wrote to Constantius, assuming a tone that perhaps no one else would have dared to assume. Vigorously defending Athanasius, he even chided the emperor for sending "threatening letters" to him. He reminded Constantius how he had assisted the latter's father in bringing peace to the Church. In this remarkable letter, Hosius became perhaps the first major Christian figure to assert explicitly the independence of the Church from the all-powerful Roman state. Thus did Bishop Hosius of Cordova dare to write to Constantius II:

> Cease, I entreat you, and remember that you are a mortal. Fear the day of judgment and keep yourself pure against it. Intrude not yourself into the business of the Church and give no commandment to us regarding it but learn it instead from us. God has placed in your hands the empire: to us he has committed the administration of the Church. And as he who would steal the government from you opposes the ordinance of God, even so do you fear lest by taking upon

yourself the conduct of the Church, you make yourself guilty
of a grave sin. It is written: "Render unto Caesar the things
that are Caesar's, and unto God the things that are God's."
Therefore it is not permitted to us to bear rule on earth, nor
have you the right to burn incense. I write this out of anx-
iety for your salvation. (Quoted by Athanasius, *Historia
Arianorum*, 44)

Constantius would not forget this bit of defiance. Although he had not yet secured the consent of either Liberius
or Hosius, he had effectively convinced, or otherwise effectively neutralized by exile or other means, the other bishop-
upholders of Nicaea. The emperor thus felt that he was finally
in a position to move openly against Athanasius, whom he
had allowed to return to Alexandria a decade earlier only
because of the strong insistence of his brother and co-
emperor, Constans, who possesed superior power in the empire at the time.

On the night of February 8, 356, while the bishop of Alexandria was presiding at night prayer in a church, imperial
soldiers forced their way into the church with trumpets blar-
ing and swords drawn. Several people were killed in the fray
that ensued. Athanasius was immediately surrounded by his
loyal monks and other members of the Alexandrian faithful.
Quickly spirited from the church and into hiding in the Egyptian desert, he disappeared for the next few years. From his
place of hiding, he issued a stream writings on which much
of our knowledge of these events is based.

As had been the case seventeen years earlier when the Arianizing bishops had imposed the Arian Gregory of Cappadocia on the see of Alexandria as bishop, once again the
same party of Eastern bishops illicitly ordained George of
Cappadocia, another Arian, and by means of military force
installed him in the see of Alexandria. About this same time,

in distant Gaul, Saturninus, the Arian bishop of Arles, was chairing a synod that tried, condemned, deposed, and banished the two pro-Nicene Gallic bishops, Rhodanius of Toulouse and St. Hilary of Poitiers. During his exile in Asia Minor, Hilary studied the Greek Fathers, became thoroughly grounded in the whole Arian controversy, and composed his great work *De Trinitate*, "On the Trinity".

At this point, organized opposition to the imperial imposition of Arianism on the whole Church appeared to be at an end: the bishop-defenders of Nicaea were in exile (or, like Athanasius, in hiding); other bishops had submitted and signed. A disinterested observer in the year 356 would have concluded that the victory of Constantius and Arianism was complete.

Yet there was more—and worse—to come. The agents of the Arianizing party were not finished; they were determined to break the holdouts, Hosius and Liberius. Although questions have been raised about the authenticity of the documentation concerning the breaking of these two bishops—some of it may have been forged either by adherents of the Arianizing party or by ultrastrict Catholics critical of the behavior of their leaders. Most probably, both Hosius and Liberius did give in—each in a different way.

As for the aged bishop of Cordova, in 357 he was again summoned to appear before the emperor. This time he had to travel to distant Sirmium in the Balkan peninsula (modern Mitrovica), where he was subjected to relentless, unbearable pressure, perhaps even torture. Dazed, he is said finally to have subscribed to one of the Arianizing creeds that the anti-Nicaea forces kept coming up with. St. Hilary of Poitiers styled this particular creed "the blasphemy of Sirmium". It was a creed that not only did not include but explicitly forbade any mention of "substance", the *homoousios* of Nicaea.

Although Hosius is said to have yielded in the matter of this doctrine, no amount of pressure, apparently, could compel him to condemn Athanasius. At length his tormentors released him, no doubt concluding that they had gotten out of him what they could. He returned to Spain to die a year or so later (ca. 358) at around the age of a hundred. Before his death, he is said to have repented of his subscription under torture to a faulty creed.

As for Pope Liberius, the rigors of exile began to tell on him, too, after a time. Apparently Bishop Demophilus of Beroea played a role in persuading him that he could yield something without essential harm to his position or office. He finally conceded that the pseudocouncil of Tyre had been justified in condemning Athanasius in 335—the action that marked the launching of the whole Arianizing drive to take over the Church with the support of the emperor.

In a letter ascribed to Liberius and written to Bishop Vincent of Capua—whom earlier Liberius had reproached for "treachery"—he is represented as stating that he had "retired from the struggle over Athanasius". In another letter attributed to him and written to some Eastern bishops Liberius is represented as saying that he had only defended Athanasius "because my predecessor, Bishop Julius, of honorable memory, had received him". We do not know whether Liberius actually authored these letters or not. Historians disagree. It is interesting that contemporaries could characterize this whole affair as a "struggle over Athanasius".

Liberius went further than merely retiring from that struggle, apparently even accepting communion with the likes of Valens of Mursa and Auxentius of Milan for the sake of peace in the Church. He also subscribed to one of the substitute creeds that omitted any mention of the *homo-ousios* of Nicaea. In 358 the Eastern bishops asked him to subscribe to yet another creed omitting reference to the *homo-ousios,* and he agreed to do so. These creeds, while not formally heretical in the sense of stating false doctrine, nevertheless failed to state the doctrine of the Church in its fullness, since by then the *homo-ousios* had been definitively decided upon by the Church at Nicaea.

Shortly afterward. Liberius was allowed to return to Rome, where he was still considered a hero—and where no one seems to have known that his release had been contingent upon his acceptance of imperial demands. That the imperial party did not immediately proceed to discredit him forever is one of the reasons documentation against him is thought by some historians to have been forged. Liberius would again be found upholding Nicaea later in his pontificate; but he remained strangely passive for a period after his release and return to Rome. There can be no question that the experience of imprisonment and exile had affected and demoralized him deeply.

XVIII.

During the course of the Arian controversy, a number of creeds were prepared and promoted as possible substitutes for the controversial Creed of Nicaea. It was certainly controversial for the Arians and Arianizers, who refused to subscribe to the *homo-ousios;* but it was also considered too controversial by many otherwise orthodox bishops who did not like the term because it was considered unscriptural (and probably for still others who disliked it precisely because it *had become* so controversial).

Detailed discussion of these alternative creeds is beyond the scope of our present inquiry concerning the primacy of

Rome in the early Church. So is detailed discussion of the contending schools of thought in the Arian controversy. These included the Arians, semi-Arians, and Arianizers, as well as various shades of orthodoxy ranging from those who did not think the matter important enough for all the trouble it was causing to those who, like Athanasius, Hilary of Poitiers, and the popes in their official pronouncements, understood that maintaining the *homo-ousios* of Nicaea was *necessary* for maintaining the integrity of the Catholic faith as a whole.

Cutting across all party lines, too, was the only-too-common assumption that opposition to imperial commands, especially those of a *Christian* emperor, was unthinkable. This attitude was reenforced when the alternative to acceptance of the imperial wishes was coercion or exile. Looking back over the many centuries that separate us from the middle of the fourth century, we find it hard to understand some of the passions that were generated and, especially, how a Constantius *could* have been so adamant about trying to impose his view on the Church. In some ways this son of Constantine comes across almost as a modern totalitarian, not content with mere outward compliance, but insistent that everybody agree with his decisions even if he had to resort to torture.

Hard and unyielding as Constantius seems to have been, he was not entirely inflexible about what he regarded as necessary for the peace of the empire. At one point Constantius came under the influence of a bishop of Ancyra, Basil, who belonged to the school of the *homo-i-ousians* ("similar to the Father", rather than Nicaea's "the same as the Father"). Later, St. Athanasius himself would come to an understanding with this particular school of thought, when its members were driven back toward Nicaea by the extremism of the so-called Anomoeans ("unlike the Father"!). These extremists at one point actually succeeded in taking over the important sees of Antioch and Constantinople, alarming many who had not been engaged up to then, and serving to drive not a few of those who had attempted to be compromisers, or "moderates", back toward the necessity of upholding Nicaea.

Most pertinent to our inquiry about many of these long-forgotten controversies is whether in subscribing to creeds that failed to include the *homo-ousios* of Nicaea, Pope Liberius actually fell into error or heresy. It has always been the claim of the Church of Rome that its bishops, the popes, have never deviated in any essential from holding and teaching the authentic faith of Christ.

The ancient Roman claim to freedom from error in teaching the authentic Catholic faith—what is today officially called the doctrine of the infallibility of the pope—was considered then, as it was defined in 1870 by the extraordinary Magisterium of the Catholic Church at Vatican Council I, to be an integral part of the doctrine of the primacy of the pope. Papal infallibility has always attracted more attention than the doctrine of the primacy; but infallibility was defined at Vatican I wholly within the framework of the council's definition of the pope's "full and supreme power of jurisdiction over the whole Church, not only in matters pertaining to faith and morals, but also in matters pertaining to the discipline and government of the Church throughout the whole world" (Vatican I, *Pastor Aeternus*, III).

The case of Liberius, though, does raise some questions. Did Liberius compromise the position of Rome by acquiescing in the condemnation of Athanasius and, especially, by agreeing to communion with Arians as well as apparently subscribing to a creed that did not include the *homo-ousios*? The case of Liberius was one that the Fathers of the First Vatican Council were obliged to examine with special care while solemnly defining the primacy and infallibility of the pope. Their conclusion was that the known facts in the case of Liberius did not preclude the issuance of the definition that they in fact issued.

For one thing, the decisions about ceasing to defend Athanasius and accepting communion with heretical bishops were expedients in the practical order that did not compromise the Church's teaching. For another thing, the creed(s) to which Liberius apparently subscribed—unlike, for instance, the blasphemy of Sirmium—are susceptible of an orthodox interpretation even if they fall short of what the Church had by then decided was necessary, namely, the inclusion of the *homo-ousios*.

Whatever Liberius subscribed to, whatever his failures may have been, he was acting under duress. Already in ancient times, St. Athanasius rendered the judgment about Liberius that we surely must accord to him today:

> But Liberius gave way, after he had been two years in exile, and subscribed for fear of threatened death. Yet this shows only their [the Arians'] violence and Liberius' hatred of heresy and support of Athanasius as long as he had a free choice. For that which men do under torture, against their original intention, ought not to be considered the will of these terrified persons but rather that of their tormentors. (*Historia Arianorum*, 41)

On the grounds of duress alone, Liberius, as "pastor and teacher of all Christians", using Vatican I's terminology, was not guilty of teaching error. As we have noted, hardly anyone at the time even seems to have been aware of his reputed lapse.

Nevertheless, it cannot be denied that the whole sad Liberius affair was unfortunate for the Church and the papacy. The lesson of Liberius is this: how unfortunate it can

be for the Church when the primacy *fails* to function properly or is *prevented* from functioning properly by an external
power. As a result of the lapse or failure of Liberius in 357
and 358, it was left to such as St. Athanasius of Alexandria
and St. Hilary of Poitiers to carry the torch until the successor of Peter "turned again" (cf. Lk 22:32).

In 359, in the aftermath of the breaking and neutraliza-
tion of Liberius, Emperor Constantius convened two councils, one at Rimini in Italy and the other at Seleucia in Asia
Minor. The bishops at these assemblies were not allowed to
object to or debate what was proposed; they were simply
obliged to accept and subscribe to the creed that Constantius had had drawn up. The four hundred bishops assembled
at Rimini were not allowed by the imperial Praetorian Prefect to leave the city until they did subscribe to this imperial
creed. Eventually they all did, recalling the hour when Jesus
was taken into custody: "Then all of the disciples forsook
him and fled" (Mt 26:56).

The same result was obtained in Seleucia. The creed the
bishops were required to sign at Rimini and Seleucia contained the following explicit rejection of the Nicaean Creed:

> [T]he term "essence" [*ousia*] has been taken up by the Fathers
> rather unwisely, and gives offence because it is not under-
> stood by the people. It is also not contained in the Scrip-
> tures. For these reasons we have decided to do away with it,
> and that no use at all should be made of it for the future in
> connection with God, because the divine Scriptures no-
> where use it of the Father and the Son. But we say that the
> Son is like the Father in all things, as the Holy Scriptures say
> and teach. (Quoted by Athanasius, *De Synodis*, 8)

Acceptance of this defective creed by the bishops of both
East and West prompted the famous statement of St. Jerome:

"The whole world groaned and was amazed to find itself Arian" (*Contra Luciferianos*, 19). The same creed was solemnly proclaimed the next year, 360, at the dedication of the great Basilica of Hagia Sophia in Constantinople, where an extreme Arian, Eudoxius, was then the bishop; he had been transferred there from Antioch. The Arian triumph over orthodoxy seemed to be complete, and the pope had meanwhile been reduced to silence (only temporarily, as it turned out).

The triumph of heterodoxy lasted only as long as the all-powerful heterodox emperor lived. Constantius died suddenly in 361 on his way to do battle with his distant relative Julian, who had been acclaimed emperor by the Roman army in Gaul. Julian, who then became sole emperor, is known to history as Julian the Apostate, since he would shortly repudiate Christianity entirely. Julian, never a sincere Christian, wanted to revive paganism in the empire and had no ambitions to dictate to the Church. Upon his accession to supreme power, he issued an edict allowing the return of all the bishops Constantius had banished; and the worship of God in any mode whatever was henceforth again legally permitted in the empire.

In Alexandria, the people rose up against the Arian bishop, George of Cappadocia, and threw him into prison, where he was later put to death. St. Athanasius returned from exile in triumph to his see—for the third time. A synod held in Alexandria provided for the rehabilitation of bishops who had lapsed, simply upon their reaffirming the Creed of Nicaea. This was a wise move, since attempting to impose penalties on the bishops who had signed the creed of 359 in Rimini and Seleucia would have meant penalizing practically all the bishops of the Church.

At this time both the *homo-ousians* and the *homo-i-ousians* rallied behind the rehabilitated Nicene Creed, setting the stage for the definitive triumph of Nicene orthodoxy over the next two decades. There would still be some further imperial interference in these creedal matters before 380, when the sincerely Catholic Emperor Theodosius I decreed universal acceptance of the Nicene Creed—and, not incidentally, communion with the bishop of Rome as well. But the days of the Arianizers were now numbered.

Theodosius also convoked the Council of Constantinople, in 381, the year after decreeing acceptance of the Nicene Creed. This ecumenical council would issue the complete Niceno-Constantinopolitan Creed professed in the Church to this day.

The nightmare of the Arianizing Emperor Constantius was over, and the Church urgently needed to restore orthodoxy and normality. In Rome, Pope Liberius broke a silence that had lasted for nearly four years and resumed his former tone of positive Roman leadership as if there had never been any lapse on his part. There seems to have been no resentment on the part of St. Athanasius over Liberius' failure to support him while he was in exile.

Liberius quickly sent to Alexandria his endorsement of the Alexandrian plan of restoring bishops everywhere upon their simple affirmation of the Nicene Creed. This plan represented a typical lenient Roman stance similar to positions taken earlier by the apostolic see when Christians had lapsed in the face of oppression or persecution. (In this case, as in those earlier cases, some people were prepared to accuse Rome of undue laxity.)

Later, Pope Liberius seems to have sent out instructions about restoring bishops upon their simply reaffiring the Creed of Nicaea. In the last year of his life, 366, Liberius was engaged in reconciling a group of *homo-i-ous*ian Eastern bishops upon acceptance by them of Nicaea and their promise to submit future disputes to judges approved by Rome. Thus, the papacy seems not to have suffered undue or permanent damage as a result of the exile and subsequent weakness of Liberius.

Perhaps there is even a benevolent Providence to be discerned in the fact that, reduced to silence, the Roman see at least took no part in the scandalous and disgraceful Councils of Rimini and Seleucia in 359. It seems unlikely that any papal legates could have prevented Constantius from working his will at those gatherings. In the very next pontificate, that of Pope Damasus, Roman documents would already be speaking of Rimini as an illicit council *because* the see of Peter had taken no part in it!

Clearly the Arianizing Emperor Constantius II wreaked untold damage and misery on the Church during the years when he was exercising his own imperial "primacy" in the Church. Constantius did not succeed in destroying the real primacy of the bishop of Rome, although surely not for lack of trying!

XIX.

During the pontificate of Pope St. Damasus I (366–384), the primacy of Rome in the Church came to be exercised more confidently and definitely than at any previous time in the Church's history. This primacy was also expounded more clearly and sharply than ever before. Damasus was the first pope to employ the term "the apostolic see"; and with him the primacy reached a fully developed stage that not only came to be recognized throughout the Church but was ratified in an imperial edict in 380.

Henceforth, nonrecognition of the Roman primacy, rejection of it, or disobedience to it would become a deviation from what was clearly established and promulgated by Church authority—presumably once and for all.

Pope Damasus, born in Rome, had been a deacon under Pope Liberius. A man of varied interests and talents, he reorganized the papal archives, composed Latin verse, and had many examples of his work celebrating the martyrs inscribed on slabs. Very interested in scriptural exegesis, he befriended St. Jerome, who served for a time as his secretary. It was Damasus who commissioned the new translation that became the St. Jerome's Latin Vulgate Bible.

Pope Damasus also seems to have been a fairly able ecclesiastical politician and maneuverer. The very fact of his election shows that he was successful in attracting supporters among the increasingly numerous Roman clergy. He also made his share of enemies: his election was immediately countered by the election of an antipope, Ursinus (366–385), who outlived him.

This antipope seems to have been elected by the ultrastrict faction among the Roman clergy. Following the elections of these two rivals, riots and armed clashes, not without loss of life, took place between the adherents of Damasus and those of Ursinus. The prefect of the city of Rome had to be called in to restore order.

Damasus would continue to be undermined by Ursinus and his supporters throughout his pontificate, and further clashes occurred. The Ursinians in due course lost the battle and eventually were banished from Rome by state authority.

In view of the confused situation that obtained during most of his pontificate, it is not easy to evaluate the character of Damasus. Various accusations were lodged against him, including one of adultery (he would have been in his seventies at the time!). Another characterized him as a murderer. These may simply have been slanders originating with his enemies.

In the atmosphere of the times, simply to uphold the faith—as it was Damasus' duty to do—made enemies of those determined that their sectarian version of it ought to prevail. We do not know all the facts in this case, but, on general principles, we should be wary of crediting uncritically the accusations lodged against him.

There is no confusion about the position of Damasus on the Roman primacy. He frequently convoked Roman synods that issued clarifications on doctrinal questions and in some cases made pronouncements on the questions of the day as well. One of these Roman synods, in 378, addressed a petition to the two joint Western emperors asking that the jurisdiction of the Roman bishops over the other bishops of the West be formally established in Roman law. Italian bishops would be directly subject to the bishop of Rome; bishops elsewhere would be subject in the first instance to their metropolitans, whether in Arles, Carthage, Lyons, or wherever. The metropolitan bishops would be directly subject to Rome or to judges appointed by Rome.

It was surely a mark of the de facto recognition that the Roman bishops had by then acquired that the Western emperors, Gratian (359–383) and Valentinian II (375–392), actually issued a rescript in 378 essentially establishing in law this Roman appellate jurisdiction over the other Western bishops.

During the pontificate of Damasus, the Church was slowly recovering from the long nightmare of state-imposed Arianism. As a result of the sad experience of the previous half century, the tide was by this time running strongly, not only for the Creed of Nicaea, but for the Roman primacy as well. Bishops in the East regularly petitioned Rome to help them recover from the ravages of the Arianism that had afflicted them; those bishops, like the Churches they led, wanted help in replacing the Arian or Arianizing bishops who remained.

The position of those Eastern bishops was complicated by the fact that while Rome enjoyed the patronage of orthodox co-emperors between 366 to 378, the East was still being ruled by an Arian emperor, Valens (364–378), who continued to interfere in Church affairs as Emperor Constantius II so vigorously had done. In this situation, some of the Eastern bishops saw the Roman see, and even the Western emperors, as weapons against the Arian yoke they were trying to throw off.

An extensive correspondence exists between Rome and Alexandria and bishops such as St. Basil of Caesarea in Cappadocia, in which he strongly pleads for Western help and support. In particular, a disputed succession in the apostolic see of Antioch saw one claimant, Paulinus, favored by Rome and Alexandria while St. Basil championed another claimant, also orthodox, Meletius. The dispute was quite complicated, and we are unable to go into detail about it here. Some historians have not been kind to Pope Damasus because he replied to the large-hearted Basil's pleas with what they saw as rigid demands that the doctrine and discipline laid down by Rome be observed without question. From our point of view, Pope Damasus upheld the Roman primacy in his handling of those pleas from the East—whether or not he handled them in the best possible way.

It is not clear that any Roman intervention whatever could have solved the knotty succession problems in the East that had resulted from more than a half century of Arian turmoil. Surely the bishops of the East had some responsibility for helping to find satisfactory solutions to their own problems. At a minimum, there had to be some disposition to accept what Pope Damasus was correctly prescribing for them—correct in broad terms at least.

Rome could not have been in possession of all the facts in such a case. Damasus undeniably acted throughout in concert with the bishop of Alexandria, Peter, who had succeeded his brother, St. Athanasius, after his death in 373. Peter was closer to the Eastern scene and presumably in better command of the facts, and Damasus tended to follow his lead.

For a brief period under the Eastern emperor Valens, Bishop Peter was obliged to take refuge with Pope Damasus in Rome as his brother, St. Athanasius, had done earlier with Pope Julius. In the course of the fourth century, Rome and Alexandria almost always acted in concert in defense of Nicene orthodoxy; nor does this close alliance seem to have been affected unduly by the temporary defection of Liberius. On the election of Damasus as pope, for example, Athanasius immediately wrote to the new bishop of Rome, reminding him of his special responsibility for ridding the Church of Arianism and its effects. Rome's record of steady insistence upon correct doctrine based on the Nicene Creed cannot be faulted in principle.

The perennial claim is that the Church of Rome has never erred in matters of faith. Pope Damasus upheld that claim. Many Eastern bishops were ready to agree with it as long as they continued to groan under Arian oppression; under those circumstances, they often pleaded eloquently with the pope not to allow the faith to be extinguished in the East, where it had originated.

As soon as some of these bishops were free of immediate oppression, however, they reverted to the old Eastern stance of questioning why the standard of faith should now be issuing from an area to which it had originally been carried from the East.

One of the greatest Eastern prelates managed to put that question into the proper context: "Was it not in the East that Christ was born?" St. Gregory of Nazianzus (d. 389) asked rhetorically. "And it was also in the East that he was slain", the saint and one-time bishop of Constantinople replied, significantly, to his own question. There was always important recognition of the position of the Church of Rome in the East in those years. In 379, for example, 153 bishops from Syria and Asia Minor met in Antioch and subscribed unconditionally to the faith prescribed by Pope Damasus for the East.

For other Eastern bishops, the fact that the see of Rome was the see of Peter was often conveniently glossed over in some formulations, even though it was not forgotten in the Church as a whole. Indeed, the primacy of Rome was at this time about to be enacted into secular law by a Catholic emperor, and shortly afterward the primacy would be recognized in one of the canons of the general Council of Constantinople.

In August of 378, the Arian emperor Valens was killed fighting the Goths at Adrianople (modern Edirne, Turkey). The Catholic emperor in the West, Gratian, then elevated to the purple a Spanish general, Theodosius, and assigned him to rule the Eastern half of the empire. Theodosius I, also called Theodosius the Great (379–395), was a sincere Catholic. Recovering from an illness in Thessalonica, he heard tales of woe concerning the plight of the Arianized Church in his new domains that contrasted greatly with his own experience of the vigor and stability of the Church in the West under the leadership of Catholic bishops in communion with the pope. Theodosius therefore decided to "establish" the Catholic Church throughout the East as well.

On February 27, 380, Theodosius accordingly issued the following edict in his own name and in the name of his West-

ern co-emperors, Gratian and Valentinian. It is worth repro-
ducing in full:

> It is our will that all the peoples subject to the government
> of our clemency shall follow that religion which the holy
> Peter delivered to the Romans, as pious tradition from him
> to the present times declares it, and as the pontiff Damasus
> manifestly observes it, as also does Peter, bishop of Alexan-
> dria, a man of apostolic sanctity; that is, that in accordance
> with the apostolic teaching and gospel we should believe in
> the deity of the Father and the Son and the Holy Spirit, of
> equal majesty, in sacred Trinity. Those who follow this law
> we order shall be included under the name of Catholic Chris-
> tians. All others we pronounce mad and insane and require
> that they bear the ignominy of teachers of heresy; their con-
> venticles shall not receive the title of churches; they shall be
> chastised first by divine vengeance, and then by the punish-
> ment of our indignation, with divine approval.

The "religion which the holy Peter delivered to the Romans ... as the pontiff Damasus manifestly observes it...."
Such was the common understanding of the primacy of Rome
in the Church near the end of the fourth century, as set down
in an imperial rescript and enacted into secular law.

This imperial enactment in no sense *created* the Roman
primacy; the popes themselves had steadily and with increasing clarity been making claim to the primacy quite apart
from, and usually in spite of, the laws of the Roman Empire.
Given the kind of world the Church was obliged to live in as
the fourth century drew to a close, there were advantages for
the Church in this new official imperial recognition—now
the enemies of orthodoxy were being called "mad and in-
sane", rather than the upholders of orthodoxy, as had been
the case during the Arian years. The see of Rome had come

a long way from its obscure origins under the outlaw Fisherman, Simon Peter.

XX.

Important as imperial recognition of the doctrine of the Roman primacy was in some respects, from the Church's own point of view, the recognition of the primacy that was included in one of the canons of the ecumenical Council of Constantinople was even more important. The same emperor, Theodosius I, who, in 380, decreed the establishment of the Catholic Church along with the primacy of the pope, also summoned the Council of Constantinople to meet in 381.

As we explained in chapter 3, the Council of Constantinople would issue the Creed destined to become the definitive Creed of the Church. Primarily because it issued this Creed, this council came to be considered ecumenical, as the Council of Chalcedon would declare in the following century, a judgment generally ratified by the pope.

The Council of Constantinople began as a purely Eastern gathering. There were no Roman legates present. Peter of Alexandria had died before the council convened, and his successor, Timothy, did not arrive until near the end. Yet this council enacted a canon that recognized the Roman primacy.

From another point of view, however, the canon that the Council of Constantinople enacted in this regard was troublesome. "The bishop of Constantinople", the canon read, "shall have precedence after the bishop of Rome, for Constantinople is the new Rome." Thus, while undeniably recognizing that Rome came first in precedence, the canon was troublesome precisely because it placed Constantinople after Rome and thus ahead of the more ancient apostolic sees of Alexandria and Antioch. This was no doubt the express intention of the bishops who participated in this council, which was, after all, being held in Constantinople; but it was destined to create strife in later years as rivalries between the great sees intensified, especially over the Councils of Ephesus and Chalcedon, which followed in the fifth century.

From the perspective of apostolicity, the see of Constantinople was an upstart. Originally it was merely a suffragan see of the Church of Heraclea, but when it was made the new capital of the Roman Empire, the city became much more important. This was one reason why this canon placing the city second after Rome in ecclesiastical precedence proved to be so problematic. It meant that the importance of the see was primarily based on the secular importance of the city in which it was located—Constantinople was "the new Rome"—as if the primacy of Rome had been based on the fact that old Rome was the capital of the empire rather than on Christ's commission to Peter to feed the sheep and strengthen the brethren.

We do not know with certainty whether Pope St. Damasus I objected at the time to the form in which this first conciliar canon affirming the Roman primacy was enacted by the Council of Constantinople. We do know that a Roman synod held the very next year, in 382, made clear in unmistakable language that Rome's claim to the primacy in the Church was based exclusively on the foundation of the Church of Rome on Saints Peter and Paul and the succession of the Roman bishops from St. Peter, and not on the secular importance of the erstwhile capital of the empire.

(This Roman Synod of Pope Damasus issued a list of the books of Scripture accepted as canonical by the Church; more than a thousand years later, the Council of Trent (1545–1563) would promulgate exactly the same list.)

In the following century, Pope St. Leo the Great wrote to Emperor Marcian and to the patriarch of Constantinople, Anatolius (451), explaining that "the basis of things secular is one, and the basis of things divine is another, and there can be no sure building save on the rock which the Lord laid as a foundation" (*Epistolae*, CIV). By then it was plain that Rome could not accept this particular canon of the Council of Constantinople in the form in which it was framed.

Ironically, then, the see of Peter was unable to approve the first formal recognition of its own primacy by an Eastern council. For if it had recognized this canon, it would also have been accepting Constantinople as standing in second place to Rome. The Holy See was not prepared to violate the Church's firm tradition. Not until the truly apostolic sees of both Alexandria and Antioch had been submerged in a Muslim sea for more than two centuries would Roman legates at the Fourth General Council of Constantinople, 869–870, finally put their names on a document recognizing Constantinople as the second see of Christendom.

From the standpoint of our present inquiry concerning the primacy of Rome in the early Church, though, it is of considerable significance that a wholly Eastern Church council formally and solemnly did recognize and subscribe to the Roman primacy in the year 381, even if it did so in a way that Rome itself could not ultimately accept. The fundamental fact of this Eastern recognition of the Roman primacy cannot be altered or abolished by subsequent Eastern attempts to modify or deny or evade the consequences of the validity of an entirely canonical Eastern Church action. The Roman primacy was recognized by an Eastern Church council that soon came to be considered the second ecumenical council of the whole Church. The authority of that council is recognized today by all Christian Churches, or communions, that accept the Nicene Creed.

Actually, it was not at all strange in the context of the times that the First Council of Constantinople in 381 should have recognized the primacy of Rome. Just about everybody was coming to recognize the Roman primacy in the course of the fourth century—with relief. The controversies of the Arian era had proved all but insoluble in the absence of a clearly recognized central doctrinal authority in the Church. The Arian troubles had demonstrated only too vividly what the alternative to the Roman primacy was: it was division; it was chaos.

At the same time, there was no other possible claimant to the supreme authority—the ultimate power to decide—in the Church. The idea that a general council might possess supreme authority was still many centuries in the future; at that time there was only an emerging, still vague recognition of what a general council was. Only two of them had taken place, and the second was not yet even recognized as a general council. Nor could the Church's experience with councils up to that time give anyone much confidence that these unwieldy gatherings effectively could exercise supreme authority in any practical way, especially in the shadow of an interested Roman emperor ready to apply pressure to get the outcome he wanted.

Nor, as far as individual Churches were concerned, was there any other see that could rival Rome. During much of the fourth century, the apostolic see of Antioch, like the newcomer see of Constantinople, was in the hands of Arian or Arianizing bishops. Similarly, the apostolic see of Alexandria was for many of these years in the hands of Arian bishops, even if they had been imposed by outside force. The same thing would be true of these other sees at various times in the future: they did in fact fall under the control of heretical bishops. From this perspective, even the temporary lapse of Pope Liberius tends to dwindle into insignificance.

By the second half of the fourth century, the unvarying, unbroken Roman record of preserving the authentic faith of Christ was accepted by practically everyone. We need to cite only a few witnesses to confirm this point. The testimony of St. Jerome and St. Ambrose will serve as well as any.

St. Jerome (c.347–420?), one of the great Latin Fathers of the Church and translator of the Latin Vulgate Bible from the Hebrew and the Greek, was a partisan of Pope Damasus. He knew him personally, had been favored by him, and had served as his secretary for a time. Nevertheless, St. Jerome was notoriously independent-minded and certainly not naïve. Yet, in a letter to Pope Damasus himself, he had the following to say about Damasus' position in the Church:

> Because the East is shattered by the ancient, fierce antagonisms of its peoples and is rending into tiny fragments the undivided and woven tunic of the Lord and the wolves are destroying Christ's vineyard, so that, amid these dry pools that hold no water, it is difficult to know where is the fountain sealed and the garden enclosed: therefore I have thought best to turn to the see of Peter and to the faith that was praised by the apostle's lips, to ask now food for my soul from the source where once I received the raiment of Christ.... You alone preserve unspoiled the heritage of the Fathers....
>
> Away with jealousy of the Roman pre-eminence, away with ambition! I speak to the successor of the Fisherman and to the disciple of the Cross. I follow no one as chief save Christ, but I am joined in communion with your blessedness, that is, with the see of Peter. Upon that rock I know the Church is built. Whoever eats the lamb outside that house

is profane. He who is not in Noah's ark will perish when the flood overwhelms all. . . . (*Epistolae*, XV)

This is an important testimony from one of the premier minds of the day. Then there is the testimony of the great St. Ambrose of Milan (340–397?). From the time that he succeeded the Arian Auxentius in the see of Milan in 374, St. Ambrose was the dominant Church leader in the West throughout the remainder of the pontificate of Pope Damasus and most of the succeeding pontificates as well. Since Milan rather than Rome was being used by the emperors as their Western capital during this period, it was the bishop of Milan rather than the bishop of Rome who most often had to interact directly with the imperial government.

St. Ambrose is perhaps best known today for the incident in 390 in which he threatened Emperor Theodosius I with excommunication unless he agreed to do public penance for his hotheaded order of a massacre of a group of citizens in the circus in Thessalonica. They had been responsible for murdering a commander in the emperor's army, but Theodosius went too far. In dramatic testimony to the ascendancy that the Church had come to exercise over the minds of the time, Theodosius laid aside his imperial insignia at the behest of the bishop and did humble penance for his rash and evil act. That a Roman emperor could be obliged to do this by a Catholic bishop was a dramatic event never to be forgotten in Christendom.

The theory of St. Ambrose matched his practice. He was one of the first major theoreticians of the independence of the Church from the state. As a normal thing the Roman emperors possessed virtually absolute power. This seemed natural; it was hard for people living then to imagine how there could be anything not subject to the Roman emperor. The bishops and the pope as well were all considered the emperor's subjects.

For St. Ambrose the faith the Church had from Christ was self-evidently beyond the jurisdiction of any worldly ruler. In the words of this great bishop of Milan, the crime that stamped the Arians as the worst of all heretics had been that "they were willing to surrender to Caesar the right to rule the Church" (*Isti imperatori volunt dare ius Ecclesiae*). For him, "the emperor [is] within the Church, not above the Church" (*imperator enim intra Ecclesiam, non supra Ecclesiam*)(*Sermo contra Auxentium*).

St. Ambrose was such a preeminent figure in the Church during the last quarter of the fourth century that some historians have even pointed to his stature as a way of belittling the primacy claimed by Rome. Milan clearly outshone Rome in these years. But then the Roman primacy is in no way dependent upon whether the popes shine or not. Ambrose accepted the Roman primacy without question; he was a strong proponent of it. We can examine several things he said about it, beginning with his famous aphorism *Ubi Petrus, ibi Ecclesia* ("Where Peter is, there is the Church"; *Enarr. in ps. XL*, 30).

In 379, for example, preaching the funeral sermon for his own brother, Satyrus, St. Ambrose noted how his brother, when seeking baptism, had inquired whether the local bishop "was in agreement with the Catholic bishops, that is to say, with the Roman Church". Writing about the party of the antipope Ursinus, who had never stopped agitating against Pope Damasus, Ambrose observed:

> They have not the inheritance of Peter, who have not Peter's seat, but rend it by wicked schism and who, furthermore, deny in their rebelliousness that sins can be forgiven in the Church, even though it was said to Peter, "I will give you the keys of the kingdom of heaven." (*De Poenitentia*, I, 7, 33)

A provincial council presided over by Ambrose at Aquileia on the Adriatic in 381 included among its acts a reference to "the Roman Church, head of the whole Roman world, and the sacred faith of the apostles, whence issue the laws of our own venerable communion for everyone" (*Epistolae*, XI).

Like Jerome, Ambrose provides a powerful witness for the Roman primacy, which had become clear to just about everyone by the end of the fourth century. By then it was seen as the necessary and providential remedy for the schisms and heresies that—with the help of the emperors—had almost succeeded in tearing the Church apart; it was seen as literally providential because it was founded upon the faith of the holy apostles Peter and Paul.

The successor of Pope St. Damasus I was Pope St. Siricius (384–399), who had served both Damasus and Liberius as a deacon. The evidence is clear that Siricius was vividly conscious of holding the primacy. He seems to have conducted his affairs in a style that later centuries would recognize as distinctly papal. Siricius is the first pope from whom we have the text of a papal decretal, an instruction or directive having the force of law and couched in the formal chancery style of the imperial edicts of the day. Liberius may have begun the practice of sending out decretals, but the earliest extant text issued from Siricius.

This Sirician decretal is dated February 11, 385. Addressed to Himerius, bishop of Tarragona, Spain, it contains rulings on such questions as the readmission of former heretics to communion with the Church, the proper seasons for baptisms, the age and qualifications for ordination, and clerical continence and celibacy. In tone and substance, the instructions issued by Pope Siricius to a Spanish bishop in this fourth-century decretal could have issued from the Holy See in almost any subsequent century.

By the end of the fourth century, the popes were fully conscious both of their special primatial mission and of many of the things they had to do to carry it out. They seem never to have looked back—except perhaps to the apostle Peter, from whom, as they had all along affirmed, they derived their special authority in the Church; and to the words and acts of their predecessors, Peter's successors, who by this time had already formed a very long and impressive line.

XXI.

Events related to the long conflict over Arianism that beset the Church during the greater part of the fourth century tend to obscure the fact that, in other parts of the Church, developments were proceeding apace. In Africa, as we have noted, the Donatist heresy raged on and would not see its term until the Vandal invasions of the fifth century ravaged both Catholics and Donatists alike. This heresy would not disappear entirely until the Muslims invaded and conquered North Africa in the seventh century—when the Church in Africa was also effectively destroyed.

In the second half of the fourth century, one of the principal results of attempts to contend with the continuing Donatist troubles was a greater realization, also among the Catholics in Africa, of the need for a center of unity in the Church. The necessity was recognized for authoritative decisions regarding the incessant and interminable doctrinal schisms and quarrels that otherwise seemed irresolvable.

Just as the persistence of Arianism helped convince many Eastern bishops that the Roman primacy was indispensable, the persistence of Donatism in Africa convinced many, including Optatus (fl. ca. 370), bishop of Mileve, a town in the

Roman province of Numidia, of the same basic truth. Bishop Optatus composed a treatise on the schism of the Donatists, *De Schismate Donatistarum,* answering all the claims of the Donatists going back to the beginning of their movement. He concluded that unity under the leadership of the Church of Rome was a necessity.

Donatism, it will be recalled, had arisen in Numidia during the days of Constantine. The first Donatists had stigmatized the bishop of Carthage, Caecilian, as having been among those who had betrayed the faith during the persecution of Diocletian. According to them, he was therefore unworthy, indeed no longer *able*, to administer the sacraments. As far as they were concerned, his lapse had nullified his episcopal ordination.

This inability to administer the sacraments extended to all who had been ordained by him as well, according to the Donatists. We saw earlier how even Emperor Constantine had attempted to reconcile the Donatists to the Church. The Donatists, however, rejected all attempts to deal with them that failed to grant their theses. By the time of Optatus in the second half of the fourth century, the Donatists had their own separate network of bishops and churches extending throughout North Africa.

We do not know very much about Optatus, but his treatise on the Donatists was a clear, strong contemporary affirmation of the primacy of Rome in the early Church. Optatus was one of the first to put in definite form the *ex opere operato* explanation of the sacraments that the Church has retained to this day, namely: the sacraments are efficacious in and of themselves and confer the grace they signify. The Church of Rome had always upheld this doctrine, for example, by her steady refusal to *re*baptize, but the theology behind this practice had never, up to then, been as clearly formulated as it was by Optatus. "The sacraments are holy through themselves", Optatus insisted in the second half of the fourth century. "Not through men.... It is God who cleanses, not man" (*De Schismate Donatistarum*, V, 4).

On the subject of the primacy of the bishop of Rome dating back to Peter, Optatus provided one of the strongest formulations up to that time, claiming that the see of Rome, founded by Peter, was the *first* bishopric in the Church, thereby ignoring the temporal priority of Jerusalem and Antioch over Rome, as far as the succession of the bishoprics founded in the Church went. We quote here from a pertinent passage in which Optatus addresses the Donatists:

> We must note who first established a see and where. If you do not know, admit it. If you do know, feel your shame. I cannot charge you with ignorance, for you plainly know. It is a sin to err knowingly, although an ignorant person may be blind to his error. But you cannot deny that you know that the episcopal seat was established first in the city of Rome by Peter and that in it sat Peter, the head of the apostles.... So in the one seat unity is maintained by everyone, that the other apostles might not claim separate seats, each for himself. Accordingly, *he who erects another seat in opposition to that one is a schismatic and a sinner*
>   ... Peter was the first to sit in that one seat, which is the first gift of the Church. To him succeeded Linus. Clement followed Linus. Then [Ana]cletus Clement.... After Damasus, Siricius, who is our contemporary, with whom our whole world is in accord by interchange of letters in one bond of communion. Do you, if you would claim for yourselves a holy Church, explain the origin of your seat....
>   (*De Schismate Donatistarum*, II, 2–3, emphasis added)

Bishop Optatus of Mileve evidently got the order of the earliest popes wrong here, but there can be no doubt concerning the position in the Church in which he placed the see of Peter and Peter's episcopal successors: for Optatus this see provided the guarantee of the unity of the whole Church "in one bond of communion". Anyone who might presume to erect another center of authority in the Church—even the "other apostles" were forbidden to establish "separate seats"!—was obviously "a schismatic and a sinner".

By the end of the fourth century, this belief had become nearly universal in the Church. Optatus is just one of many witnesses for it, and not the least significant one.

Another African bishop, the great St. Augustine (354–430), also writing against the Donatists, would shortly repeat the claim concerning the same Bishop Caecilian who had been traduced by the Donatist sect. In spite of this, according to Augustine, Caecilian continued to be the legitimate bishop of Carthage, principally because he was "joined by letters of communion to the Roman Church, in which the primacy of the apostolic see has always obtained" (*Ep.* XLIII).

XXII.

Although the doctrine of the primacy of jurisdiction and the doctrinal infallibility of the pope were not to be formally defined by the Catholic Church until 1870, these fundamental Church doctrines were already substantially developed by the end of the fourth century. Henceforth it would simply be a matter of how successive popes exercised and elaborated on their almost universally recognized primacy (and infallibility).

We therefore cite only a few further examples demonstrating how acutely conscious the popes would henceforth be of their possession of the primacy, how they generally acted on their understanding of it, and how this primacy was understood and accepted throughout the Church.

We saw in chapter 3 how dramatically different were Nicaea and Constantinople, the first two ecumenical councils in the fourth century, in which the popes were relatively passive, from the fifth-century councils of Ephesus and Chalcedon, in which the interventions of Popes St. Celestine and St. Leo were all-important. These two popes are famous for their acute consciousness of the leadership role they were obliged to play in those two great councils, helping to fashion the Church's critical definitions of the Trinity and of the person and natures of Christ. It would be difficult to illustrate the case for the papal primacy (and infallibility) more plainly than these two great popes did in connection with these two councils.

St. Leo, however, was not the only fifth-century pope through whom Peter "spoke". Elected in 401, Pope St. Innocent I (401–417) outdid his predecessors Julius I and Damasus I in asserting and exercising the Roman primacy. Although he happened to be outside Rome at the time, Innocent I was pope in the year 410, when the city fell to the barbarian leader, Alaric the Goth, and was brutally sacked. (As historian Edward Gibbon so memorably recorded in his *Decline and Fall of the Roman Empire*: "Eleven hundred and sixty-three years after the foundation of Rome, the imperial city, which had subdued and civilized so considerable a part of mankind, was delivered over to the licentious fury of the tribes of Germany and Scythia. . . .")

But if the Roman empire was falling, the papacy was rising; if the civilized European world was descending into barbarism, the popes were trying to maintain and preserve order and civilization, even though their primary task was to promote the faith of Christ. Pope St. Innocent I is known for having issued a series of decretals to various bishops on doctrinal and disciplinary issues, insisting that "the Roman custom" was the proper norm for all the Churches. In a letter to Bishop Vitricius of Rouen written in 401, the year of Innocent's election, he declared that all *causae maiores* ("greater cases") needed to be referred to Rome. This principle would increasingly recur in papal documents.

In addition to carrying on what were by now ordinary papal actions, such as issuing decretals, Pope St. Innocent I carried out a number of other extraordinary actions. He actually excommunicated an Eastern Roman emperor, Arcadius, a bishop of Constantinople, Atticus, and a bishop of Alexandria, Theophilus—and saw all of these extraordinary actions vindicated in the end. These admittedly drastic actions were all taken in connection with the well-known case of the great preacher St. John Chrysostom ("Golden mouth"), ca. 347–407, a bishop of Antioch and later of Constantinople.

In 403 St. John Chrysostom was deposed from the see of Constantinople through the machinations of a bishop of Alexandria, Theophilus. Although the rivalry between Alexandria and Constantinople stemmed from multiple causes, the precedence accorded to Constantinople by the council held in that city in 381 had created continuing bitterness in Alexandria.

The sorry business of the deposition of John came about after some monks who had been expelled by Theophilus from Egypt appealed to the emperor in Constantinople against their bishop. Since the accused, Theophilus, was himself a bishop, Emperor Arcadius at first did not want to judge the case. He referred it to the bishop of Constantinople, St. John Chrysostom. John scrupulously declined to take the case, since judgment of Theophilus properly belonged to the bishops of Egypt, according to the custom of the Church. The emperor, not to be put off by ecclesiastical niceties, ended summoning Theophilus to come from Alexandria to Constantinople to face trial.

The Alexandrian bishop arrived in Constantinople in 403 accompanied by twenty-nine of his suffragan bishops from Egypt—and a not inconsiderable supply of Egyptian gold for purposes of bribery. By then Theophilus was absolutely determined to get St. John Chrysostom deposed, since this bishop of Constantinople had not favored his cause. In due course, Theophilus was able to organize a council, or synod, at the Palace of the Oak across the Bosphorus from Constantinople. Together with his suffragan bishops, and along with some other Church malcontents in the capital—whom he had bribed—he organized the so-called Synod of the Oak, which deposed St. John Chrysostom from the see of Constantinople.

Incredibly, Emperor Arcadius, influenced, perhaps, by his empress, Eudoxia, ratified the sentence. Eudoxia believed that she had been personally embarrassed by the fiery preaching of the saintly bishop of Constantinople. Through a subsequent series of maneuvers, the sentence against John was first withdrawn, then reimposed; he was banished from the city, returned, then banished again.

Meanwhile, St. John Chrysostom appealed his case to the bishop of Rome, Pope St. Innocent I. Innocent wrote back condemning the false Synod of the Oak and endorsed St. John's suggestion that a bishop of Constantinople should be judged by an impartial assembly of bishops from both East and West. The Western emperor, Honorius (395–423), endorsed this plan, but messengers from the West bearing the words of the pope and the Western emperor were not allowed to enter the city of Constantinople.

The condemnation of St. John Chrysostom was upheld, meanwhile, and he was banished to the far eastern reaches of the Anatolian peninsula (modern Turkey), where, worn out, he died on September 14, 407. At this point Pope Innocent I resorted to the extraordinary measure of excommunicating the

Eastern emperor and the bishops of Constantinople and Alexandria for their part in John's unjust condemnation and exile.

The pope stuck to his guns with typical Roman intransigence for years thereafter, until all parties finally came around to a just view of the matter. "Communion, once broken off," this pope insisted, "cannot be renewed until the person concerned gives proof that the reasons for which communion was broken off are no longer operative."

This was a constant Roman position on such matters. As often as not, even to our own day, the "intransigence" of the popes has often been criticized, and their "absolutist" positions deplored. Why the popes are not instead admired and praised for consistently sticking to the principles they profess is a question critics of the papacy will have to answer for themselves. An examination of many of the cases of papal intransigence in history will often reveal the great willingness of the popes to go on negotiating, sometimes long after there is any chance whatsoever of reaching agreement.

There are some principles and positions that the popes will and should *never* give up. Any competent authority obliged to uphold established principles and positions is bound to be seen as intransigent by those who disagree. But even the open enemies of the Church ought to credit the popes with being consistent with their own principles.

Another dramatic example illustrating the position the see of Rome had achieved by the pontificate of Pope St. Innocent I concerns the condemnation of the heretic Pelagius by two provincial councils in Africa. Pelagius, a British monk, lived for a number of years in Rome, where he acquired a reputation as a moralist and spiritual director. He came to espouse a viewpoint that unduly exalted human free will and downplayed the role of divine grace, essentially denying the Catholic doctrine of Original Sin.

The views of Pelagius proved to be quite popular among many people and continued to spread, inevitably arousing opposition. The great St. Augustine of Hippo composed a number of incisive tracts against Pelagianism. In due course, two councils held in different parts of Africa condemned the views of Pelagius; in 416, one African council expressly renewed a condemnation of Pelagius that had been decided upon by an African council in 412. The African bishops then forwarded their judgments to Rome.

Pope St. Innocent I replied to the African bishops the following year, accepting the decisions of the two African councils. Concerning this reply, St. Augustine wrote: "Already two synods have sent to the Apostolic See concerning this affair. The rescripts have come from there. The cause is finished (*causa finita est*). Would that at last the error were finished too!" (*Sermo* CXXXI).

This incident was ostensibly the origin of the widely quoted statement regularly attributed to Augustine: *Roma locuta est, causa finita est* ("Rome has spoken, the cause is finished"; meaning, the matter is settled). It should be evident from both the text and the context that what St. Augustine actually said was slightly different than what the statement is generally taken to mean. Augustine seems to have been referring to the whole process: two African councils had considered the views of Pelagius and correctly judged him to be in error. Following this, the only possible court of appeal, the bishop of Rome, confirmed the judgment of the African councils; the appeal process was accordingly exhausted, and it was time for the heretics to desist as well—they stood no chance of ever persuading the Church of their aberrant views in the face of a Roman judgment upholding a legitimate Church synod.

The matter was indeed settled—not *just* because "Rome had spoken", but because the whole Church process for arriving at correct doctrine had been gone through and the result had gone against the Pelagians. Thus, what Augustine actually meant in this case was more nuanced than what is usually meant when the saying *Roma locuta est, causa finita est* is quoted.

The meaning generally attributed to the saying is not thereby to be considered false. It is true; it expresses the plain meaning of the ultimate power of decision in the Church that is necessarily inherent in the Roman primacy. It was almost inevitable that the saying would be perpetuated because it *does* express the basic meaning of the Roman primacy so accurately.

Nor is the adapted saying in any way false to the facts of the case out of which it arose. For the African referral to Rome in this case elicited from Innocent I perhaps the strongest and clearest statement up to that time asserting the supremacy of the Roman *teaching authority*, or Magisterium. The actual words of what Augustine called the "rescript" that came back from Rome are very significant in the development of the papal teaching office. This is what Pope St. Innocent I wrote to the African bishops in the case of Pelagianism:

> [We approve your action] that nothing which was done even in the most remote and distant provinces should be taken as *finally settled* unless it came to the notice of this see, that any just pronouncement might be *confirmed by all the authority of this see*, and that other Churches might from thence gather what they should *teach*. . . . (*Epistolae* XXIX, January 417; emphases added)

Because of both the manner and the matter of his words and actions, Pope St. Innocent I has sometimes been referred to as "the first pope". That is certainly far from the case: there were many such popes before him. The words and actions of Pope Innocent were *typical* of many of his predecessors, as was his understanding of the nature of the authority conferred by Christ on Peter as it had developed in the history of the Church of Rome.

Innovativeness is generally *not* among the salient characteristics of the see of Peter. Consistency in preserving and handing on what had been handed down from Jesus Christ, however, has been a hallmark of the incumbents of the Roman see, and this was eminently true of Pope St. Innocent I.

The immediate successors of Pope St. Innocent I in the early part of the fifth century continued along the same lines. Pope St. Boniface I (418–422) wrote, "It has never been lawful for what has once been decided by the apostolic see to be reconsidered." Years later, Pope St. Hilarus (461–468) circulated a decretal emphasizing the Roman primacy throughout the entire East, confirming the Councils of Nicaea (325), Ephesus (431), and Chalcedon (451), as well as the *Tome* of Pope St. Leo the Great.

Actions of this kind were by then habitual for the popes. By that time, *all* of the popes regularly functioned as had these fifth-century popes. The primacy of Rome was an established, well-documented fact throughout the Catholic Church.

XXIII.

To conclude this chapter on the primacy of Rome in the early Church, we look at those pontiffs who were involved in the so-called Acacian schism of the late fifth and early sixth centuries. It is instructive to see how this particular crisis was handled. Papal authority was very much a factor in the whole affair.

The Acacian schism involved a break in relations between the Church of the East and Church of the West that lasted from 484 to 519. The schism spanned five pontificates and constituted a very interesting kind of dress rehearsal for subsequent schisms between East and West that would culminate in the final break, in 1054, which unfortunately endures to our own day (although the mutual excommunications of 1054 were rescinded by Pope Paul VI and Patriarch Athenagoras of Constantinople when they met together in Jerusalem in 1964).

The Acacian schism came about as a result of the efforts of the Eastern emperors to become reconciled with their Monophysite subjects, especially those residing in Egypt and Syria. Many Christians in both countries had continued to resist the Chalcedonian Catholic orthodoxy that had been the official religion of the empire—as well as of the Church!—since the 450s. Successive Christian emperors encountered continuing and sometimes bitter opposition to the decisions of the Council of Chalcedon from some of their subjects; sometimes this opposition seemed based on nationalism rather than on religious differences.

The Monophysites in Egypt, for example, viewed the deposition by Chalcedon of Bishop Dioscoros as a deep national humiliation. They viewed the banishment of his successor, Timothy Aelurus ("the Cat"), the same way. Egypt and Alexandria, after all, had earlier fought successfully against nearly the entire empire for Nicene orthodoxy and the cause of St. Athanasius; Egypt and Alexandria had triumphed at the Council of Ephesus with St. Cyril (acting under a mandate from Pope St. Celestine I).

The irony was that the Alexandrians, heirs of St. Athanasius, were fighting, no longer for the cause of Catholic orthodoxy, but mostly for their tradition, for pride. This basic difference between their actions and the earlier actions of an Athanasius and a Cyril seems to have escaped the Egyptian Monophysites of this later period. What seemed to move them most strongly was the humiliation they felt. Their resentment was often directed more against Constantinople and the empire than against Rome; yet once they had embraced the Monophysite heresy, the break with Rome was inevitable, as was the break with Constantinople.

Questions of truth and doctrinal orthodoxy were not always the main concern of Constantinople. Almost from the time of the adoption of Christianity as the religion of the empire, the Christian emperors often were prepared to sacrifice the authentic truth of Christ—as verified in the decisions of the bishops of Rome and the general councils of the Church—for the sake of expediency and for the order, peace, and concord of the empire. This tendency was especially pronounced in the period we are now discussing and would continue as long as the eastern Roman Empire endured.

Emperors who were orthodox Catholics were willing enough to impose Catholic orthodoxy by political means. Less orthodox emperors were equally prepared to use political means to enforce *their* versions of the faith upon their subjects, even when these versions diverged widely from Catholic orthodoxy. Imposing a variant faith on the Church by means of state power certainly did not accord with Christ's promise that the gates of hell would not prevail against the Church (cf. Mt 16:18). Rather, it confirmed, time and time again, the wisdom of Christ in committing the cause of Christian truth into the hands of Peter and his successors rather than allowing it to be subject to those who happened to hold political power—or who were in a position to influence those in power.

For more than twenty years after the Council of Chalcedon, the Eastern emperors, principally Leo I (457–474), enforced Chalcedonian orthodoxy throughout the empire and banished dissident bishops. After Leo's death in 474, riots and disturbances broke out in various places. These uprisings convinced the usurper of the imperial throne, Leo's successor, Basilicus, that the Monophysites had to be accommodated. He reverted to the policy of the Arianizing emperors of the previous century: he imposed official state solutions to deal with religious disagreements.

In this particular case, Basilicus decided to recall the deposed Alexandrian Monophysite bishop, Timothy the Cat (so-called on account of his feline features). Basilicus also presumed to annul the decisions of Chalcedon by his imperial authority and to decree the return of the Church to Nicaea as the sole declared standard of faith.

Accordingly, Basilicus circulated an imperial letter, the *Encyclion*, in which he wrote, "We decree that all the bishops of the world shall anathematize, and give to the flames, the *Tome* of [Pope St.] Leo and all that was done at Chalcedon in the matter of faith." While approving of Nicaea and Ephesus, this imperial usurper also approved of the Robber Council (*Latrocinium*) of Ephesus of 449; at the same time, he condemned the doctrine of Eutyches, the archimandrite in Constantinople who had been one of the principal proponents of early Monophysitism.

The doctrine of Basilicus was a hodgepodge. Nevertheless, every bishop was commanded to add his signature to the *Encyclion*, and in the twenty months (475–476) that Basilicus controlled the imperial throne, hundreds of bishops did. Many sincerely Catholic bishops signed because they understood the document simply to be condemning Monophysitism in condemning Eutyches; and as had been the case with Nicaea and its *homo-ousios* a century and a half earlier, many of them were not convinced that the terminology of Chalcedon was essential to the integrity of the faith.

In the meantime, many Monophysite or Monophysite-tending bishops were also willing to sign because they no longer identified their position narrowly with that of Eutyches—and the *Encyclion*, after all, did condemn Chalcedon, the council to which most of them objected. It was a document expressly crafted by the usurper to be a consensus, or compromise, document, and, as is so often the case with such documents, it prescinded from the question of authentic doctrinal truth. The point was to gather as many signatures as possible and thus achieve "agreement" and "peace" by papering over existing differences.

In 476, a rightful emperor, Zeno (d. 491), regained the imperial throne. He too was determined to impose peace. On the advice of the new bishop of Constantinople, Acacius, he proposed to deal with the religious question by means slightly less crude than those of Basilicus but that nevertheless represented another solution decided on by the emperor on his sole authority, neither consulting with nor seeking the agreement of the Church's bishops or any authoritative Church body.

The solution suggested by Bishop Acacius and imposed by Emperor Zeno was another irenic formula, the *Henoticon*, issued by the emperor in 482. The *Henoticon* condemned by name both Eutyches and Nestorius, approved the Twelve Anathemas St. Cyril of Alexandria had drawn up against the latter, and declared that "one of the Trinity was incarnate". The document avoided any mention of either one or two natures in Christ and concluded by anathematizing any heresy, "whether advanced at Chalcedon or at any synod whatever". This formulation simply left open the *essential* question of whether there had been, or could have been, any heresy advanced at Chalcedon. Signatories of the *Henoticon* could decide for themselves whether or not the general Council of Chalcedon fostered heresy—in other words, whether or not it was even a legitimate ecumenical council of the Catholic Church. This was surely an early example of private theological judgment espoused by a Christian emperor!

This papering over of the differences between the parties was somehow supposed to satisfy all sides. It was a typical imperial compromise, fastened upon the Church from outside; it was in no sense a true Church decision.

All parties involved in theological disputes were at least agreed on the importance of doctrinal truth, of correctly expressing what God had revealed in Christ about his own persons and nature. But there was disagreement, strong and sometimes violent, about where the authority *to define* the authentic teaching of Christ was to be found.

No one who has followed our inquiry up to this point will be surprised at the reaction of the bishop of Rome to the *Henoticon* of Emperor Zeno and Patriarch Acacius. (By this time, the term *patriarch* was being applied to the incumbents of the great apostolic sees of Alexandria and Antioch and of "the New Rome", Constantinople; the pope had meanwhile been regularly called "the Patriarch of the West". The term *pope*, indicating precisely his primacy over the whole Church, had only recently been applied exclusively to him.)

Reigning at the time of Zeno's *Henoticon* was Pope St. Felix II (483–492). The patriarch of Alexandria was another Monophysite, Peter Mongos ("the Hoarse"). The deposed, rightful Egyptian patriarch, John Talaia, like a number of his predecessors, had been forced to take refuge with the pope in Rome. Similarly, the patriarch of Antioch around this time was yet another Monophysite, Peter, surnamed "the Fuller".

Considering the tendencies of these incumbents, it is not surprising that the emperor was seeking some compromise formula that could satisfy all parties. From the point of view of Catholic doctrine, the gravity of the situation made the definition and promulgation of the authentic truth of Christ even more essential.

Understandably concerned about so many developments unfavorable to Catholic orthodoxy, Pope Felix II dispatched simultaneous letters to Emperor Zeno and to the patriarch Acacius in Constantinople. In his letter to the emperor, the pope called for the deposition of the Alexandrian Monophysite Peter Mongos and the restoration of Chalcedonian orthodoxy. He also asked for assistance from the emperor for the Catholics of North Africa, who were being terribly persecuted by Arian Vandal invaders.

In his letter to Acacius, Felix strongly reproached the Eastern prelate for his support of Peter Mongos and of Emperor Zeon's *Henoticon*. In a subsequent letter, the pope actually summoned Acacius to Rome to answer the grave charges the deposed Alexandrian Catholic patriarch, John Talaia, had lodged against him.

However, the ambassadors Pope Felix despatched to Constantinople themselves failed, apparently after torture, to uphold the pope's position. Among other things, during the public celebration of the Eucharist, the papal legates stood by while Acacius included the Monophysite Peter Mongos in the diptychs—the names of the living and the dead being publicly prayed for by the Church. This inevitably created the impression that the pope approved of both Peter Mongos and the *Henoticon*—exactly the impression Pope Felix wanted to avoid.

Pope Felix responded to the failure of his own embassy to Constantinople by convening a Roman synod, which met on July 25, 484. As a result of the deliberations of this synod, the pope decided to excommunicate the patriarch of Constantinople, Acacius, along with his own legates. It must be remembered that the popes possessed no significant material power at this time; if they could not, by moral suasion, motivate the emperor and the state authorities to act in support of the Church and orthodox doctrine, the popes had little recourse.

Acacius, who enjoyed the patronage of the emperor, reacted to his excommunication by Pope Felix by dropping mention of *him* from the diptychs—in effect, excommunicating the pope! The patriarch of Constantinople on this occasion expressly preferred communion with the Monophysite Alexandrian patriarch, Peter Mongos, to communion with Pope St. Felix II. The Acacian schism between East and West had begun. It would last thirty-five years.

Acacius died in 489, unreconciled and apparently unrepentant. Zeno, who had imposed his compromise solution to the Monophysite problem crafted by Acacius, followed the latter to the grave two years later. Zeno was succeeded by another emperor with Monophysite sympathies, Anastasius I (491–518). Pope Felix died the following year, 492, wholly unsuccessful in his efforts to counter a renegade archbishop of Constantinople supported by a renegade Christian emperor.

XXIV.

Pope St. Gelasius I (492–496), who followed Pope St. Felix II, was one of the great successors of Peter during this period. Born in Rome, although of African descent, Gelasius was the first pope to be called "the Vicar of Christ",

having been given this title by a Roman synod in the year
495. Gelasius, a very active pontiff, issued numerous decretals and composed several theological tracts; his reign, however, was relatively short.

Pope Gelasius articulated the teaching that it was the pope's
prerogative, a function of the primacy, to ratify the acts of
Church councils, insure that they were carried out, and defend them if and when they were neglected or challenged.
According to Gelasius, the pope "judges the whole Church
and himself stands before no tribunal, and no judgment can
be passed on his judgment, nor can his decision be abro-
gated" (PL 59.28B). It would be difficult to make the case
for the Roman primacy more clearly than in that papal statement dating from the end of the fifth century.

Pope Gelasius was also one of the great theoreticians of
the Ambrosian idea of freedom of the Church from the absolutism of the Roman imperial government. His often-
quoted letter to the Byzantine emperor Anastasius I on this
subject is deservedly famous:

> There are, most august Emperor, two powers by which this
> world is chiefly ruled: the sacred authority of the popes and
> the royal power. Of these the priestly power is much more
> important, because it has to render account for the kings of
> men themselves to the divine tribunal. For you know, our
> very clement son, that although you have the chief place in
> dignity over the human race, yet you too must submit your-
> self faithfully to those who have charge of divine things, and
> look to them for the means of your salvation.... (Letter *Duo
> Quippe Sunt*, 494)

Only by a fortunate historical chance was Gelasius able to
write in this vein to the emperor and to pursue the idea of
the freedom of the Church with such clarity and vigor. This

was because, temporarily, the popes were no longer subjects of the Roman emperor in Constantinople. Between 476 and 536, barbarian Gothic kings ruled Italy, including Rome; although they were Arians, they were tolerant for the times, and the popes were able to operate in relative freedom during this period.

Except for these few years at the end of the fifth and the beginning of the sixth centuries, the popes were *always* subjects of the all-powerful, Roman emperor. This was true until the eighth century. The early popes were not rulers as the medieval popes came to be. The fact that, while continuing to be subjects, the popes were nevertheless able to establish the Roman primacy in the Church and to succeed in getting it accepted throughout the Church is not the slightest of miracles in the Church's history.

As regards the continuing Acacian schism, Pope Gelasius had little sympathy for the ambitions of Constantinople to rule in the Church. He refused to be reconciled with the patriarch Euphemius (489–495) because, although otherwise orthodox, Euphemius nevertheless continued to include the names of Acacius and other signers of the *Henoticon* in the diptychs. (It would have been difficult for any patriarch of Constantinople to drop them when the emperor was determined to retain them.)

The immediate successor of Gelasius, Pope Anastasius II (496–498), took a slightly more conciliatory line. He wrote to Emperor Anastasius, actively seeking to heal the Acacian schism. This pope had an ulterior motive: he wanted the barbarian ruler of Italy, Theodoric the Ostrogoth, to be officially recognized as ruler by the emperor. And the pope did succeed in getting this recognition for Theodoric in the course of his short reign, but his efforts to heal the schism came to nothing.

The efforts exerted by the next pope, Pope St. Symmachus (498–514), also came to nothing. Symmachus was distracted during his tenure by the activities of an antipope, Lawrence, elected by a faction of the Roman clergy in part because of disagreements about whether or not to take a hard line in dealing with Constantinople. Nothing Rome could have done would have availed, for the attitude of Emperor Anastasius had so hardened that he was determined to impose Monophysitism on the Church everywhere he could. And he had a formidable ally in the newly installed patriarch of Antioch, Severus, who had been elevated to that see after a long career as a determined theological opponent of Chalcedon.

The efforts of Emperor Anastasius to impose Monophysitism ceased only with his death in 518, although continuing failure to reconcile the Monophysites may have changed his viewpoint somewhat toward the end of his life. In both 515 and 517 he agreed to receive Roman delegations again. These delegations were sent by Rome when the emperor, in difficulties because of his ecclesiastical policy, fell back once again on the imperial policy of calling a council. The pope was willing to discuss this; here was one more case in which Rome proved ready to talk if anything might come from talking. The familiar Roman intransigence normally surfaced only when a basic principle or doctrinal orthodoxy was at stake.

Nothing came of these Roman delegations. The healing of the Acacian schism and the restoration of communion between East and West were only destined to come about when a staunch Catholic who subscribed to the Council of Chalcedon became the new emperor. This was Emperor Justin (518–527), who had been prefect of the Praetorian Guard under Anastasius.

Pope St. Hormisdas (514–523), an Italian despite his name, which was apparently of Persian origin, sent two unsuccessful delegations, in 515 and 517, to treat with Anastasius. He was ready and willing to reach a suitable agreement with the new emperor.

Justin, like his nephew and better-known successor, the great Emperor Justinian (527–565), was anxious to achieve a settlement. These emperors needed the restoration of peace and communion with the Holy See in order to undertake the reconquest of the Western empire from the barbarians—an enterprise that, although never completed, was to be one of Justinian's many great works.

Just six days after the coronation of Justin in 518, an excited congregation in Sancta Sophia demanded that the emperor and the new patriarch of Constantinople restore Chalcedonian orthodoxy and depose the Monophysite patriarch of Antioch, Severus. Shortly afterward, a synod in the capital accepted an appeal from some monks to allow all the exiled Chalcedonians to return. More significantly, the new emperor, Justin, invited Pope Hormisdas to come to Constantinople to proclaim the restoration of Catholic orthodoxy in the East.

In time-honored Roman fashion, Hormisdas sent five papal legates to Constantinople in his place; they included a Greek-speaking deacon, Dioscurus, two bishops, a priest, and another deacon. The delegation carried a document containing the terms of the "settlement" of the Acacian schism drafted in Rome. Like the *Tome* of Pope St. Leo the Great before the Council of Chalcedon, this document was not drawn up as the basis for any negotiation.

The Formula of Hormisdas (519) contained perhaps the clearest and strongest statement of the primacy of Rome in the Church ever. The instructions given to the papal legates by Pope Hormisdas demanded unconditional acceptance of this document by Constantinople as the sine qua non of reunion. There was to be no discussion; signatories to the document were required to agree that if they should ever go back on their acceptance of the document, they would become accomplices of the very heresies and heretics condemned in the document.

The Formula of Hormisdas is of such importance in the history of the Church that it merits being reproduced in full here:

The first condition of salvation is to keep the norm of the true faith and in no way to deviate from the established doctrine of the Fathers. For it is impossible that the words of our Lord Jesus Christ, who said, "Thou art Peter, and upon this rock I will build my Church," (Mt 16:18), should not be verified. And their truth has been proved by the course of history, for in the Apostolic See the Catholic religion has always been kept unsullied. From this hope and faith we by no means desire to be separated and, following the doctrine of the Fathers, we declare anathema all heresies, and, especially, the heretic Nestorius, former bishop of Constantinople, who was condemned by the Council of Ephesus, by Blessed Celestine, bishop of Rome, and by the venerable Cyril, bishop of Alexandria. We likewise condemn and declare to be anathema Eutyches and Dioscoros of Alexandria, who were condemned in the holy Council of Chalcedon, which we follow and endorse. This Council followed the holy Council of Nicaea and preached the apostolic faith. And we condemn the assassin Timothy, surnamed Aelurus ["the Cat"] and also Peter [Mongos] of Alexandria, his disciple and follower in everything. We also declare anathema their helper and follower, Acacius of Constantinople, a bishop once condemned by the Apostolic See, and all those who remain in contact and company with them. Because this Acacius joined himself to their communion, he deserved to receive a judgment of condemnation similar to theirs. Furthermore, we condemn Peter ["the Fuller"] of Antioch with all his followers together with the followers of all those mentioned above.

Following, as we have said before, the Apostolic See in all things and proclaiming all its decisions, we endorse and approve all the letters which Pope St. Leo wrote concerning the Christian religion. And so I hope I may deserve to be associated with you in the one communion which the Apostolic See proclaims, in which the whole, true, and perfect security of the Christian religion resides. I promise that from now on those who are separated from the communion of the Catholic Church, that is, who are not in agreement with the Apostolic See, will not have their names read during the sacred mysteries. But if I attempt even the least deviation from my profession, I admit that, according to my own declaration, I am an accomplice to those whom I have condemned. I have signed this, my profession, with my own hand, and I have directed it to you, Hormisdas, the holy and venerable pope of Rome. (*The Church Teaches*, pp. 70–71)

None of the ancient patriarchates of Alexandria, Antioch, or Constantinople emerged unscathed from this severe Roman judgment, which clearly equates orthodoxy with what the Roman see has defined or endorsed, as it equates communion with the Apostolic see with being in the Catholic Church in the full sense—as St. Irenaeus had contended in the second century.

The Formula of Hormisdas was destined to have a continuing influence in the history of the Church. It would be invoked or quoted in subsequent centuries. It served as a basis for the famous *Dictatus Papae* of the great medieval Pope St. Gregory VII in 1075 ("The Roman Church has never erred, nor, by the testimony of Scripture, will it ever err"). It was also one of the sources for the 1870 definition given

by the First Vatican Council concerning of the primacy and
infallibility of the pope. Vatican I quoted the Formula at some
length, saying that "in the Apostolic See the Catholic religion has always been kept unsullied" and that "the whole,
true, and perfect security of the Christian religion resides
[in] ... the one communion which the Apostolic See proclaims" (*Pastor Aeternus*, IV).

But how was the Formula of Hormisdas received in Constantinople in the year 519? The document was subscribed to
as written—not without some initial hesitation—by the Eastern emperor, Justin, by the patriarch of Constantinople, John,
and by some 250 Eastern bishops. John of Constantinople added
a gloss in signing the document, not modifying the text itself
but claiming for his see the second rank among the sees of
Christendom—which the Council of Constantinople had accorded to it but Rome had never recognized up to that point.

Thus, in 519, all the leaders of the Eastern Church, whatever their motives or the pressures weighing on them, *officially subscribed to and affirmed the primacy of Rome in the Church
of Christ*; in other words, *the Eastern Church officially and ca-
nonically accepted the primacy of the pope.*

No modern reader with even the slightest acquaintance
with the history of the Church will imagine that this agreement was destined to hold. It did not even hold for very
long. Nevertheless, history records that there was a time in
the early Church when both East and West affirmed in most
solemn terms the primacy of Rome.

If, as some still argue today, the periodic instances of Eastern opposition to the papal primacy somehow tend to prove
that the Roman primacy based on Christ's commission to
Peter was not a divinely willed feature of the Church of Christ,
then the contrary phenomenon, this solemn adherence of
the leadership of the Eastern Church to the wholly canon-

ical Formula of Hormisdas ought to tell in favor of the Roman primacy. It is impossible to have it both ways.

More than that, the Fourth General Council of Constantinople, 869–870—called by the Byzantine emperor in time-honored Eastern fashion—adopted an only slightly modified version of the Formula, which was agreed to by all of the Eastern participants. Later, in what was becoming a a different Eastern pattern, Constantinople IV ceased to be recognized in the East as ecumenical—in part *because* it had solemnly reaffirmed the Roman primacy.

The Roman primacy was reaffirmed at two more ecumenical councils—although not recognized as such by the Eastern Church: the Second General Council of Lyons, in 1274, and the Council of Florence, 1438–1445. There was Eastern representation at both of these councils, and the acts proclaiming the Roman primacy were agreed to by the Eastern participants. By this time, though, the principal Eastern motive for participating in or agreeing to the acts of these Western general councils seems to have been the desire of the Byzantine emperors to secure Western military assistance against the always rising Muslim and Turkish threat.

Back home among their own people, however, the subjects of the emperor seem to have hated the Latins even more than they feared the Turks—an antipathy greatly intensified following the brutal conquest and sack of Constantinople by the Western crusaders in the year 1204. After that unfortunate event, whatever the Byzantine emperor or patriarch of Constantinople might find expedient to agree to at councils held in the West was likely to be a dead letter in the East. Such are the unhappy consequences of historical sins of Christians.

Nevertheless, subsequent councils held in the West were authentic ecumenical councils, all of them expressly referenced and quoted in the famous 1870 Dogmatic Constitution of Vatican I, *Pastor Aeternus*, defining forever the doctrine of the primacy and infallibility of the pope. As noted above, Vatican I's *Pastor Aeternus* incorporated verbatim several propositions from the Formula of Hormisdas of 519.

Even at the time, the principles enshrined in the Formula were also incorporated into the great civil code of laws of Justinian of 529, the *Corpus Juris Civilis*, in which Justinian included an enactment dating from the time of Emperor Valentinian III (425–455). It read as follows:

> Since the primacy of the Apostolic See has been confirmed by the merits of St. Peter, the prince and the crown of the episcopacy, by the dignity of the city of Rome, and also by the authority of the holy synods, no one should presume to attempt to do anything illicit outside the authority of this see. For the peace of the Churches will finally be preserved everywhere when the whole Church is subject to its supreme ruler. (Quoted in Davis, *The First Seven Ecumenical Councils*, pp. 226–27)

This was the civil law. As we have noted, the Church herself never grounded the Roman primacy in the dignity of the city of Rome. However, Justinian and the lawyers who helped him draft his great Code, conscious of the need to make the case for Constantinople on account of its "dignity", could not have failed to include a reference to the (former) secular position of Rome along with the reference to Christ's commission to Peter. Included in the Code was the following:

> [T]he most holy pope of ancient Rome is the first of all the hierarchs and . . . the holy bishop of Constantinople—the new Rome—occupies the second see, after the holy and apostolic see of Rome, but with precedence over all other sees.

Even in the Justinian Code, the bishop of Rome is "the first of all the hierarchs": the bishop of Rome enjoys the primacy in the Church. Even though the Eastern Church has long since receded from the position to which it solemnly agreed in 519 and after, we can conclude our inquiry at this point, confident that the see of Peter did enjoy the primacy in the early Church, and did so with the agreement of substantially the whole ancient, undivided Church—the One, Holy, Catholic, and Apostolic Church of the Creed.

XXV.

Our review of the earliest available historical data allows us to conclude that the bishops of Rome were conscious of possessing a very special authority in the Church of Christ—the primacy—which they did not fail to exercise in accordance with the means available to them.

Since the Church of Christ was an illegal, often hounded, and generally despised entity for roughly the first three centuries of her existence, it is not surprising that the historical record testifying to the primacy of Rome in the early Church is sparse. Nevertheless, on the basis of the historical data, we can assert that there is much that points to the conclusion that Rome did indeed possess this primacy and was generally understood in the Church at large to possess it—even though the primacy had not yet achieved the development that it would later have.

There was no other possible candidate than Rome for the primacy. All of the other apostolic sees, like so many of the other sees, were more than once in the hands of heretical bishops.

All available historical data show that the developed doctrine of the Church today, handed down from the time of the apostles, never could have been handed down intact if, time after time, the bishops of Rome had not seen fit to intervene to preserve the integrity of "the catholic faith that comes to us from the apostles", as the Roman Canon of the Mass expresses it today.

In particular, the collegial method of Church government characteristic of the early local and provincial synods and councils proved to be incapable of maintaining by itself either the Church's unity or her authentic teaching. Similarly, national Churches everywhere proved equally incapable of maintaining and handing on intact the full, authentic teaching of Christ.

A study similar to ours, of later centuries in the history of the Church, would yield many comparable instances of what we have seen in the early Church, in which papal interventions were absolutely essential to the preservation of the Church's authentic life and doctrine. Advocates of a universal Church of Christ without a recognized successor of Peter at her head need to recognize and admit that, on the basis of the data reviewed here, they are advocating an ecclesiology originally devised and practiced by such as the Montanists, Donatists, Arians, Nestorians, and Monophysites, who on more than one occasion almost succeeded in destroying the Church of Christ—except that the bishop of Rome was always there.

It is time—and it is also fair—to ask those Christians who oppose the pope and the papacy: Why *not* a Roman primacy? Christ undeniably made his promise to Peter. Why should the primacy not continue to reside in the successors of Peter in the see of Rome? This particular model of the Church has worked better in the history of Christianity than any other, just as the—in one sense, very mysterious—preeminence of the Catholic Church continues among the communions and communities that still claim the name of Christ today.

If Christ called out Peter and set him and his successors apart to perform a special mission to insure the perpetuation of his word and his work and the unity of his followers in this very divided and sinful world, then the actual history of the see of Peter provides evidence of how that mission, time after time, has been fulfilled. Just as the history of the great ecumenical councils of the Church sometimes gives us a sense that, despite the turmoil and even chaos that often accompanied them, these gatherings were directed from "elsewhere" toward their essential goal. The history of the see of Peter also gives us the sense that the incumbents of the Roman see were nearly always protected and somehow mysteriously guided from "elsewhere".

In an 1817 book on the phenomenon of the papacy, *Du Pape* (*On the Pope*), Joseph de Maistre collected many examples of how the see of Peter down through the centuries mysteriously functioned exactly the way any institution possessing a primacy over sister institutions *would* function. This author was a diplomat and close observer of public affairs during a lifetime spanning the French Revolution and the Napoleonic Wars. This was a period in history that saw the physical abduction by armed soldiery of two popes in succession, Pope Pius VI and Pope Pius VII. Each of these popes was forcibly removed from Rome and transported north of the Alps—the first of them to die a painful death there—to serve the secular agenda of the new imperial power that had arisen in Paris. Napoleon Bonaparte initially viewed the pope as playing a useful chaplain's role in his new empire; like Constantius II in antiquity, he aimed to bend the Church to his purposes, not allowing her the freedom to pursue hers.

In this aim Napoleon was ultimately no more successful than Constantius had been, but, while he was engaged in trying to reduce the head of the Church to a subservient status in the French Empire, the outcome of the whole affair for the Church was long in doubt; observers at the time could not fail to be seized by the titanic clash taking place between pope and emperor. Astute observer that he was, Joseph de Maistre did not fail to draw important lessons about the nature and function of the papacy from observing the conduct of Pope Pius VII under these unusual circumstances. Even though the pope was at one point the prisoner of Napoleon, by virtue of being the head of the worldwide Church, he eventually won out (just as he had earlier obliged Napoleon to conclude a concordat). Napoleon found that he simply could not proceed with his imperial plans *against* the Church.

It was Pius VII who abolished, with the stroke of a pen, the entire hierarchy of France, hopelessly decimated and compromised by the French Revolution, and appointed a new French hierarchy in its place to carry out the concordat that he had concluded with Napoleon. Nobody then knew that the pope possessed the authority to abolish an entire national hierarchy—any more than anybody before the end of the second century knew that Pope St. Victor I had the authority to excommunicate entire Churches over the question of the proper celebration of Easter. Victor was responding to the failure of the system of the early local and regional synods to resolve the problems faced by the Church, just as Pius VII was responding to the failures of the bishops who had proved unable to carry out their commission from Christ under the relentless tyrannies of the French Revolution and Napoleon.

The papacy, always there by the will of Christ, managed to survive the French Revolution and Napoleon, just as it had survived Constantius II more than fourteen hundred years earlier. Observing this improbable and uncanny ability—in every age—of the see and bishops of Rome to survive the most amazing ordeals, Joseph de Maistre came to believe that something more than human was involved. And why not?—if indeed it was Jesus Christ, the Son of the living God, who had made a promise to that effect to one Simon Peter, a Galilean fisherman who went on to other things following Jesus Christ's command and ended his career as head of Christ's Church in Rome.

Joseph de Maistre was not insensible to the charge, frequently heard, that "absolute" authority, such as the popes', inevitably results in its own kind of tyranny. This witness to the tyranny of the "general will" of the French Revolution astutely points out, however, that the pope's authority, though supreme, is far from absolute: the pope is strictly bound by, and cannot deviate from, Catholic tradition. The pope is, in effect, bound by the authentic acts of all of his predecessors in the see of Peter!

As the Second Vatican Council pointed out, the pope's supreme teaching authority, or Magisterium, is bound by sacred Scripture and sacred tradition:

> This Magisterium is not superior to the word of God, but is its servant. It teaches only what has been handed on to it. At the divine command and with the Holy Spirit, it listens to this devotedly, guards it with dedication and expounds it faithfully. All that it proposes for belief as being divinely revealed is drawn from this single deposit of faith. (Vatican Council II, Dogmatic Constitution on Divine Revelation, *Dei Verbum*, no. 10)

The quotation above is an apt description of the consistent tradition of the Church of Rome. We close this chapter by quoting these words of Joseph de Maistre, pertaining roughly to the period covered in this chapter:

> An invisible law raised up the see of Rome. We can say that the head of the universal Church was born a sovereign. From the scaffold of the martyrs he mounted a throne which at first no one could see, but which became formed and developed imperceptibly, as indeed all truly great things do. From the earliest times this throne was enveloped with a grandeur created by no humanly assignable cause.
>
> Did the Roman pontiff have need of wealth? Wealth flowed to him. Did he have need of influence? An indefinable aura of influence and splendor always surrounded the throne of St. Peter. This was true to such an extent that, already in the fourth century, one of the great lords of Rome, the prefect of the city, in fact, said only half-jokingly to St. Jerome: "Promise to make me the bishop of Rome and I will immediately become a Christian myself!"
>
> ... [T]he world often witnessed the popes sending out legates and issuing orders and making themselves obeyed from afar—without the world ever being able to give a name to the kind of supremacy that the popes somehow did enjoy. Providence itself had not yet given it a name.
>
> In pagan Rome, the Roman pontiffs made even the Roman emperors nervous: they never really were subjects of the emperors. The emperors may have enjoyed absolute power over the pope; and meanwhile he had no power against them. Nevertheless, in the end, it proved impossible for them to remain in the same place where the pope was.... A hidden hand "expelled" them from the Eternal City, leaving it to the head of the Eternal Church.... The same enclosure could not contain both the emperor and the pope. Constantine, in effect, ceded Rome to the popes.... Nothing has ever really been more historically true in one sense than "the Donation of Constantine...." (*Du Pape*, 2, VI)

Chapter 5

THE EARLY CHURCH WAS THE
CATHOLIC CHURCH

Did Jesus Christ establish the Catholic Church as we know her today? The answer is no, not exactly, for the Church has undergone many changes in her two-thousand-year history.

Nevertheless, the Catholic Church as we know her today is the same Church that Jesus Christ established on Peter and the other apostles, investing them and the successors they would appoint with authority to teach, rule, and sanctify those who would become members of "his body, the Church" (cf. Col 1:18) to the end of time.

The Church Christ founded in ancient Palestine as described in the New Testament *became* the Catholic Church we know today. The early Church became today's Catholic Church in the course of her life on earth of fulfilling the mission committed to her by Jesus Christ—always with the promised assistance of the Holy Spirit. The Church became what she is today by struggling despite many vicissitudes to remain faithful to Christ's original commission to her.

The many "developments" the Church has undergone in her history were mostly implicit in the infant Church. In the present study, many of these developments have been shown to have been logical and legitimate, even inevitable. If we were to trace the Church's history beyond the early centuries, we would discover many similar developments. The Church, like all living organisms, exhibits movement, change, and growth. Her composition steadily changes as new members are baptized into her; this comes about in a way similar to how the cells of a person's body also change over time. The Church's leaders also change. New ones are ordained to replace those who have passed into eternity with Christ. The goal of all Christians, after all, is to continue to live the life of Christ in heaven.

The Church's Magisterium is similarly a living thing. Through the authoritative decisions of popes and councils and with the assistance of the Holy Spirit, the Church is able to bring new meanings and applications out of the original deposit of revelation in order to help the faithful in each generation deal with an ever-changing world. This living Magisterium is able to deal with moral questions posed by strictly modern developments, such as nuclear warfare or artificial contraception. A living Magisterium is able to deal with such questions in a way that sacred Scripture alone, even though inspired, could never do.

Just as the Church's doctrines have developed out of the original revealed deposit of faith and possess new aspects and implications, the practices, structures, and institutions of the Catholic Church today have similarly developed out of the original practices and institutions of the apostles.

Jesus did not lay down in minute detail what the life of Christian perfection was to consist of when he enjoined his followers to "be perfect" (Mt 5:48). Yet the ways of achieving a life of perfection that were fostered by a St. Benedict, a St. Dominic, a St. Francis of Assisi, and a St. Teresa of Avila in and through the religious orders they founded or reformed represent legitimate elaborations of Jesus' call for us to be perfect.

Many examples of developments in the early Church have been noted in these pages, and many others could easily be cited. Neither the episcopacy nor the papacy appeared full-blown at the time of Christ's original commission to Peter and the other apostles; nevertheless, from the undeniable evidence of the New Testament, Christ *did* commission both Peter and the other apostles (cf. Mt 16:18–19; 18:18–19) in such a way that the papacy and episcopacy followed logically—and *inevitably*. As was understood in ancient times, Peter and the other apostles would be succeeded by subsequent popes and bishops who would shepherd the flock of Christ as Peter and the apostles had done.

Our examination of the data concerning the early Church confirms that *Catholics can entirely rely on the Church's own account of herself.* What the Church today teaches and practices with regard to her own foundation, her sacraments, her priesthood, her hierarchy, the apostolic succession, her Magisterium, the Scriptures she has included in the sacred canon—all these things and many more can be accepted on faith by intelligent people and acted on; the confidence of the believer that the Church is the ark of salvation and the teacher of truth is well founded. No historical, scientific, or scholarly data seriously call into question or contradict the Church's own account of herself—what she is and what she does.

It is vain to imagine that our faith in Jesus Christ has to be validated by what scholars or experts think they may have discovered about him from historical records. The entire enterprise of modern Scripture scholarship in no way really modifies what the Church has from Christ and interprets and hands on with the help of the Holy Spirit. But all the "evidence" in the world can in no way be considered the basis or foundation of our faith. No: we believe that what God has revealed is true, "not because its intrinsic truth is perceived only by the natural light of reason, but because of the authority of God who reveals, and who can neither deceive nor be deceived" (Vatican Council I, Dogmatic Constitution on the Catholic Faith *Dei Filius*, III).

Nevertheless, it is reassuring to know that the faith we profess is entirely credible by rigorous evidential standards; it has in no way been disproved by modern science and scholarship; rather, it is entirely defensible in the face of the doubts and disbelief so common today. These doubts can be cogently answered; disbelief is no foregone conclusion for modern man.

This is certainly the case as regards the evidence we have covered concerning the early Church. On the basis of what we have reviewed in this book, we can with great confidence continue to profess our firm belief in the One, Holy, Catholic and Apostolic Church of the Creed. The Church named in the Creed is the visible, worldwide Catholic Church headed by the pope in Rome and by Catholic bishops in union with him throughout the world.

Our examination of the historical data concerning the early Church establishes that the early Church was the Catholic Church; the One, Holy, Catholic, and Apostolic Church of the Creed is identical to the visible, living communion headed by the pope and the bishops in union with him who teach, govern, and sanctify the members of his "body, the Church" (cf. Col 1:18).

Appendix I

THE NAME OF THE CATHOLIC CHURCH

The Creed we recite on Sundays and Holy Days speaks of "one holy catholic and apostolic Church". As everybody knows, however, the Church referred to in this Creed is more commonly called just "the Catholic Church". It is *not* properly called "the Roman Catholic Church", by the way, but simply "the Catholic Church".

The term *Roman Catholic* is not used by the Church herself; it is a relatively modern term, confined largely to the English language. The English-speaking bishops at the First Vatican Council in 1870 conducted a successful campaign to insure that the phrase "Roman Catholic" was nowhere included in any of the Council's official documents about the Church herself.

Nowhere in the sixteen documents of the Second Vatican Council is *Roman Catholic* found. Pope Paul VI signed all the documents of the Second Vatican Council as "I, Paul, Bishop of the Catholic Church." There are references to the Roman Curia, the Roman Missal, the Roman Rite, etc., but when the adjective *Roman* is applied to the Church herself, it refers to—the diocese of Rome! Cardinals are styled "Cardinals of the Holy Roman Church"; but that designation chiefly means that in being named cardinals, they thereby become honorary clergy of the Holy Father's home diocese,

A longer version of this article appeared in *The Catholic Answer*, May/June, 1995.

the diocese of Rome. Each cardinal is given a titular church in Rome, and in electing a new pope, the cardinals are participating in a process that in ancient times was carried out by the clergy of the diocese of Rome.

Although the diocese of Rome *is* central to the Catholic Church, this does not mean that the Roman Rite (or, as is sometimes said, "the Latin Rite") is coterminous with the Church; this would also mean forgetting or neglecting the Byzantine, Chaldean, Maronite, and other oriental rites that are all part of the Catholic Church. In our day, greater emphasis has been given to these non-Roman rites. The Second Vatican Council devoted a special document, *Orientalium Ecclesiarum*, to the Eastern Rites of the Catholic Church. The *Catechism of the Catholic Church* similarly gives considerable attention to the distinctive traditions and spirituality of these Eastern rites.

So the proper name of Christ's Church is *not* "the Roman Catholic Church". That term caught on in English-speaking countries; it was promoted for the most part by Anglican supporters of the "branch theory" of the Church, namely, that the "one holy catholic and apostolic Church" of the Creed was supposed to consist of three major branches, the Anglican, the Orthodox, and the—so-called—Roman Catholic. To avoid that interpretation, the English-speaking bishops at Vatican I warned the Church away from ever officially using a term that could too easily be misunderstood.

Today, in an era of widespread dissent in the Church and equally widespread confusion regarding what an authentic Catholic identity is supposed to consist of, many loyal Catholics have recently taken to using the term *Roman Catholic* in order to affirm their understanding that the "catholic" Church of the Sunday Creed is the same Church that is united with the Vicar of Christ in Rome, the pope.

This understanding is correct. Such Catholics should nevertheless beware of using the term because of its dubious origins in Anglican circles intending to suggest that there just may be some other Catholic Church around somewhere besides the Roman one; also because the term is often used to suggest that the Roman Catholic Church is something less than the catholic Church of the Creed. The term is commonly used by some dissenting theologians who consider "the Roman Catholic Church" just another contemporary Christian denomination rather than the "one holy catholic and apostolic Church" of the Creed.

The proper name of the Church, then, is "the Catholic Church", never "the Christian Church". Although the prestigious Oxford University Press currently publishes a useful reference book called *The Oxford Book of the Christian Church*, there has never been a major entity called by that name. The Oxford University Press has adopted a misnomer.

There is a Protestant denomination in the United States that calls itself by that name, but that denomination is hardly what the Oxford University Press had in mind when assigning the title to its reference book. The title appears to be just one more instance of declining to admit that there is one—and only one—entity in the world that can possibly be designated "the Catholic Church". This entity is the very visible, worldwide Catholic Church, in which the 263rd successor of the apostle Peter, Pope John Paul II, teaches, governs, and sanctifies, along with some three thousand other bishops around the world, successors of the apostles of Jesus Christ.

The New Testament does mention that the followers of Christ early became known as "Christians" (Acts 11:26). The name *Christian*, however, was never commonly applied to the Church herself. In the New Testament, the Church is simply called "the Church". There was only one. There were not yet any breakaway bodies substantial enough to be rival claimants of the name, and from which the Church needed to distinguish herself.

Very early in post-apostolic times, the Church did acquire a proper name—precisely in order to distinguish herself from rival bodies that were beginning to form. The name the Church acquired then was the one by which she has been known ever since: the Catholic Church. The name appears in Christian literature for the first time around the end of the first century, in the Letter to the Smyrnaens of St. Ignatius of Antioch. By the time it got written down it had certainly already been in use, and everybody then understood exactly what was meant by the name.

Thereafter, mention of the name became more and more frequent in the written record. It appears in the oldest account we possess outside of the New Testament of the martyrdom of a Christian for his faith—the martyrdom of St. Polycarp, bishop of Smyrna, which took place about 155 A.D.

Catholic, of course, simply means "universal". Employing it in these early days, St. Ignatius of Antioch and St. Polycarp of Smyrna were referring to the Church that was already "everywhere", as distinguished from sects, schisms, or splinter groups that grew up here and there. The term was understood even then to be an especially fitting name because the Catholic Church was also for everyone, not just for such adepts or enthusiasts as might have been attracted to a particular sect.

It was already understood that the Church is "catholic" because she possesses the fullness of the means of salvation. She was also destined to be universal in time as well as in space, and to her is applied the promise of Christ to Peter and the other apostles that "the powers of death shall not prevail" against her (Mt 16:18).

The *Catechism of the Catholic Church* sums up the reasons why the name of the Church of Christ is "the Catholic Church": "The Church is Catholic", the *Catechism* teaches, [because] "she proclaims the fullness of the faith. She bears in herself and administers the totality of the means of salvation. She is sent out to all peoples. She speaks to all men. She encompasses all times. She is 'missionary of her very nature'" (CCC no. 868).

At the first ecumenical council of the Church, held at Nicaea in Asia Minor in the year 325, the bishops were legislating in the name of the universal body they called "the Catholic Church". This was the council that formulated the basic Creed in which *catholic* is one of the four notes of the true Church of Christ. The same name is to be found in all sixteen documents of Vatican Council II.

Back in the fourth century St. Cyril of Jerusalem (ca. 315–386) wrote, aptly:

> Inquire not simply where the Lord's house is, for the sects of the profane also make an attempt to call their own dens the houses of the Lord; nor inquire merely where the "church" is, but where the Catholic Church is. For this is the peculiar name of this Holy Body, the mother of all, which is the Spouse of Our Lord Jesus Christ. (*Catecheses*, xviii, 26)

The same inquiry needs to be made in exactly the same way today, for the name of the true Church of Christ has not been changed. It was inevitable that our present-day *Catechism of the Catholic Church* would employ the same name that the Church has had throughout her long history: the Catholic Church.

Appendix II

LIST OF THE EARLY POPES

(Includes name, commonly accepted place of birth or origin, date of accession to the papacy, and date of the end of the reign, which is generally also the date of death.)

1. St. Peter (Simon Bar-Jonah): Galilee; d. 64 or 67.

2. St. Linus: Tuscany; 67–76.

3. St. Cletus (or Anacletus): Rome; 76–88.

4. St. Clement: Rome; 88–97.

5. St. Evaristus: Greece; 97–105.

6. St. Alexander I: Rome; 105–115.

7. St. Sixtus I: Rome; 115–125.

8. St. Telesphorus: Greece; 125–136.

9. St. Hyginus: Greece; 136–140.

10. St. Pius I: Aquileia; 140–155.

11. St. Anicetus: Syria; 155–166.

12. St. Soter: Campania; 166–175.

13. St. Eleutherius: Greece; 175–189.

14. St. Victor I: Africa; 189–199.

15. St. Zephyrinus: Rome; 199–217.

16. St. Callistus I: Rome; 217–222.

17. St. Urban I: Rome; 222–230.

18. St. Pontian: Rome; July 21, 230 to Sept. 28, 235.

19. St. Anterus: Greece; Nov. 21, 235 to Jan. 3, 236.

20. St. Fabian: Rome; Jan. 10, 236 to Jan. 20, 250.

21. St. Cornelius: Rome; Mar. 251 to June, 253.

22. St. Lucius I: Rome; June 25, 253 to Mar. 5, 254.

23. St. Stephen I: Rome; May 12, 254 to Aug. 2, 257.

24. St. Sixtus II: Greece; Aug. 30, 257 to Aug. 6, 258.

25. St. Dionysius: Rome; July 22, 260(?) to Dec. 26, 268.

26. St. Felix I: Rome; Jan. 5, 269 to Dec. 30, 274.

27. St. Eutychian: Luni; Jan. 4, 275 to Dec. 7, 283.

28. St. Caius: Dalmatia; Dec. 17, 283 to Apr. 22, 296.

29. St. Marcellinus: Rome; June 30, 296 to Oct. 25, 304.

30. St. Marcellus I: Rome; May or June 308 to Jan. 16, 309.

31. St. Eusebius: Greece; Apr. 309 or 310 to Aug. 309 or 310.

32. St. Miltiades (Melchiades): Africa; July 2, 311 to Jan. 11, 314.

33. St. Silvester I: Rome; Jan. 31, 314 to Dec. 31, 335.

34. St. Marcus: Rome; Jan. 18, 336 to Oct. 7, 336.

35. St. Julius I: Rome; Feb. 6, 337 to Apr. 12, 352.

36. Liberius: Rome; May 17, 352 to Sept. 24, 366.

37. St. Damasus I: Spain; Oct. 1, 366 to Dec. 11, 384.

38. St. Siricius: Rome; Dec. 384 to Nov. 26, 399.

39. St. Anastasius I: Rome; Nov. 27, 399 to Dec. 19, 401.

40. St. Innocent I: Albano; Dec. 22, 401 to Mar. 12, 417.

41. St. Zosimus: Greece; Mar. 18, 417 to Dec. 26, 418.

42. St. Boniface I: Rome; Dec. 28 or 29, 418 to Sept. 4, 422.

43. St. Celestine I: Campania; Sept. 10, 422 to July 27, 432.

44. St. Sixtus III: Rome; July 31, 432 to Aug. 19, 440.

45. St. Leo I the Great: Tuscany; Sept. 29, 440 to Nov. 10, 461.

46. St. Hilary: Sardinia; Nov. 19, 461 to Feb. 29, 468.

47. St. Simplicius: Tivoli; Mar. 3, 468 to Mar. 10, 483.

48. St. Felix II: Rome; Mar. 13, 483 to Mar. 1, 492.

49. St. Gelasius I: Africa; Mar. 1, 492 to Nov. 21, 496.

50. St. Anastasius II: Rome; Nov. 24, 496 to Nov. 19, 498.

51. St. Symmachus: Sardinia; Nov. 22, 498 to July 19, 514.

52. St. Hormisdas: Frosinone; July 20, 514 to Aug. 6, 523.

Appendix III

GLOSSARY OF HERESIES IN THE EARLY CHURCH

Adoptionism. Adoptionism held that Jesus was not really God but merely a man to whom special graces had been given and who achieved a kind of divine status at his baptism. This idea that Christ as a man was only the "adopted" son of God proved to be a persistent heresy. It was condemned by Pope St. Victor I, who excommunicated Theodotus of Byzantium for Adoptionism. The same heresy was condemned in 785 and again in 794 by Pope Adrian I. Revived by Peter Abelard in the twelfth century, Adoptionism was again condemned by Pope Alexander III in 1177.

Anomeanism. A radical variant of Arianism (see below), Anomeanism held that the Son was "unlike" (Greek: *animoios*) the Father.

Apollinarianism. This heretical doctrine of Apollinaris (310–390), bishop of Laodicea in Asia Minor, held that Christ had a human body but only a sensitive soul—and no rational human mind or human free will, these having been replaced in Christ by the divine Logos, or Word of God. This theory was condemned by Roman synods in 377 and 381 and by the ecumenical Council of Constantinople in the latter year.

Arianism. A major heresy that arose in the fourth century and denied the divinity of Jesus Christ. First effectively advanced by Arius (256–336), a priest of Alexandria, who denied that there were three distinct divine Persons in

God. For Arius, there was only one Person, the Father. According to Arian theory, the Son was created ("There was a time when he was not"). Christ was thus a son of God, not by nature, but only by grace and adoption. This theory logically evacuates the doctrine of the Incarnation of God in Christ of all meaning: if God did not become man, then the world has not been redeemed and the faith itself eventually dissolves. Arianism was formally condemned in 325 by the first ecumenical Council of Nicaea, which formulated and promulgated the original version of the Nicene Creed; but Arianism and Semi-Arianism (see below) nevertheless continued to prevail in its original form in many areas for more than a century. Arianism was combatted by the great St. Athanasius of Alexandria (296–373) among others; but the heresy nevertheless persisted, especially among the barbarians, for several centuries.

Donatism. A fourth- and fifth-century African heresy holding that the validity of the sacraments depends upon the moral character of the minister of the sacraments and that sinners cannot be true members of the Church or even tolerated by the Church if their sins are publicly known. Donatism began as a schism when rigorists claimed that a bishop of Carthage, Caecilian (fl. ca. 313), was not a true bishop because he had been ordained by a bishop who had been an apostate under the Diocletian persecution. The Donatists ordained their own bishops, one of whom was Donatus, for whom the heresy is named. Donatism was condemned by Pope Miltiades (311–314) and by the (local) Council of Arles in 314, but it nevertheless persisted in North Africa until the Muslim conquest in the seventh century. The great St. Augustine (354–430) wrote extensively against Donatism.

Gnosticism. The heretical theory that salvation comes through some special kind of knowledge, usually knowledge claimed by a special elite group. Gnostic theories existed before Christianity, and the Gnostics adapted the Gospels to their own views and for their own purposes, even composing pseudogospels embodying their particular ideas and doctrines. Gnosticism held matter to be evil and hostile to the human spirit; it also essentially denied the truths of Christian revelation. Secular historian Jacob Burckhardt described the Gnostics as "speculative enthusiasts" who embraced Christianity only as a platform for Platonic and Oriental ideas. Gnosticism as an organized sect or body of beliefs has long been extinct, but Gnostic ideas persist and surface in some form in nearly every major heretical version of the Christian faith.

Macedonianism. A heresy named after Macedonius, an Arian bishop of Constantinople (d. ca. 362) whose followers denied the divinity of the Holy Spirit: the Spirit was declared by them not to proceed from the Father but to be a creation of the Son. Macedonianism was condemned in 381 by the ecumenical Council of Constantinople, which added to the Nicene Creed an affirmation of belief in the divinity of the Holy Spirit and the consubstantiality of the Holy Spirit with the Father and the Son.

Marcionism. A second-century heresy of Marcion (fl. ca. 140) and his followers, who rejected the Old Testament and much of the New Testament, except for the Gospel of Luke and ten of the Letters of St. Paul. The Marcionists claimed to preach a purer gospel after the manner of St. Paul; for them Christianity was purely a gospel of love to the exclusion of any law. Only virgins, widows, and celibates were baptized by the Marcionists; married people could not advance beyond the catechumenate.

Modalism. A form of Trinitarian heresy of the second and third centuries, Modalism held that there is only one Person in God, who manifests himself in various ways, or modes. Sabellianism (see below) was a form of Modalism, as was Priscillianism (see below).

Monophysitism. A fifth-century heresy holding that in Christ there is only one nature (Greek: *mono*, single; *physis*, nature), a divine nature. Thus, Monophysitism denies the true human nature of Christ; this human nature is absorbed into Christ's divine nature, according to Monophysitism. This heresy arose primarily in reaction to Nestorianism (see below). Monophysitism, though condemned by Pope St. Leo the Great in his famous *Tome* of 449 and by the ecumenical Council of Chalcedon in 451, persists to this day in parts of the East.

Monothelitism. A heresy that arose in the seventh century as a result of Byzantine imperial efforts to accommodate the Monophysites (see above). Monothelites accepted the orthodox doctrine of the two natures, divine and human, in the Person of Jesus Christ but held that these two natures had only "one will" (Greek: *monos*, single; *thelein*, will). This heresy was condemned by the Sixth General Council of Constantinople in 681.

Montanism. A second-century heretical movement that professed belief in a new "Church of the Spirit". The Montanists believed they enjoyed the direct inspiration of the Holy Spirit. This claim meant that their fanatically rigorous views concerning morality superseded the authentic revelation of Christ that had been handed down in the Church. The heresy of Montanism, which claimed the great Tertullian (160–220) himself, was condemned by several Eastern synods and, finally, by Pope Zephyrinus around the year 202.

Nestorianism. A fifth-century heresy claiming that there are two distinct Persons in the Incarnate Christ, one human and one divine. The Church teaches that Christ was and is a divine person who took on a human nature. According to Nestorianism, it is unthinkable that God was born, crucified, and died; nor could Mary really have been the mother of God, but only the mother of a human being conjoined to God. Nestorianism, which took its name from Nestorius, a bishop of Constantinople (d. ca. 451), was condemned by the ecumenical Council of Ephesus in 431. Overemphasizing the humanity of Christ, Nestorianism is the opposite heresy from Monophysitism (see above), which overemphasized Christ's divinity.

Novatianism. A schism that became a heresy. It originated with Novatian, a Roman priest who became an antipope, claiming the papacy in 251 in opposition to the true pope, St. Cornelius. The Novatianists adopted a moral rigorism similar to that of Donatism (see above). Those guilty of grave sin were excluded from the Church permanently, and absolution was refused to those guilty of the sins of murder and adultery.

Pelagianism. A heretical doctrine on divine grace taught by Pelagius (355–425), a monk from the British Isles who first propagated his views in Rome in the time of Pope Anastasius I. Pelagius argued against the Church's teaching that in order to do good, divine grace in the soul was necessary. This canceled human free will. Pelagianism included a cluster of other beliefs and essentially entailed a denial of the Church's doctrine of Original Sin. It was condemned by local councils in Africa in 416 and 417, and also by Pope St. Innocent I in the latter year. It was condemned again in 418 by his successor, Pope St. Zosimus. Semi-Pelagianism, a related heresy, was condemned by the local Council of Orange in 529 but has long persisted among those who question Original Sin and the supremacy of divine grace.

Priscillianism. A fourth-century heresy originating in Spain and combining forms of both Modalism and Gnosticism (see above). It denied Christ's divinity and real humanity, holding that human souls were united to bodies in punishment for their sins.

Sabellianism. A third-century heresy named after a theologian, Sabellius (fl. ca. 215). The Sabellians believed that there was only one Person in God, with three "modes", or aspects, of manifesting himself: as Creator, Redeemer, and Sanctifier. It was thus a form of Modalism (see above). Jesus Christ was merely a temporary manifestation in the flesh of the eternal God. This heresy was also known by the name of Patripassianism, since it held that it was the Father who suffered on the cross. It was condemned by Pope St. Callistus I, but as a form of Modalism it has persisted in history in connection with other heresies.

Semi-Arianism. A modified form of Arianism (see above) that flourished after the Council of Nicaea had condemned Arianism in 325. The Semi-Arians were often "moderates" who wanted to forge a "compromise" between those who held to the Church's strict teaching concerning the divinity of Christ and Christ's consubstantiality with the Father and those tempted by Arianism to deny many great truths. Sometimes referred to as Arianizers, the Semi–Arians also included those who wished to substitute *homo-i-ousios* ("of like substance") or *homoios* ("similar") for the orthodox Nicene *homo-ousios* ("one in being" or "consubstantial") with the Father. There were a number of differing positions that fell within the general category of Semi-Arianism; their common theme was an unwillingness to accept that the Nicene term *homo-ousios* was necessary to the Church's orthodox doctrine of the Holy Trinity.

Subordinationism. A general name for all the fourth-century heresies that admitted only God the Father as God. See the entries above for Arianism, Anomeanism, Macedonianism, Modalism, and Semi-Arianism; all of these heresies are forms of Subordinationism.

Valentinianism. A form of the ancient heresy of Gnosticism (see above) based on the teaching of one Valentinus, who lived in Rome between 136 and 165. The Valentinians claimed that the visible world had been created by the God of the Old Testament but that only the invisible world was real. According to them, Christ came to deliver mankind from its bondage to matter and the physical world; most of mankind, however, wholly engrossed in matter, would nevertheless end in eternal perdition. The great St. Irenaeus (ca. 125–ca. 202) inveighed against Valentinianism in particular in his magisterial work *Against the Heresies*.

Bibiography

Attwater, Donald. *The Penguin Dictionary of Saints*, 2d ed. Penguin Books: Harmondsworth, Middlesex, England, 1986.

Balthasar, Hans Urs von. *The Office of Peter and the Structure of the Church*, trans. Andrée Emery. San Francisco: Ignatius Press, 1986.

Barry, Colman J., O.S.B., ed. *Readings in Church History*. volume one: *From Pentecost to the Protestant Revolt*. New York: Newman Press, 1960.

Battifol, Pierre. *Primitive Catholicism*, trans. Henri L. Brianceau. New York: Longmans, Green, 1911.

Bettenson, Henry, ed. *Documents of the Christian Church*, 2d ed. London: Oxford University Press, 1963.

Broderick, John F., S.J. *Documents of Vatican Council I*. Collegeville, Minn.: Liturgical Press, 1971.

Burckhardt, Jacob. *The Age of Constantine the Great*, trans. Moses Hadas. New York: Dorset Press, 1989.

Carmody, James M., S.J., and Thomas E. Clarke, S.J. *Word and Redeemer: Christology in the Fathers*. Glen Rock, N.J.: Paulist Press, 1966.

Catechism of the Catholic Church, 2d ed. New York: Vatican City: Libreria Editrice Vaticana, 1997.

Chadwick, Henry. *The Early Church*. New York: Dorset Press, 1986.

The Church Teaches: Documents of the Church in English Translation, trans. the Jesuit Fathers of St. Mary's College. Rockford, Ill.: Tan Books, 1973.

Daniel-Rops, Henri. *L'Eglise des apôtres et des martyrs*. Paris: Artheme Fayard, 1948.

Davis, Leo Donald, S.J. *The First Seven Ecumenical Councils (325–787): Their History and Theology*. Collegeville, Minn.: Liturgical Press, 1983.

Duffy, Eamon. *Saints and Sinners: A History of the Popes*. New Haven: Yale University Press, 1997.

Durell, J.C.V. *The Historic Church*. New York: Krause Reprint Co., 1969 (reprint of 1906 Cambridge University Press ed.).

Eusebius. *The Ecclesiastical History of Eusebius Pamphilus*, trans. with Introduction by Christian Frederick Cruse. Grand Rapids, Mich.: Baker Book House, 1977.

Flannery, Austin, O.P., ed. *Vatican Council II: The Conciliar and Post Conciliar Documents*. Northpoint, N.Y.: Costello Publishing Company, 1975.

Fortescue, Adrian. *The Early Papacy to the Synod of Chalcedon in 451*, 3d ed. Ed. Scott M.P. Reid. Southampton, England: Saint Austin Press, 1997.

Fox, Robin Lane. *Pagans and Christians*. San Francisco: Harper and Row, 1988.

Fremantle, Anne, ed. *A Treasury of Early Christianity*. New York: New American Library, 1953.

Gibbon, Edward. *The Portable Gibbon: The Decline and Fall of the Roman Empire*, ed. with Introduction by Dero A. Saunders. New York: Viking Press, 1957.

Grant, Michael. *Constantine the Great: The Man and His Times*. New York: Barnes and Noble, 1993.

Hardon, John A., S.J. *Modern Catholic Dictionary*. Garden City, N.Y.: Doubleday, 1980.

Hughes, Philip. *A History of the Church*. Volume I: *The World in Which the Church Was Founded*, rev. ed. New York: Sheed and Ward, 1949.

Hughes, Philip. *The Church in Crisis: A History of the General Councils, 325–1870.* Garden City, N. Y.: Doubleday, 1960.

Jedin, Hubert, *Ecumenical Councils of the Catholic Church: An Historical Survey,* trans. Ernest Graf, O. S. B. New York: Herder and Herder, 1960.

Kelly, J. N. D. *The Oxford Dictionary of Popes.* Oxford: Oxford University Press, 1986.

Lebreton, Jules, S. J., and Jacques Zeiller. *The Triumph of Christianity.* Book IV of *A History of the Early Church,* trans. Ernest C. Messenger. New York: Collier Books, 1962.

Maistre, Joseph de. *Du Pape.* Geneva: Librairie Droz, 1966.

Newman, John Henry. *An Essay on the Development of Christian Doctrine.* New York: Doubleday, Image Books, 1960.

O'Connor, James T. *The Gift of Infallibility: The Official Relatio on Infallibility of Bishop Vincent Gasser at Vatican Council I.* Boston: Daughters of St. Paul, 1986.

Ratzinger, Joseph. *Called to Communion: Understanding the Church Today,* trans. Adrian Walker. San Francisco: Ignatius Press, 1996.

Richardson, Cyril C., ed. *Early Christian Fathers.* Newly Translated by Cyril C. Richardson, in collaboration with Eugene R. Fairweather, Edward Rochie Hardy, and Massey Hamilton Shepherd, Jr., New York: Macmillan, 1978.

Schatz, Klaus, S. J. *Papal Primacy: From Its Origins to the Present,* trans. John A. Otto and Linda M. Maloney. Collegeville, Minn.: Liturgical Press, 1996.

Schimmelpfennig, Bernhard. *The Papacy,* trans. James Sievert. New York: Columbia University Press, 1992.

Shotwell, James T., and Louise Ropes Loomis. *The See of Peter.* New York: Octagon Books, 1965.

Stanley, David M., S. J. *The Apostolic Church in the New Testament.* Westminster, Md.: Newman Press, 1965.

INDEX

Acacian Schism, 275–81,
  283–87
Acacius, 278–81, 286
Adoptionists, Adoptionism,
  174, 198, 311
Adversus Haereses. See *Against the Heresies*
Against the Heresies (Irenaeus),
  55–56, 156–58, 317
Agatho, Pope St., 97–98
Alaric the Goth, 268
Alexander of Alexandria, 78
Alexander Severus, 169–71
Ambrose, St., 196, 261–63
Anastasius I (emperor), 281–85
Anastasius II (pope), 283
Anicetus, Pope St., 169–71,
  176
Anomeans, Anomeanism, 243,
  311
Apollinarianism, 86, 311
apostles
  appointing successors, 123,
    127, 129, 157, 162
  commissioned by Jesus, 20
  at the Council of Jerusa-
    lem, 32, 80
  powers of, 31, 43–44

apostolic, meaning of, 35
Arianism
  condemnation of, 224–25,
    253
  Council of Nicaea and, 75,
    78–79
  creeds and, 79–80, 242–
    44
  definition of, 311–12
  growth and spread of, 75,
    83, 224, 239–40, 247
  heretical beliefs of, 74–76
  origins of, 75, 78, 198
  role of Eusebius of Nico-
    media, 76–78, 83, 224
Arians. *See* Arianism
Arius, 75, 78, 83, 87, 224
Athanasius, St.
  and the Council of Nicaea,
    78–81
  defense of, 202–3, 228, 230,
    236–39
  exiles and returns of, 225,
    233, 247–48, 253
  and *homo-i-ousios*, 79–80,
    243
  on the name of the Church,
    80–81